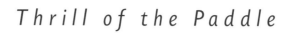

Thrill of the Paddle

THRILL ^{OF THE} PADDLE

The Art of Whitewater Canoeing

PAUL MASON AND MARK SCRIVER

FIREFLY BOOKS

For my father and mother, who set me on the path I have taken.
PAUL MASON

For Marilyn, Ian and Paul, who put up with and share my enthusiasm for paddling.
MARK SCRIVER

A FIREFLY BOOK

Published by Firefly Books Ltd. 1999

First Printing

LIBRARY OF CONGRESS CATALOGUING IN PUBLICATION DATA

Mason, Paul
Thrill of the paddle : the art of whitewater canoeing / Paul Mason, Mark Scriver.–1st ed.
[192] p. : ill. col.; cm.
Summary: Illustrated guide to canoeing in extreme (class 3 or 4) water conditions.
ISBN 1-55209-451-0
White-water canoeing. 2. Canoes and canoeing. I. Scriver, Mark. II. Title.
797.1/22 –dc21   1999   CIP

Published in the United States in 1999 by
Firefly Books (U.S.) Inc.
P.O. Box 1338, Ellicott Station
Buffalo, New York, USA
14205

Published in Canada in 1999 by Key Porter Books Limited.

Electronic formatting: Heidi Palfrey
Cover and interior design: Peter Maher
Front cover photograph: Simone French
Author photograph: Jen Buck

Printed and bound in Canada

CONTENTS

Acknowledgments 6
Introduction 7

1 River Morphology / 8
International scale of river difficulty, 9; River morphology, 10; Anatomy of a surfing wave, 13; Anatomy of a surfing hole, 13; River morphology–Nasties, 14; River rescue, 18

2 Equipment / 20
Canoe design, 20; Classic canoes, 22; Tandem playboats, 22; Solo playboats, 22 ; Paddles, 27; Clothing for cold weather, 31; Clothing for warm weather, 33; Footwear, 34; Hoods and toques, 36; Accessories, 36; Helmets, 38; Personal Flotation Devices, 40; Rescue systems, 41; Customizing Your Canoe, 43; Outfitting, 44; for your knees, 46; for your feet, 48; anchors, 49; Repairs, 52

3 Tandem Classic / 54
Skills–Strokes, 55; Backpaddling, 58; Rolling, 60; Maneuvers–Front surfing, 60; Back surfing, 64; Back-Ferry versus Speed and Front-Ferry, 66; Side Surfing, 68; Flat Spins in a Hole, 69

4 Solo Classic / 70
Skills–Forward strokes, 70; Backpaddling, 71; Bracing strokes, 72; Rolling, 73; Maneuvers–Front surfing, 74; Back surfing, 79; Side Surfing, 82; River Running Skills–Punching Holes, 84; Staying Dry, 85; Crossing the Grain, 86; Boofing, 90

5 Tandem Playboat / 92
Skills–Strokes, 94; Rolling, 96; Maneuvers–Front surfing, 97; Using the foam pile, 103; Back surfing, 104; Hole surfing, 107; Flat spins in the hole, 108; River-running skills, 109; Boofing, 110

6 Solo Playboat / 114
Introduction, 114; Skills–Pivot strokes, 115; Steering strokes, 118; Forward strokes, 122; Backpaddling, 124; Bracing strokes, 126; Self-rescue, 128; Emptying your canoe, 129; Rolling, 130; Maneuvers–Eddy Turns, 134; Ferrying, 141; Front surfing, 142; Blasting, 147; Back surfing, 148; Backsurf strokes, 150; Flat spins, 152; Shredding the foam pile, 153; Hole riding, 156; Vertical moves, 160; River-running skills, 168; Boofing, 169; How to hit rocks, 174; River reading, 175; Visualizing, 177; Punching holes, 178; Creeking, 179; Crossing the grain, 180; Sneak routes, 182; Hair boating, 184; The Holtzbox, Inn River, Austria, 185; Test Yourself: Solution, 186

Glossary 188
Bibliography 189
Index 190

INTRODUCTION

This book is designed for, but not limited to, intermediate and advanced canoeists. Do you fit that category? If you read my late father's book *Path of the Paddle* and it made sense, and if your canoeing skills have progressed to where you approach front and back ferries with probable, rather than possible, success, you're now ready for *Thrill of the Paddle*. Each chapter starts out with a review of the basics and ends with more challenging moves for the hard-core expert (see especially the rodeo and creeking moves covered in the Solo Playboat chapter).

There's no need to rush out to buy a new boat to experience really fun basic playboating maneuvers. The book begins with tandem classic boats, which refers to a regular tripping canoe. Some classic canoe designs are more suited to playing than others (see Chapter 2, the section on Canoe Design). Minor alterations in outfitting your canoe for performance and safety reasons have been suggested. These are also covered in Chapter 2, in the section Outfitting.

Once you've experienced the thrill of playboating, you'll quickly reach a point where your classic canoe will start hampering your learning curve. Then it's time to consider a tandem or solo playboat. Read the chapters on these craft to get an idea about what kind of boat will suit you. Granted, your playboat design ideals will be based on my opinions and Mark's, but rest assured we've spent a huge amount of time formulating these ideas in a quest to satisfy our addiction called "playboating."

Mark and I were introduced to playing in rapids when we ran them during wilderness trips. Playing in the whitewater honed our skills, which we then applied in rapid-running situations. I recall executing a do-or-die (or at least, a get-very-wet-and-scared) front surf on the Little Nahanni in the Northwest Territories one summer. My partner and I were chasing an overturned canoe through a relatively "busy" canyon. The canoe had a fair headstart on us, as we'd been preoccupied with rescuing another boat when it drifted by. All of the swimmers were out of the water, but since the canoe carried a full load of gear for our three-week trip, it was a pretty valuable prize. We gave chase, hoping to catch it before it reached the last rapid, which was unrunnable, even with our spray covers. We arrived in the river-right eddy above the rapid, but no canoe was in sight. The high-water conditions and steep canyon walls left only one option: surf across a small wave at the brink, then smash the bow into the shale on the opposite shore, which would cause the stern to quickly swing in so we could run a slot backward. The slot ended in a ledge, but I figured it was shallow enough that the canoe would grind to a halt before the ledge. From the look on my bow partner's face I could tell she was a little skeptical about the plan. Fortunately, it worked. Having learned to surf for fun, we were equipped with the skill to perform this difficult maneuver in "real life." Being confident in our surfing ability gave us the means to extract ourselves from a sticky situation. (P.S. We didn't catch up with the runaway canoe until the following evening when we found it grounded on a gravel bar.)

On the other hand, I can't think of a single river-running situation that would call for such an advanced maneuver as a vertical 360-degree pirouette. Are we then entering the realm of learning new skills solely to enjoy whitewater for the sake of plain old fun? Perhaps, just be aware that it is all too easy to develop a narrow field of vision focusing only on running rapids rather than the stuff in between sets that allows you time to enjoy the river environment as a whole.

Those of you who are already experienced play-boaters will enjoy the later chapters on tandem and solo playboating. The advanced skills are explained in the same comprehensive style with which my dad introduced the art of white-water canoeing in *Path of the Paddle*.

See you on the river.

PAUL MASON

On the many drives to and from the river, Paul and I spend countless hours discussing why some moves work and some don't, how to improve the design of the latest canoe, and what new moves or lines we need to try. I know just enough physics to develop little theories about why a new move should work but not always enough to convince Paul of its validity. This sort of stuff fascinates me. The discussions while away the hours and occasionally lead to the enlightenment of either or both of us.

In this book, the maneuvers are described and illustrated in enough detail that you can try them if they are new to you or refine them if it's a move with which you're already familiar. But perhaps more importantly, we also discuss the reason why these moves work, and relate some of the stories of us "paying our dues," learning these things the hard way. Hopefully, we can pass on not only the skills and little tricks that we've learned but also the fascination we have for the interaction between the canoe and whitewater.

Although we've paddled together and have similar skills, Paul and I often have different approaches to solving the challenges the river presents. Watching other paddlers is always educational, but with Paul as a paddling partner I have a mentor, a coach and a fellow competitor who shares my love of paddling and learning. I think neither of us on our own would have developed the skill level we now possess, or the motivation and interest that keeps boating fun for both of us week after week, year after year.

MARK SCRIVER

ACKNOWLEDGMENTS

When the idea of an open-canoe playboating book first came up, it seemed only natural that I co-write it with Mark Scriver. We paddle together a lot and share a desire, or curse, to always want to know how and why a particular maneuver works. We discuss technique continually, but even so, during the process of proofreading each other's text, there was the occasional "Hey, you never told me that trick" phone call.

To try to capture some of the flavor that my late father, Bill Mason, worked into his book *Path of the Paddle*, I used the same writing technology that he did. I have my mom, Joyce Mason, to thank for typing out my long-hand scrawls. (Mom, I promise to learn how to type–really!)

I was also fortunate to have my mother-in-law, Olive Seaman, and my mom watching our two daughters so that my wife, Judy, and I could get out for the tandem-canoe photo shoots. Of course I am deeply indebted to Judy for putting up with the silliness that seems to spring out of a project like this– ideas such as, "I'm sure someone at the party will want to stick his or her head in a bucket and be held underwater so he or she can get an underwater shot of us rolling a canoe. All the snow is gone and it *is* a pool party, after all."

To all those folks who did not have to put their head in a bucket but who were coerced into shooting photos anyway, a big thank you.

Ken Buck was our primary photographer for the instructional photographs. Additional photos were shot by Sue Buck, Jenny Buck, Andrew Westwood, Colin Seaman, Don Beckett, Joyce Mason, Alan Dunne, Mark Rab, Garry Donaldson, Sharon Bryce, Gillian Currie, Ian Holmes, Joe Langman, Jim Risk, Carolyn Pullen, Chris Pullen, Phil Green, Patrick Fournier, Matt Bender, Don Holmes, Bob Holmes, Gillian Wright, Marilyn Scriver, Maryke Van Oosten, Kevin Schultz, Judy Mason, Ed Hanrahan, Kevin Varette, and Rick Matthews (slalom photo).

Thank you, as well, to the friends who helped out with things such as holding the bucket down on the camera person's head. They are Fred Bryce, Ben Bryce, Bill Sheffield, and Peter Selwyn.

Mark and I want to express our gratitude to Lloyd Seaman for his valiant attempt at proofreading our text. Additional proofreading was done by Alan Dunne and Ken Buck.

We have Peter Cook, a fellow cartoonist, to thank for the computer collages. Due to him, reality was not a limiting factor. But rest assured that we didn't alter photos unless for an instructional purpose.

The profile on cool paddling gear could not have happened without the generous support of the paddle-sports industry. Thanks to Dagger Canoes, Mad River Canoe, Trailhead, Palm Equipment, Albert Angenent, Grateful Heads, Lotus Design Inc., Robson Paddles, North Water Rescue and Paddling Equipment, Akona Water Sport Shoes, Salamander Inc., Aqualung, Sport Helmets Inc., Brooks Wetsuits Ltd., Dupont, Lightning Paddles, Grey Owl Paddles, Primex of California, Headwaters Inc., Whites and Outfitting by Mikey.

Finally, thanks to our editors, Clare McKeon and Mary Ann McCutcheon, and Key Porter Books for gambling on the hope that two boaters could stay off the water long enough to write about it.

1 RIVER MORPHOLOGY

1 Ah... wilderness.

2 Destination paddling.

3 What class of difficulty is this rapid?

Where to Start

When you start to consider actually playing in a rapid rather than simply descending it safely, your perspective changes radically. Instead of looking for the easiest line down, you start looking for the juiciest play spots.

Initially, you're bound to be nervous about playing in the river features you've always tried to avoid. However, paddling with a group can remove some of this trepidation. Usually, someone in the crowd can show you the potential for playing, plus help you more quickly determine whether a particular spot is safe.

Or you can learn by taking lessons. Accessible learning sites can lead to a different kind of "eddyline" on busy weekends.

Crowded eddies are not conducive to learning anything, except how to cope during river festivals. The best way to avoid the masses is to paddle during non-peak days or seasons. Mid-week in late fall won't look anything like the "circus" at this popular paddling spot (see photo 1).

Meeting other paddlers and swapping stories is all part of the fun of playboating. It also means you can agree to rescue one another; by making use of a "buddy" system there's less chance you'll get into trouble unnoticed. And it's much easier to learn how to playboat when you receive some feedback on what you're doing.

Destination Paddling

Destination paddling means you're not seeking the river-running experience; you're going to hang out at a particular play spot. This approach obviously misses much of what most of us think of as canoeing. On the other hand, it makes possible the discovery of many more paddling places than you knew existed. Sometimes this is a little drop hidden away on a river that you wouldn't normally be on. Sometimes it's a surfing wave at the discharge pipe of an old mill (see photo 2). The place shown here was really spooky because the water was coming out of a tunnel, forming a wave right at the mouth. This meant surfing with the bow almost in the tunnel. Boils surged out of the dark, making the surf really dynamic. *Urban boating*, as we call it, offers some unique, even bizarre, experiences. Mark and I wouldn't recommend most of them, but if you *are* exploring urban areas, make darn sure you know which way and where the water is going and remember that it could rise at any moment.

Rating Rapids

Rating the difficulty of rapids is highly subjective. However, the American Whitewater Association (AWA) surveyed paddlers to establish benchmarks based on well-known rapids. This is pretty much what you would do when getting information about an unknown river from a friend. As well as finding out what rating they would give the river, you would find out how they rate a river you both know, which tells you whether your friend rates a rapid easier or harder than you do.

Of course, your rating of a rapid will inevitably be influenced by your likes, dislikes and phobias. Here's a case in point. Mark and I boat together often, and occasionally we get out with another experienced paddler named Marc Rab. Even though we paddle much of the same water, we often give different ratings to serious whitewater–for example, the falls and rapids in photo 3. Mark says it's a class 4-, I call it a 4 and Marc Rab calls it a 4+. This really isn't a big deal if you can portage the rapid, but if you're contemplating a run that has few portaging options, you could be in over your head, with no choice but to run the rapids.

Sometimes paddlers who are more skilled than you can lead you astray. They may make the lines look easy, by using proper technique and superior river reading skills to take advantage of every micro-current or wave. They appear to be easily floating through the rapid. Indeed it is easy, because they are on line. But if an unsuspecting paddler strays off that line, it may be difficult to compensate and lead to serious consequences.

International Scale of River Difficulty

The International Scale of River Difficulty, recently revised by the AWA, is the U.S. version of an international rating system used to compare river difficulty throughout the world. The system is not exact: rivers don't always fit easily into one class, and regional or individual interpretations may cause misunderstandings. The system is no substitute for a guidebook or accurate first-hand descriptions of a run.

If you're attempting difficult runs in an unfamiliar area, act cautiously until you get a feel for the way the scale is interpreted locally. River difficulty may change from year to year due to fluctuations in water level, downed trees, recent floods, geological disturbances or bad weather. Stay alert for unexpected problems!

As rapids become longer and more continuous, the challenge increases. Consequently, there's a definite difference between running an occasional Class 4 rapid and dealing with an entire river in this class. Also, as river difficulty increases, the danger to swimming paddlers becomes greater. Allow an extra margin of safety between skills and river ratings when the water is cold or if the river is remote or inaccessible.

Class 1: Easy.
- *Fast-moving water with riffles and small waves.*
- *Few obstructions, all obvious and easily missed with little training.*
- *Risk to swimmers is slight.*
- *Self-rescue is easy.*

Class 2: Novice.
- *Straightforward rapids with wide, clear channels that are evident without scouting.*
- *Occasional maneuvering may be required, but rocks and medium-sized waves are easily missed by trained paddlers.*
- *Swimmers are seldom injured and group assistance, while helpful, is seldom needed.*
- *Rapids at the upper end of this difficulty range are designated "Class 2+."*

Class 3: Intermediate.
- *Rapids with moderate, irregular waves that may be difficult to avoid and that can swamp an open canoe.*
- *Complex maneuvers in fast current and good boat control in tight passages or around ledges are often required.*
- *Large waves or strainers may be present but are easily avoided.*
- *Strong eddies and powerful current effects can be found, particularly on large-volume rivers.*
- *Scouting is advisable for inexperienced parties.*
- *Injuries while swimming are rare.*
- *Self-rescue is usually easy, but group assistance may be required to avoid long swims.*
- *Rapids at the lower or upper end of this difficulty range are designated "Class 3-" or "Class 3+" respectively.*

Class 4: Advanced.
- *Intense, powerful but predictable rapids requiring precise boat handling in turbulent water.*
- *Depending on the character of the river, there may be large, unavoidable waves and holes or constricted passages demanding fast maneuvers under pressure.*
- *A fast, reliable eddy turn may be needed to initiate maneuvers, scout rapids or rest.*
- *Rapids may require "must make" moves above dangerous hazards.*
- *Scouting may be necessary the first time down.*
- *Risk of injury to swimmers is moderate to high, and water conditions may make self-rescue difficult.*
- *Group assistance for rescue is often essential but requires practiced skills.*
- *A strong Eskimo-roll is highly recommended.*
- *Rapids at the lower or upper end of this difficulty range are designated "Class 4-" or "Class 4+" respectively.*

Class 5: Expert.
- *Extremely long, obstructed or very violent rapids that expose a paddler to added risk.*
- *Drops may contain large, unavoidable waves and holes or steep, congested chutes with complex, demanding routes.*
- *Rapids may continue for long distances between pools, demanding a high level of fitness.*
- *What eddies exist may be small, turbulent or difficult to reach.*
- *Several of these factors may be combined at the high end of this class.*
- *Scouting is recommended but may be difficult.*
- *Swims are dangerous, and rescue is often difficult even for experts.*
- *A very reliable Eskimo-roll, proper equipment, extensive experience and practiced rescue skills are essential.*
- *Because of the large range of difficulty that exists beyond Class 4, Class 5 is an open-ended, multiple-level scale, designated Class 5.0, 5.1, 5.2, etc. Each level is an order of magnitude more difficult than the previous one. For instance, the increase in difficulty from Class 5.0 to Class 5.1 is a similar order of magnitude as the increase from Class 4 to Class 5.0.*

Class 6: Extreme and Exploratory.
- *Comprises runs that have almost never been attempted and often exemplify the extremes of difficulty, unpredictability and danger.*
- *The consequences of errors may be very severe and rescue may be impossible.*
- *For teams of experts only, at favorable water levels, after close personal inspection and taking all precautions.*

River Morphology

All river formations are caused by either a change in gradient or a change in direction of the current. A basic understanding of river formations is a prerequisite for whitewater. *Path of the Paddle* explains the classic formations you see on a river and a few of their variations. You need to know what an eddy is, for example, to do an eddy turn. As your skill increases, examining the nuances of the current will help you take better advantage of the power of the water and will make your maneuvers more efficient. For the most part, we see rivers in two dimensions—now try to imagine what the riverbed looks like and how the water flows under the surface, so you can predict what the water will do to a boat.

Eddy

Eddies occur when an obstruction changes the direction of the current. Water fills in the void behind the obstruction to form an eddy. The relative difference in speed between the main current and the eddy current is important. We'll call that the *current differential*. If the flow is slow or the change in direction is small, such as a slight bend in the riverbank, the current differential will be weak. However, if the flow is fast or the change in direction is steep, which makes the flow fast, the current differential will be strong.

Eddylines   The components of an eddy are very visible. The eddyline is the transition zone between the current going downstream and the current in the eddy rushing back to the obstruction and exiting again into the main current. Identify the sweet spot of the eddyline. That is the point with the strongest current differential and the zone that you normally would use to do an eddy turn. It is near the top of the eddy. At the top of the eddy, the water slows as it hits the obstruction. Near the bottom of the eddy, the water is going into the eddy, so you have a wider eddyline and below that, the water starts spilling downstream out the bottom of the eddy. The depth and the contour of the river bottom have a significant influence on the character of the eddyline. Squirt boaters who perform maneuvers below the surface of the water think of the eddyline as a three-dimensional wall—with currents going vertically as well as horizontally. If the riverbed drops away or the water becomes deeper along an eddyline, currents will travel downward, and whirlpools may form if there is a lot of volume. Whirlpools form sporadically and then move downriver along the eddyline. If you sit on the eddyline or cross it slowly and wait for a whirlpool to form, you can stick your bow or stern in the whirlpool and sometimes the end becomes slightly elevated. It's kind of fun to be spun around by strong currents. Be aware, however, that all the water in the vicinity is descending, and in big whirlpools an upside-down boat or swimmer may have trouble reaching the surface until the whirlpool dissipates. If the vortex of the whirlpool is more than six inches below the surface, find something smaller to play in until you're familiar with the forces involved. If the depth of water in the eddy is less than in the main current, water will be coming to the surface to form a wide boiling eddyline. It's more difficult to control the angle of the boat in boils, so generally you will want to cross those eddylines aggressively. If the water is deep all around the eddy, the eddyline will be narrow and distinct and there will be a strong current differential, even if there isn't a lot of gradient change.

Tongues

Tongues and standing waves are caused by a change in the gradient of the riverbed. Where the riverbed is steep, the flow speeds up; the water stretches out and has a smooth undisturbed surface known as a *tongue*. Tongues can be steep and long, as shown in photo 4, or shorter with less gradient. If there are obstructions above an increase in gradient, the current will be deflected and a reactionary wave will be created going diagonally from the obstruction into the tongue. An eddy will be created behind the obstruction, but the steeper the gradient the less water there is available to fill in the eddy. These reactionaries will define a V in the undisturbed tongue, with the apex downstream. The tongue has solid, unaerated green water, and as long as it is deep enough you can get effective strokes to accelerate, to alter your angle or to maintain momentum while crossing the grain. Remember that the water is speeding up, so you'll have less time to alter your course than on the flatter water above the tongue. Also, on a steeper tongue, gravity will have a greater effect and will try to pull you straight down the fall line. At the end of the tongue or V, the gradient will either increase into a waterfall or decrease and form a hole or standing waves.

4 *Tongues.*

Standing waves

Standing waves are formed when the gradient decreases and the water slows down. Fast-moving water rushes into the slower-moving water and piles up to form smooth-peaked waves. There will be a series of waves that are the same distance apart and diminishing in height. The more abrupt the gradient change, the shorter the distance or period between them. The greater the volume of water, the higher the waves.

The key to reading a standing wave is to first look at the surface of the water as if it wasn't moving. The wave often has ribs that extend farther upstream, with steeper sections or shallower parts in the crest. Boaters seek standing waves for surfing or to assist in ferrying. They look for standing waves that are connected to each other or close enough that you can use them. Ask yourself, if the water were clay, where would a marble roll? Also consider the direction that the water is flowing in relation to the peak of the wave. A standing wave may be perpendicular to the shore but have water going through it on an angle. It will be easy to ferry from the upstream end of the wave to the downstream end of the wave and more difficult or impossible to ferry in the other direction.

Breaking wave

A breaking wave is similar to a standing wave but is caused by a more abrupt drop, which produces a steeper wave. The abrupt drop can be caused by a boulder or simply a depression in the riverbed. Water falls down the upstream side of the wave as a white, aerated foam pile. The more abrupt the drop or depression, the farther down the wave you'll find the foam pile, or break. Only a matter of degrees separate a standing wave from a breaking wave, and some waves will be standing for a while, then breaking, then standing once more. If you surf on a wave like that, the extra turbulence you create will "mush out" the wave and cause it to break. The breaking water travels upstream and can help a boat to stay on a wave.

A very abrupt drop or depression causes a large foam pile and is considered a *hole*. Arbitrarily, we say that if the green water is descending when it meets the foam pile, it is a hole; if the green water reaches the bottom of the trough and starts back up before it meets the foam pile, it is a breaking wave (see photo 5).

Slide

We refer to a sloping rock without enough water to actually float a boat as a *slide* (photo 6). Rock climbers might refer to some of the routes I have seen Paul run

as moist 5.8's. The more water or algae or the smoother the rock, the less friction there will be and the more vinyl will remain on your boat.

Hole

When water flows over an abrupt drop it will tend to continue downward. This down-rushing green water resurfaces downstream as a boil similar to the peak of a wave. The void between the boil and the down-rushing green water is filled by water from the peak of the boil (see photo 7). This water recirculates upstream and when it meets the green water it goes down and resurfaces at the boil line. The point where the recirculating water meets the down-rushing current is the hole, since it is the lowest point of the formation. This can be a great place to play with vertical moves, but if the hole is strong, it can be difficult to exit, whether you're in a boat or swimming. The more green water going into the hole, the stronger the recirculation. A boil line located more than a few feet from the deepest part of the hole indicates a strong recirculation. The greater the height from the peak to the deepest part of the hole, the more violent the hole. The ends of the hole are important features in determining suitability for play. If the ends meet the shoreline, rocks or a dam abutment, it will be hard to exit the hole. It will also be hard to exit if the lowest part of the hole is much

5 Breaking wave.

6 Slide.

7 Hole.

below the surface of the water rushing past the end of the hole. If the hole angles downstream, it will be easier to exit than if the hole points upstream. Try to assess the depth of water at the hole. For rodeo moves, you want the hole to be deep enough to avoid hitting the ends of your boat (too much). At the 1995 Rodeo Worlds in Augsburg, Germany, we thought that our boats would fall apart before we finished the practice sessions; however, even though the hole was a bit shallow in places, it was still great, and by experimenting, we found spots deep enough for good vertical moves.

Woodall Shoals

Holes need a pretty close examination to determine how sticky they will be. Some of the biggest and nastiest-looking are the hardest to stay in (or, depending on your perspective, the easiest to exit). One of the longest visits I had with a hole was in Woodall Shoals, on section 4 of the Chattooga river on the Georgia–South Carolina border. I scouted it first, then watched as a couple of kayakers ran a tight line skirting it. I recognized the hole was one I didn't want to experience, but the line looked do-able. As I started charging down the rapid, I suddenly remembered that this was the first time in a year or more that I had been in a kayak and the kayakers making the line look easy were among the best in the southeast United States.

My line sent me through the left edge of the hole. Things still looked under control at that point; I told myself to just lean forward, plant the paddle and punch the hole. Sitting down with your feet up in front of you is a good position for watching whitewater videos, but when it comes to punching serious holes, I think sitting up high with your knees on the bottom of the boat is the only way to be. And you can forget about those little nine-foot boats that look like they've been run over by a truck. They're great when you have

to tie six boats on a car, but for charging through holes, give me that big ol' open boat.

I back-endered. Still no panic—I like holes. I rolled up to find I was still in the hole but not completely in my kayak; I don't know how you're supposed to stay in those things without thigh straps.

I would just get myself reorganized and settled back in my boat, when that low-volume end would once again dip underwater. I would have been happy if I could have gotten rid of one of the blades on my paddle. You need only one to roll with, and the other one seemed to be getting in the way. Throughout this washing-machine thrashing, I kept thinking that I would have been a lot happier in my open boat. The kayak must have sensed this and we soon parted company. Without my floundering strokes, the kayak left the hole quickly. I, however, remained. Simultaneously, I had that sense of almost being able to touch the bottom and almost being able to get my head out of the water. The treading water maneuver that I'd learned as a child just wasn't doing anything for me, so I chose a more proactive approach. I shoved myself to the bottom to get a good push-off to the surface. The first two attempts replenished my air supply and the third sent me downstream.

In my open boat I would have been stuck, as well, but I think that things happen slower in an open boat. People who actually know how to paddle a kayak could probably have used those low-volume ends to their advantage, started cartwheeling and worked out of the hole. I think that in some holes, the greater volume of the open boat can be an advantage over kayaks. The open boater has more leverage and a longer reach to pull one end up and out of the hole for an ender—plus the boat's extra weight provides more momentum to punch the hole in the first place. I'm not ready to declare that it's easier to get out of a hole with an open boat than it is with a kayak, but on that day, in that hole, my second wish would have been for an open boat instead of a kayak.

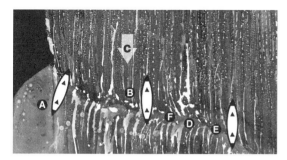

8 Surfing wave, side view.

9 Surfing wave, top view.

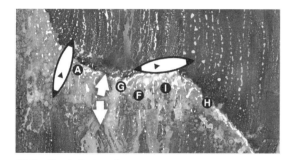

10 Surfing hole, side view.

11 Surfing hole, top view.

Anatomy of a Surfing Wave

To read a surfing wave you need to be able to recognize more than just whether it is a curling or a standing wave.

Sweet spot

This is that mythical area of the wave that is best for whatever maneuver you are attempting. It may be the steepest part, or it may be the slope that just happens to suit the length and rocker of your canoe.

Shoulder

(Illus. 8, fig. A)   These are the sides of the wave that slope away from the peak. The shoulder may curve away downstream, causing you to fall off the wave during a front surf (illus. 9, fig. E) or the shoulders may curve upstream, helping you to stay on but, more important, assisting you in catching the wave.

Trough

(Illus. 8 and 9, fig. B)   This is the lowest point of the wave, at its upstream base. For example, the lowest point between two standing waves.

Foam pile

(Illus. 8 and 9, fig. F)   The foamy white stuff on top of a breaking wave. Often a smooth wave will develop a foam pile when your canoe is on it.

Current

(Illus. 8–10, fig. C)   River current generally flows downhill, but it changes directions, for example, in an eddy and when it forms a wave. The water on the face of a wave definitely goes up.

Backside

(Illus. 8 and 9, fig. D)   Every wave has a backside, or downstream side. Surfing too far down the wave will cause the bow of the canoe to hit the backside of the preceding wave (illus. 8). This will fill up the canoe or send you careering off the wave.

Anatomy of a Surfing Hole

To really work a hole you need to know its strengths and weaknesses. Most diagrams show you how to escape from a hole, but we're interested in how to enter and stay in it.

Shoulder

This is the edge of the hole, and it may lead into the hole (illus. 11, fig. A), making it difficult to exit. Or the shoulder may fall away downstream (illus. 11, fig. H), tending to push you away from the meat of the hole. But don't count on it if the trough of the hole is significantly lower than the surrounding water.

Trough, or meat, of the hole

The deepest part of the hole, usually the stickiest.

Foam pile

(Illus. 10 and 11, fig. F)   This includes the area from the most upstream edge of the foamy bit to just downstream of the boil line.

Boil line

(Illus. 11, fig. I)   You need to stay upstream of this to stay in the hole.

Backside

(Illus. 10, fig. D)   The water downstream of the boil line flowing away from the hole. Not a useful place to be.

River Morphology

12 Big water!

Slide and pour-over holes

In a slide hole, the green water enters the hole on an angle rather than vertically. The angle can be quite flat—30 degrees or less—and still form a hole if it is sliding into a pool. This type of hole is ideal for rodeo moves, since the green water is just under the recirculating, aerated layer and many rodeo moves require lots of interaction between the greenwater and the foam pile. In a pour-over hole, the slope of the green water is more vertical. This makes the layer of aerated, recirculating water much thicker.

13 Pour over.

Ledge and waterfall

A ledge or waterfall is a pour-over hole where the water falls from a greater height. A hole and a boil line will still be located downstream. The interaction between the down-flowing water and objects floating in the hole becomes greater as the volume of water and the height of the drop increase. It's sometimes hard to predict whether there are hazards such as logs or rocks located below the surface in the aerated water beneath waterfalls. The lip or the edge at the top of the drop is a critical feature if you're considering running the waterfall. The lip sometimes has a square abrupt edge, or may even be slightly upturned in what could be called a *ski jump*. If the lip is rounded and the falling water is thick, solid and not particularly vertical, we call it a *ramp*.

Boils

Boils can occur exclusive of holes where the riverbed deflects a strong current toward the surface. Boils generally occur in deep large-volume rivers. They sometimes appear, surge and disappear in places where the gradient decreases and the flow slows. Often, they occur where whirlpools do. They may also have a destabilizing effect on your boat. A seam line occurs where water flowing out from the center of the boil flows downward at its edge. Being sideways on a seam line will feel similar to side-surfing a hole.

Floods

Flood levels can provide some awesome boating conditions. But flooding rivers also offer ample opportunities to mess up big time. Newly formed holes in now unrecognizable rapids provide major hazards once the shoreline has been submerged. Eddies may be non-existent or guarded by trees that are very easy to wrap your boat around. The rapids will now tend to flow into each other with long wave trains instead of that expected calm pool. On the harder runs it is not uncommon for paddlers to lose their boats permanently if they swim. Once you bail out of your boat, you are at the mercy of the river because the strong currents will make swimming very difficult. Retrieval of your boat may be impossible as you can't expect your buddies to race headlong into unknown rapids in flood with few eddies. The difficulty is compounded by the fact that the muddy brown color of the water makes it difficult to see the rocks.

High water levels may erode the banks, causing trees to fall into the river and form sweepers. Debris moving downstream in the rapids during flood levels could be a hazard but usually it just floats in the eddies, making it hard to reach shore. As the water level drops, trees may become stranded midstream or across narrow channels. Occasionally, flash floods may even move boulders—reshaping the riverbed itself.

River Morphology–Nasties

15 Collision insurance for your canoe?

Although you can never be fully prepared for every circumstance, as this photo illustrates, you must be aware of all the various hazards found in whitewater.

We've tried to outline how to recognize each hazard and why you need to avoid it. However, the skills needed to rescue someone in trouble go beyond the scope of this book. Several good books and videos on river rescue are available, and at least one of them should make it into your library. Of course, there's no substitute for the hands-on experience gained through a river-rescue course. Certified river-rescue instructors do an excellent job of teaching the latest rescue techniques. It's well worth the time and effort.

Ice

Ice is a hazard that few of our southern paddling buddies are familiar with. Those of you who paddle in areas with a real winter, however, be aware. Surface ice can reduce the size of slow-moving eddies. Treat overhanging shore ice as you would an undercut rock. In general, the ice will only be at the surface, but chunks of ice from upstream may have broken off and become jammed beneath the overhanging shore ice. If you're contemplating running a rapid that ends with the flow going under the ice and you think you can just paddle up onto the ice, contemplate further that if you flip or slide back in you'll spend your last breath looking at a hockey rink from below.

However, winter paddling can be fun. In early winter, the thin film of ice in the eddies and on your clothing and

14 Shore ice, early spring.

paddle merely builds character. For the most part, you can ignore it. At one of our winter surfing spots, occasionally pans of ice float by. We try to avoid them, but occasionally they flow underneath us. I would definitely avoid playing in a hole where these ice pans can flip end for end, and stay away from icebergs if there are rocks or shallows where you could become caught between ice and a hard spot. After a long cold snap, the river can freeze from the riverbed up, and mushy ice builds up on rocks in the riverbed and can form ledges, holes and eddies. When it reaches the surface, islands of ice quickly form.

Here are a few tips for winter paddling. See if you can figure out the reasons behind the suggestions.

- *Don't put your car keys in a zippered pocket.*
- *Keep your hands on your paddle in the proper position as much as possible.*
- *Try to thaw the ice off your boat.*
- *Don't rely on your throwline working.*

16 Strainer.

Strainers

Strainers are trees lodged in currents whose branches literally strain the water as it passes through them, trapping all sorts of debris. The tree may be partially or completely submerged. One spring, I learned a valuable lesson on a small creek not far from home. Mark, myself and one other paddler had been really working the creek with our playboats, catching eddies and trying to surf every wave we saw. Near the end of the whitewater section the creek split into several small channels. I chose the smallest, guessing it would provide the steepest gradient and most excitement. It did. The end was totally blocked off by driftwood, causing the water to flow through the trees. Just before rejoining the creek, the water flowed over a barely submerged log about four inches in diameter, lying at about a 45-degree angle to the current. Without giving it a second thought, I gained momentum to slide over it. Unfortunately, I stalled out before I was even halfway across the log.

The current that was traveling diagonally to the log instantly grabbed my stern and swung it downstream. Fortunately, I was already leaning forward from trying to teeter-totter over the log, so I quickly shifted to what was becoming the downstream gunwale. Much to my surprise, the canoe continued to tip upstream. By diving out of my thigh straps and lying on the downstream gunwale, I managed to stop the boat from broaching on the log. I

probed the depth of the water on the downstream side of the log—and found that it was only knee-deep. I crawled out and stood up, feeling somewhat chagrined.

Such minor events aren't really worth working up a sweat about—since the water was slow moving and shallow. But when I pondered why the canoe had tipped upstream so dramatically, an important fact became apparent. When the canoe is perpendicular to the log and halfway up on it, the pivot point is in the center of the canoe, most likely at your knees. When the canoe is on top of the log and parallel to it, however, the balance point is between your knees but now the canoe teeters from side to side, and is much more unstable. Picture the canoe falling off the log sideways. It will roll off. The only way to stay upright is to slide off sideways. This won't happen in a current because the water is pushing your hull against the log, creating too much friction for you to slide back into the water on the upstream side. For the same reason, you tilt downstream *before* broaching on a rock. The difference is that unless the rock is undercut, the worst that can happen is that the canoe will wrap, probably becoming partially submerged, whereas with a log the current pushes you under the obstacle. If you can't avoid a tree and the current is strong enough that you may be unable to stay upright when you hit it, make sure you're on the way out of the boat on contact so you can get a headstart over the strainer.

17 Potholes hidden by falls.

When you find yourself in the water upstream of a strainer, the objective is to swim aggressively toward it doing a head-up front crawl so that you're going faster than the current and can launch yourself over the strainer before the current catches your legs and pulls them under. Wearing a quality personal flotation device (PFD) is essential because the impact will be considerable. During a strainer simulation exercise the impact I received as I swam over the log momentarily winded me.

Other hazards include trees at the bottom of drops and in undercuts. They become lodged at odd angles, trapping other debris and compounding the danger of the situation.

Pothole

A pothole is an eroded depression in the rock of the river bottom, usually located at the base of a steep drop. Stones that become caught in the depression act like grit, wearing away the bedrock and creating a pothole. Sometimes the side of the pothole wears away, creating a hole that the current flows through. This poses a real threat, as the passage may be too small for a swimmer to pass through. A more likely scenario is that a swimmer could catch his or her foot in a small pothole at the bottom of a steep drop. Photo 18 is of the same drop as 17 but without water. In

18 Joe Langman standing in a pot hole at low water.

photo 18, Joe Langman is standing in a pothole with his left hand on the river bottom! The pothole is about three feet in diameter. A larger pothole located at the base of a pour-over can create a strong recirculating current that makes it difficult to exit the hole.

To read first-hand accounts of near-misses with many of these hazards, check out the *Journal of the American Whitewater Affiliation.* For a little more reading that will keep you awake at night, read the *Whitewater Safety Task Force Newsletter,* published by Charlie Walbridge. Walbridge compiles paddling-related accident reports that warn of trends developing in our paddling community.

Suck hole

This river nasty is right up there among the top three in its ability to induce nightmares in paddlers. A suck hole is just what its name implies—a tunnel with water flowing through it that sucks you in. The danger is that it may become narrow at the outflow or debris may be lodged in it.

Photo 19 was taken on Cane Creek in Tennessee. The paddler pulled up to what looked like shore, only to have his canoe pulled underwater into the suck hole. Fortunately, he reacted quickly enough to hop out before things became critical. A rope attached to the end of the canoe extracted it easily from the suck hole.

Sieve

A sieve is similar to a suck hole, but is usually formed by rocks lodged in the current. The danger is that the water flows through the nooks and crannies. Debris and hapless paddlers become pinned underwater by the force of the current. Note the t-grip of a paddle sticking out of the small sieve in photo 21. As with other notable nasties, local paddlers can often alert you to known hazards. In general, the harder the run, the more likely you are to encounter formations that create these dangers. Since you're exposed to them more frequently, you begin to

19 Suckhole.

20 Suckhole, diagram.

21 Sieve.

22 Sieve, diagram.

23 Undercut.

24 Undercut at low water.

take them for granted. However, this doesn't mean that the consequences of hitting one are any less severe.

Undercuts

Anytime water flows under a rock or river bank it is said to be undercut. Undercuts can form through erosion, as in water hitting a rock face, or because of the shape of the rock itself. A large round boulder midstream will act as an

undercut since its sides curve under the water. A slab of rock resting in the stream bed can be far worse, as water may actually flow completely under it. Undercuts caused by erosion of a rock face are easier to read since the imposing rock face will likely attract your attention. The lack of water bouncing off the cliff face may also indicate the extent to which the face is undercut. Compare photo 23 with photo 24, taken at low water.

River Rescue

25 I should've gone golfing.

Experience is a great teacher, and trial and error is a great way to learn. However, in a rescue situation, you may not have time to experiment, and as a victim, you wouldn't want your paddling friends winging it. Most of us who come from a tripping background have first-hand experience at pulling wrapped canoes off midstream rocks, so we appreciate the force of the current and the potential for things to go wrong. Fortunately, conscientious paddlers and rescue professionals typically have the knowledge, techniques and experience needed to deal with most of the rescue situations you'll encounter on the river.

The river-rescue techniques described here won't teach you how to perform them. The purpose is to highlight some of the rescue techniques that have been developed. If any of this material is new to you, take the time to learn these skills. Two excellent sources are *River Rescue* by Les Bechdel and Slim Ray, published by Appalachian Mountain Club Books, and *Whitewater Rescue Manual* by Charlie Walbridge and Wayne A. Sundmacher Sr., published by Ragged Mountain Press. You'll also find a good overview of river-rescue techniques in real-life situations in the American Canoe

Association's video *Heads Up! River Rescue for River Runners*. These resources should supplement, but not replace, the hands-on experience of a river-rescue course. By taking such courses, you will realize the power of moving water and the difficulties of working in it. Persuade your paddling buddies to take the course as well. It's kind of like knowing CPR: as a victim, you hope that those around you have taken a course. Practicing the river-rescue skills and techniques you learn will keep them current and give you more experience to draw on to make effective decisions in a rescue situation.

Foot entrapment

Foot entrapment is a serious danger, especially since it is more likely to happen to novices, who assume that the easier whitewater holds no danger. The simple solution is to never, ever stand up in rapids. It's just too easy to jam your foot between the rocks and be pushed over by the current.

Rare spots are nasty enough that you could catch an arm or your clothing in them if you were swimming after a bail-out, even if you didn't attempt to push off the bottom. Local paddlers can often warn you of such spots.

Falls and pour-overs are additional hazards. As the water becomes vertical on the drop, so does the swimmer, who may then be driven to the bottom in what is essentially a standing position. The accepted coping method is to curl up in a ball so that your limbs won't get jammed into a hole or crack. Doesn't sound like fun, but let's face it, if you're swimming over a falls, your options are limited.

26 Throw rope.

Throwing a rope

This would involve throw lines and throw bags. They are used differently and each has its benefits. There are also different types of throw lines and throw bags, which also have different uses and benefits. See Chapter 2 for details. I have used throw bags to rescue swimmers more often than I have used all the other rescue techniques combined. Throw ropes are also an essential component of rescues.

Amoeba

Members of the group take turns moving in the eddy of the upstream person while they stabilize each other. This method enables a group of people to move through shallow moving water (photo 25). In deeper water you must be exceedingly careful about foot entrapment and must move the group as a unit. The *amoeba* is a fast, technology-free way of getting people out of the water quickly.

Tripod

The only equipment this method requires is low-tech–a stick. Place the stick upstream so you can lean on it. Use it to balance while changing your footing. You can do it alone, but other people standing in the eddy that you create will help to hold you steady. There tends to be a little more mayhem if the group is swept away by the current, what with folks falling on one another.

27 Strong swimmer.

Strong swimmer

There is a whole variety of land-based tethered-swimmer rescues. They require a person to be clipped into a line to assist them while they are in the current. A proper quick-release rescue harness on a personal flotation device is a must for these rescues. Although fast and seemingly simple, any rescue involving tethered swimmers is dangerous. Learn the techniques and practice them in a controlled situation.

Snag line

A snag line across the river can be used to assist victims who are entrapped. By anchoring both ends of the line it becomes a static line that can be used as a zip line. Angled downstream, the zip line can be used to ferry someone across a river.

Once, when I was participating in a river-rescue course, we decided to use a zip line to reach a simulated victim perched on a midstream rock in a Class 1 current. Although I should have known better, I attached a quick-

release waist belt to the static line. Because I had trimmed the excess webbing off the belt, it was too short to fit around my PFD at the chest, where it should have been. As I approached the victim, the current suddenly doubled me over at the waist. The pressure on my abdomen was intense. As I reached for the quick release, I slid into the eddy, gasping–and had a whole new respect for the formidable adversary that the current can be.

28 Strainer.

Strainer simulation

You'll really appreciate the foam padding that the front of your PFD provides during this exercise. Once again, practicing this maneuver opens your eyes to the strength of the current. Tether a log in the current to simulate a strainer. Using the head-up front crawl, aggressively swim downstream toward the log, propel yourself up and over it. If you float up to the log at the same speed as or slower than the current, you'll be pulled under the simulated strainer–an enlightening experience, to say the least.

Telfer lower

This time-consuming boat-based rescue requires extensive gear and rescuers. The very next day after teaching this skill to a group of instructors, we had a boat become snagged at the end of a 70-foot throw rope. The bag had become lodged between some rocks on the bottom, resulting in the 17-foot canoe doing a Moby Dick impression at the brink of the next

29 Telfer lower.

set of rapids. Although we could ferry to the canoe in a tandem canoe, we couldn't stay in position to wait for it to surface and we would be unlikely to get hold of it anyway. We were also concerned that it was surfacing so violently that it would flip us. You can imagine the glee with which the instructors sprang into action to put their new skills to the test. With the telfer lower we were able to safely retrieve our boat.

Swimming

The tactics that you decide to use once you are out of your boat and in the water will depend on the kind of water and the particular situation you find yourself in. Consider this before you run the rapid–you can waste precious time in the water trying to figure out which direction to swim. The basics should be instinct to you. But just in case they're not, here's the list:

- *get away from the boat*
- *keep your feet up*
- *try to self-rescue*

A couple of situations warrant different tactics. If you have to swim through deep, boil-infested water, hang on to your boat. It has more flotation than just you and a PFD and will help to keep your head above water. If there is danger downstream, use an aggressive heads-up front crawl to reach shore as fast as possible.

2 EQUIPMENT

Canoe Design

Canoe design used to be a compromise so canoes could be versatile. That is, the perfect canoe was one that you could paddle tandem with gear, yet take out on the weekend for some solo playing in the rapids. Recent designs, however, focus on the canoe performing just one whitewater task efficiently. This means that you may have to compromise on the range of activities you can perform with one boat. Fortunately, all of the new designs perform the basics to some degree. Boat designs, it seems, become more specialized as skill levels increase.

Canoe design is a tricky science and an intricate art. Boat designers combine many different design components that affect various performance characteristics to achieve an overall performance character. Hopefully, the characteristics they've chosen meet the needs of the paddlers they're intended for. For example, playboats aimed at first-time buyers generally have both stability and good tracking ability, while advanced playboats are responsively edgy and ender well.

As you read about each design component, keep in mind that without examining the rest of the boat's design it's hard to predict how it will affect performance. Once you understand each component, examine the photos of the different canoe shapes. These canoes are by no means the only great boats available on the market. Use them just to compare hull shapes. Incidentally it is easier and almost as much fun to actually test the canoe out on the water, rather than just speculate on how it will perform.

Rocker

A canoe with rocker that from the side looks like a banana (illustration 30) pivots easier than a canoe with a straight keel. You must just decide how much rocker

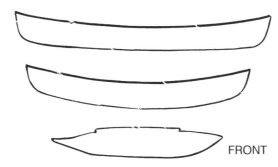

30 Rocker

FRONT

you really need. Rocker also contributes to keeping the boat dry, as it will bob rather than travel in a straight line through the face of each wave. For surfing, more rocker means less pearling on steep waves, but the slower hull speed makes it harder to catch some waves.

Length

Longer canoes usually move faster; shorter canoes turn more quickly. Because shorter canoes are lighter (less material) and have less friction (less surface area), they accelerate more quickly.

Width

The wider the boat, the more stability and volume it will have. More width will make it harder for the paddler to reach the water, tilt the boat over and go from edge to edge.

Bottom and chine

The bottom of a boat determines its stability when the boat is flat (*initial stability*) and when it is tilted (*secondary stability*). It also determines how the boat will carve, or turn, when it is moving forward, and what happens when a current hits it from the side. The *chine* refers to the transition from the bottom to the side of the canoe. A flat bottom creates a hard chine and has good initial stability. (Think of a box. When

you tilt a box on an edge, it doesn't have much secondary stability.) However, a hard chine provides more resistance and carves a turn faster than a soft chine. (See the discussion of eddy turns in the Solo Playboat chapter.) The upstream edge of a hard-chined design is more likely to catch and flip the boat in cross-currents or when side-surfing. Outside-tilt eddy turns in a solo playboat take advantage of this characteristic. A slightly arched bottom creates a soft chine, and has less initial stability (comparable to a rocking chair). When tilted, this rounded edge offers more secondary stability than a hard-chined design. A hard-chined boat demands that you pay attention, since the response of the canoe to your strokes or to a misplaced tilt is immediate. A softer-chined boat seems more predictable and forgiving.

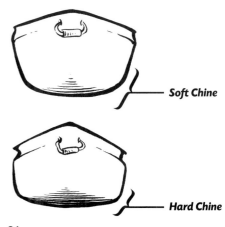

Soft Chine

Hard Chine

31

Flare

Flare is the outward curve of the hull above the chine (illustration 31). Flare at the ends contributes to dryness but makes enders more difficult. Flare in the middle improves secondary stability by softening the chine and providing a flatter surface when the boat is tilted.

Classic Canoes

Tumblehome

Tumblehome is the inward curving of the cross-section of the hull just below the gunwales. Tumblehome makes it easier to reach the water and allows you to tilt farther before water pours in. When extreme tumblehome occurs abruptly within three or four inches of the gunwale, you can have the advantages of flare and tumblehome.

Depth

One of the advantages of deep canoes is that they are drier. However, more depth also has some disadvantages. Deep canoes have more material in them and are heavier. Less depth at the end makes enders easier. When you finish a roll, a deep canoe will hold more water. Gunwales that rise dramatically at the ends hinder the boat from going all the way upside down if you flip offside.

Prospector

Prospector designs originated with the Chestnut Canoe Company. Many versions are available in glass and a few in Royalex. The shallow arch and soft chine give it a sensitive feel, good secondary stability and quickness going from tilt to tilt. It also has good speed and a nice compromise of turning and tracking ability. Although it isn't as dry and lacks the carrying capacity of some slower 16-footers, it's still a very good choice if you'll be using it for solo and tandem whitewater as well as river, or even flatwater, tripping. The 17-foot Prospector is equally versatile and performs very well in whitewater when loaded. Few other 17-footers are as responsive if you are using them empty for day trips.

Bluehole Cumberland

The Cumberland was also known as the Starburst in its aluminum gunwale version. This boat also has a shallow-arched, soft-chined hull for stable and predictable tilts. Having more rocker than the Prospector helps it turn quicker. The rocker, along with good depth, contributes to its dryness. It is a good classic boat for day trips and has good whitewater performance for tripping but lacks speed.

32 Prospector

Mad River Freedom

The success of the Mad River Explorer led Mad River to design the Freedom specifically for whitewater. The shallow-V, soft-chined hull offers excellent initial and secondary stability. Flare above the waterline at the ends gives it both dryness and carrying capacity. It is very forgiving and predictable, and its dryness and carrying capacity are big assets for river tripping.

Dagger Legend

The Legend has a harder chine in the middle and softer chines at the ends. This results in responsive, yet forgiving and predictable, turns. It has very good initial and secondary stability. The large full ends keep the boat dry when you're surfing or when you hit standing waves, plus it has good carrying capacity for river tripping. It's faster than it looks, although it isn't a fast boat.

33 Bluehole Cumberland

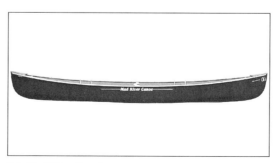

34 Mad River Freedom

35 Dagger Legend

Tandem Playboats

Mohawk XL 15

Mohawk's XL series evolved from Nolan Whitesell's Piranha and Scamp designs. Mohawk started with the XL 13, then made 15-, 14-, 12- and 11-foot versions of the same hull. The boats have a shallow arch and soft chine, and a moderate amount of rocker. The XL 15 turned out to be a crossover between a river tripper and tandem playboat. Without as much rocker as more specialized playboats of the time, such as the Dagger Dimension, it is slower to turn, yet predictable, forgiving and fairly responsive. Its full ends compensate for its shortness as a river tripper, but it is slow compared with 16-foot boats.

Dagger Caption

The 14-foot Caption is a fun tandem playboat. It has a shallow-arched, soft-chined hull with quite a bit of rocker. It handles for two people the way a soft-chined, solo playboat handles for one person. Some people choose to paddle it as a solo boat. Lots of rocker and full ends make it an easy-turning surfing machine. The quick-turning ability of this tandem boat makes tight creek moves possible for experienced paddlers on Class 4 water.

Mad River Synergy

At 15 feet, the Synergy is a quick-tandem playboat. It is a shallow-arched, soft-chined boat with lots of rocker. Turns carve quickly and predictably. It doesn't turn as quickly as the shorter Caption, but it is faster and tracks better. The full ends are quite dry when running big water. This boat is ideal for tandem day trippers who want a responsive, smooth-turning boat for Class 2–3 water without sacrificing speed.

36 Mohawk XL 15.

37 Dagger Caption.

38 Mad River Synergy.

Solo Playboats

The evolution of solo playboat design

Unless you've had your helmet pulled down too far, you've probably noticed there are a lot more kayaks than open canoe playboats on the river. Classic canoes still outnumber kayaks and arguably are more suited to whitewater tripping than kayaks. But when it comes to day trips, open canoe playboats are a minority. There are advantages to that (less competition at the rodeos), but the disadvantage is that it is hard for the manufacturers to justify new designs every year for such a small market. In the rodeo category alone, between the 1995 and 1997 World Championships there have been 16 new rodeo kayak designs, while the Massive Aire (a glass production boat), a prototype by Frankie Hubbard, a prototype by Jeff Richards and several "one of" cutdown versions of the Dagger Ocoee were the only new open boats. Including all solo whitewater playboats, there have been six new solo and two new tandem designs between 1993 and 1997. What can we open boaters do about that? Hope that the open boat designers are really clever and come up with perfect designs, buy lots of new boats and give them to our friends, and when we get bored with the existing designs, cut them up and modify them.

A bit of history

At the 1993 rodeo worlds, boat modification in the open boat class amounted to removing decks and trimming the depth at the ends. Ironically, now that the boats are shorter, long decks are back in style. At the 1995 Worlds, most of the boats had the end depth trimmed, some by as much as 6 inches, and many had an inch or two removed from the center depth. Four of the Ocoees were shortened to under 10 feet, including the eventual winner's boat. In addition to more drastic modifications, a new design was introduced. The Departure by Ian Thomson of Massive was an aptly named departure from open playboat design, and turned quite a few heads. Its depth, volume and shape were akin to decked boats, but it had gunwales, float bags and a saddle. A small wave would wash over the cockpit, but it held almost no water so it didn't really require bailing. It could potentially cartwheel and even blast as well as a kayak or C-1. Despite it being a late entry, the open boat competitors collectively agreed it should be allowed to compete. It placed eleventh. In a meeting following the competition, a consensus was reached that some standards were necessary to maintain the character of existing open boats. No one really wanted to restrict evolution in design or the ability to challenge existing ideas, but the skills of coaxing a large volume of boat to verticality and trying to keep the cockpit dry down a creek run or extreme slalom course are skills that are unique to open boats and are worthy of the recognition. Some rules were established for rodeo competition, which we will list.

At the 1997 Worlds, the 10'6" Mohawk Rodeo was the longest boat in the competition and Frankie Hubbard's 9'6" prototype was the shortest. (The rotomolded plastic prototype measured 9'2".) Between 1995 and 1997, quite a few shortened Ocoees appeared on the rivers and in the rodeos. In most cases about a foot was removed from the middle, but Ian Holmes and Joe Langman took 7 or 8 inches out of the ends with very good results. That was not as easy as it sounds. They used different ideas and numerous cuts and tapers were required to get smooth lines on the hull.

Rodeo open boat specifications

- *The depth of the boat must be at least 14 inches for the middle 2 feet of the boat.*
- *The gunwale line may not drop more than 3 inches from the center of the boat to the end.*
- *Neither deck may exceed 22.5 percent of the length of the boat.*
- *Tumblehome may not exceed 3 inches, including gunwales and foam outfitting.*
- *Flotation must be removable and attached only with cord.*
- *Completely solid bulkheads are not permitted. Bulkheads with holes for knees are allowed.*
- *There is no length restriction.*

Smaller and lighter

A boat that is a foot or two shorter is that much lighter to carry and to paddle, and has much less friction to overcome when you want to accelerate. Since this means less effort to move the boat—on the water or on the portage—shorter designs may open the sport to smaller paddlers who are frustrated with the effort required to paddle larger solo playboats.

Easier for beginners

Shorter boats may also make the sport of solo playboating more inviting to beginners. Short boats are easier to turn and surf. A short boat is much more forgiving and fun for a beginner to paddle. A beginner will have a harder time making a short boat track. However, you can learn to make a short boat go in a straight line, but even an expert can't make a long boat turn as quickly as a short boat.

How short for creek boats?

One of the problems that compounds the small market for open boaters and accounts for the reluctance of manufacturers to produce new boats is that as the sport develops and gets more specialized, the boats become less versatile, which perhaps reduces the market further. In 1997 I had a 10-foot Ocoee rodeo boat and a 10-foot Ocoee creek boat. The rodeo boat was narrower (26" at the widest point), had less depth at the ends and middle, and a bit more rocker. The lower volume ends would blast and go through vertical moves better. In my creek boat, more width (29" at the widest point) and less rocker gave me more stability, and more depth made the boat drier. I'm convinced of the benefits of a short creek boat. It turns faster, accelerates more quickly, boofs better and fits in micro-eddies. I was trying to convince Paul to shorten the full-size Ocoee that he uses for creeks while we were going down the Big Sandy in West Virginia. Our conversation was interrupted when we spied a slot move. I was ahead and just barely made it around a tight corner between a few boulders. I looked back to see that Paul had made it over the drop and had his bow and stern lodged against either end of the slot. As his boat sank beneath him, I gave him my best "I told you so" expression. There was no way that an 11-foot boat would have fit through that slot.

Whitesell Piranha

In the late 70s and early 80s, Nolan Whitesell, designer of the Piranha, along with Dave Simpson, Bailey Johnson and Robert Harrison were pioneer open boaters who challenged the hardest rivers being run by kayakers. The 14'3" Piranha is a shallow-arched, soft-chined boat that turns well due to a pivoting bulge in its center. The boat is quite stable and rolls easily. Whitesell Nolan introduced the funnel-shaped bow design, in which the ends flare quickly to provide buoyancy that lifts the bow when you're plowing into waves or going off drops. The Descender and the Whirlwind are shorter, more modern, descendants of the classic Piranha.

Dagger Encore

The Encore was one of many popular designs by Steve Scarborough. The craft introduced harder chines to creek and playboats. Its popularity was long-lasting, particularly in the southeast United States, the heart of Dagger country. Although it is no longer in production, it was at the time a significant improvement over other boats.

Dagger Genesis

Well-known paddler and instructor Bob Foote designed the 13'6" Genesis (with input from Steve Scarborough) in 1992, when playboats were moving shorter than 13 feet. It has a very shallow V in the stern, which improves tracking ability. The design is notable in that the boat carves turns nicely and is relatively responsive. Although many other boats have eclipsed it performance-wise as a solo playboat, including Foote's Dagger Rival, it is included here because it may be one of the best solo whitewater tripping boats around if you want play performance combined with tripping capacity.

39 Western Canoeing Piranha.

40 Dagger Encore.

41 Dagger Genesis.

Mad River Outrage

The Outrage is a co-design of Jim Henry, who built the ME, one of the first boats specifically designed for solo whitewater, and Tom Foster. It has a shallow-arched, soft-chined hull with lots of rocker at the end, giving it good initial and secondary stability, and it turns very easily and predictably when it is flat or tilted. Full high ends along with the rocker make it a very dry boat. It has a bit more edge than the Rival but doesn't track quite as well.

Dagger Rival

The Rival was designed by Bob Foote, with some input by Steve Scarborough. The Rival and the Mad River Outrage were first introduced when the best boaters were in the hard-chined Vipers and Ocoees. These slightly softer-chined boats were aimed at less aggressive paddlers or those who wanted a more predictable and forgiving ride. The boat is fast and holds its angle. Full ends keep it dry but prevent it from endering. Compared with the Outrage, it tracks better, and is perhaps slightly more forgiving.

Dagger Ovation

The Ovation was introduced to cater to experienced boaters who wanted a relatively short and responsive boat that would surf, play and creek well, but that didn't demand the attention that a hard-chined boat does. It has a flat middle section, soft chines and a unique second chine located just above the flat waterline. When tilted dramatically, this chine is engaged, but otherwise the forgiving softer edges don't catch the paddler unaware. Soft-chined, full and rockered ends make it easy to stay on a surfing wave but do not permit enders.

42 *Mad River Outrage.*

43 *Dagger Rival.*

44 *Dagger Ovation.*

Mohawk Viper

Frankie Hubbard designed the Viper 12 and 11 for Mohawk after designing the Edge series. The Edge designs were originally slalom racing boats, but some people favored them for creeks because of their responsive hard chines. The Vipers are flat-bottomed, hard-chined boats that lead the market in their shortness. The low-volume entry line flares quickly to a large rounded deck to accommodate Mohawk's large deck plate. The Vipers' performance has encouraged some open-boat first descents and they have dominated whitewater rodeos.

Dagger Ocoee

Frankie Hubbard worked with Dagger to design the Ocoee. The flat bottom and hard chines are similar to those of the Viper. However, the Ocoee is shorter, has a bit more rocker and has harder chines toward the end. It is even more responsive turning and quicker going from edge to edge than the Viper.

Modified Ocoee

This shorter Ocoee may not be a production boat, but was popular in the late 1990s for rodeo and creeking. Most are approximately or just under 10 feet in length. When you are cutting them you can adjust the amount of rocker, but the short length is more of a factor in turning quickness. The shorter length also allows them to surf much steeper waves. They tend to be less stable than longer boats, but again, with their varying amounts of rocker and widths, each boat handles somewhat differently. They accelerate well and have good speed on the wave but lack sustained forward speed.

45 *Mohawk Viper.*

46 *Dagger Ocoee.*

47 *Modified Ocoee.*

48 Savage Skeeter.

Massive Air

The Air design is aimed at rodeo and playboating performance. It has a shallow-arched hull with soft chines. Although it is very stable and is predictable surfing and blasting, without edges it does not carve as well as hard-chined boats. From the cockpit area, the gunwale line drops three inches at the ends. That, combined with its rocker, results in very low-volume ends that are easy to push through the vertical position and that stay retentive in the hole. But the boat doesn't get the big air that larger boats do when they ender.

Savage Skeeter

Frankie Hubbard left Dagger and developed a new 9'2" design that is being molded in polyethylene by Savage. The middle section of his Skeeter is similar to the Ocoee, with a flat bottom and hard chines. The rocker increases dramatically for the last three feet or so at the ends. The width is carried towards the ends to give more stability and a large planing surface for surfing. The ends taper quickly to a low volume that is easy to control through the vertical station. The sides flare slightly and then tuck in dramatically near the gunwale. The outfitting includes three inches of foam on the inside wall to displace water and help keep the boat stable when it is swamped. This boat has done well at rodeos, and is a reasonable creek boat.

Dagger Quake

Steve Scarborough designed the 8'10" Quake as a playboat and for all round river running. The center section of the polyethylene hull is flat bottomed with release chines that help it to flat spin. The short length and a phantom chine just below the waterline at the ends allow the boat to edge and turn quickly on an outside tilt. The flared bow is designed to keep the boat dry and avoid pearling when surfing. The flared

49 Massive Air.

50 Savage Skeeter.

51 Dagger Quake.

bow does make it harder to initiate vertical freestyle moves and control the boat in a vertical station. The stability is a real treat if you're used to an Ocoee. This is a fun boat to paddle. It surfs and flat spins well. It is responsive on creeks and boofs well.

Paddles

Hanging around the put-in, comparing paddles, is almost as much fun as arguing about the best canoe design. The variables in designing and manufacturing a canoe paddle are almost endless, and since whitewater paddles are still evolving, new designs are likely to come on the market. You'd think that because whitewater canoeing has been around since that first great paddling season when the earth had 40 days and 40 nights of rain, people could agree on the best shape of blade for a whitewater paddle. Fortunately, in the interest of lively campfire arguments, this is not the case.

The performance of your paddle is not quite as important as the performance of your boat—but almost. Any old paddle can propel or steer the boat. Sometimes, though, you need every bit of propulsion or steering you can get out of your paddle, and that's when having the very best paddle counts. The difference between a good paddle and a great paddle may be minuscule, but it may make all the difference between catching and not catching that eddy above the waterfall at dusk after you've done 1000 to 2000 strokes that day. Paddle performance is based on the criteria of stiffness, weight, blade shape, shaft shape, durability and paddle length. How we prioritize these factors will dictate our final product. A lightweight paddle can't be durable and cheap. But a heavier paddle could be durable and inexpensive. As with most of the finer things in life, once you've used a real sweet "stick" it will be hard to revert to using your old "oar."

Stiffness

Extremely flexible paddles can accentuate a slightly uneven pull and cause flutter, especially for strong paddlers. Flutter occurs when water spills off the blade unevenly during the power phase of the stroke, making the blade wobble. Paul and I prefer the stiffest possible paddle, although Paul uses a paddle with some flex for training, claiming it reduces stress on his shoulders. But water gives a bit, and stroking is not like running on pavement. When the paddle flexes, you lose some of the energy you put into a stroke and you don't get it all back in the whip at the end of the stroke.

Weight

The lighter the paddle, the quicker you can be between strokes and the less tired you'll be at the end of the day. Too bad we don't buy paddles by the pound—some of the lightest ones are the most expensive.

Blade shape

Blade shape affects your grip in the catch phase of a stroke. A curved blade offers significantly better grip. It has a disadvantage when backpaddling, because the water spills off the convex back side of the blade but makes for a more efficient forward stroke. Square tips rather than rounded ones (by design or wear) give a surprisingly improved grip for a duffek or cut stroke during an eddy turn or when ruddering on a surf. Spooned blades (cupped edges as well as curved from top to bottom) give an even better grip, but avoid them for whitewater, since they won't slice through the water straight on a duffek, cut or sculling draw. An abrupt spline on a flat blade will cause turbulence when you knife the blade through the water. (Spline is the thickest part of the blade.) If the thickness tapers smoothly to the edge, the blade will slice smoothly.

The upper edge of the blade where it curves in to meet the shaft is called the shoulder. It can be quite abrupt and squarish or more gradual, sloping in to create a *fantail*-shaped blade. Although the fantail shape reduces the blade surface area, meaning less resistance, it does allow your blade to get right under the canoe, closer to the center line of the boat, which makes for a more efficient stroke.

Shaft shape

Shafts are either oval or round. The oval shaft has a slight ergonomic advantage. In photo 53, fig. 9, the lower part of the shaft bends back toward you as you paddle, so your wrist is at a natural, less extended angle during the stroke. Below the grip, the shaft bends back to put the blade on a plane with the upper shaft. The result is less stress on the wrist, and therefore a more comfortable, more powerful stroke. The slight advantage in reach (perhaps an inch) is insignificant.

Paddle grip

Most grips are T-shaped, but grip shape is a matter of personal preference. My favorite is a round, straight, 1¼-inch diameter dowel, but some are sculpted.

Durability

Paddles inevitably abrade, wear out, or are broken. However, if you're worrying about your paddle breaking, you're not concentrating on the river. Your priorities are dependent on your activities. For example, when you're competing in rodeo or a slalom race, performance is crucial. When you're running a 10-mile creek, however, having a paddle that won't break, leaving you up that creek, is a priority. If you can't afford to break an expensive paddle or two a year, performance and value are the priorities.

Consider the following facts if you want durability in a paddle:

- *An aluminum tip offers the best abrasion resistance and doesn't slip when you're pushing off rocks.*
- *Foam-core paddles are very strong and stiff, but they don't have much protection on the edges and don't stand up well in shallow rocky situations.*

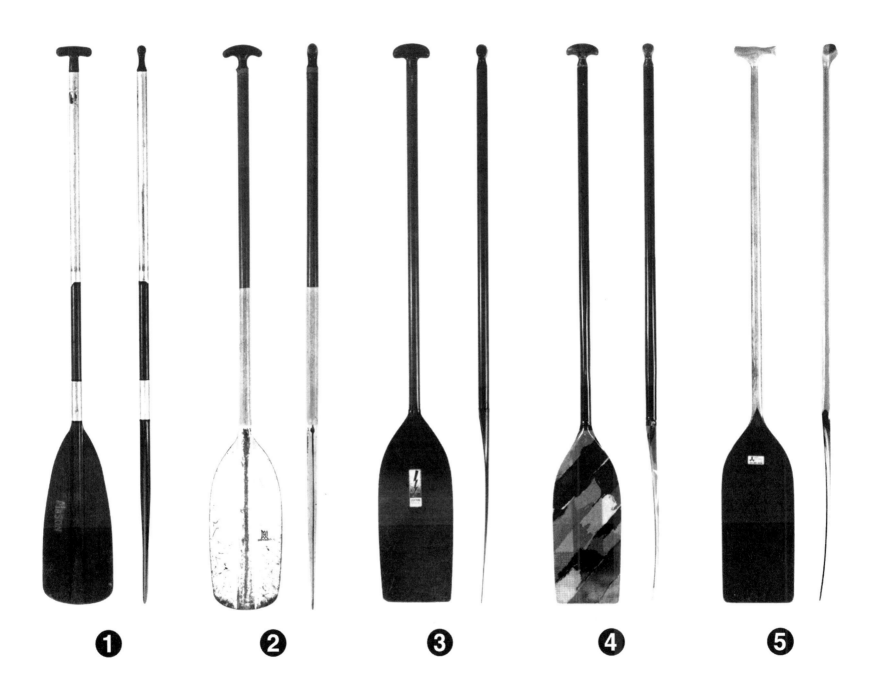

52 Paddles and sticks.

- *Wood paddles generally stand up best to being whacked on rocks in shallow rivers and creeks. When they break, you usually get a warning crack first, so the situation isn't as catastrophic as when your carbon paddle breaks.*
- *Injection-molded resin and fiber blades are strong and abrasion-resistant.*
- *Straight fiberglass or S-glass laminates are generally very strong, but the edges wear quickly.*
- *Weight and durability are closely related; so are price and durability.*

I use a carbon/foam-core/aluminum-tipped ergonomic shaft whenever I can, and a wood/carbon/aluminum-tipped ergonomic shaft on rocky creeks, and I carry a straight shaft AquaBound take-apart paddle in my boat. Paul uses a Kevlar reinforced/fiberglass/straight shaft/curve blade/aluminum tip paddle for creeks and a carbon stick for rodeo. He admits to the merit of ergonomic shafts but can't justify the expense to himself—yet.

Paddle length

When you're sitting upright in your boat with the full blade in the water, the top of the paddle should come to about your eyelid. At the beginning of your stroke, your top arm should be just above your eye. If the paddle is any shorter, your head will get in the way of the beginning of your stroke. If your paddle is any longer than this, crossing over to your offside will be more difficult and it won't improve your reach.

Here are some brands to consider when you're buying a paddle.

1. Mohawk

The most cost-effective paddles on the market have an injected plastic blade with an aluminum shaft. Several brands are available, such as the Mohawk brand paddle pictured. They are durable, good for rental programs and fun paddles to start with if you're not certain that you'll be paddling for more than two weekends a year. Many people carry them as spares, hoping they'll never have to use them. They flex a lot and the shaft insert in the blade prevents them from slicing nicely through the water, so you lose a lot of the energy you put into your strokes with this type of paddle. Stronger and stiffer aluminum shafts are available and some manufacturers use them for stiffer, reaction-injected blades. The result is a better-performing paddle. Most people, however, skip this intermediate paddle and jump to a lighter, stiffer paddle made of fiberglass, wood or carbon.

2. Harmony

This paddle has a fiberglass shaft and a fiberglass-and-epoxy blade. Only a few companies manufacture fiberglass and carbon shafts and they supply Harmony and most other paddle manufacturers. The Harmony paddle is reasonably light, quite stiff and durable. The spline causes turbulence when the paddle slices through the water, and the blade's edges abrade easily. A two-year-old Harmony paddle that I once owned had very rounded edges and a full inch worn off the length of the blade, but it was one of just a few paddles that lasted more than one year of hard use.

3. Lightening

This paddle has a similar construction to the Harmony but is molded of stronger, lighter and more expensive S-glass, with a curved blade. The Lightening is very light and the spline has a lower profile. The very thin edges drop into the water easily but can flex, which may cause the paddle to flutter on a strong stroke. Also in this category are paddles with a fiberglass shaft and an injected blade of fibers and some type of resin such as nylon. These blades may have better abrasion resistance and stiffer edges than a fiberglass epoxy paddle, but the overall blade may flex more than a composite foam core or wood paddle.

4. Robson Fiberglass

The blade of this paddle is made of epoxy and fiberglass, with a foam core and an aluminum tip. The foam core improves the stiffness compared with Harmony or Lightening paddles and allows a smooth transition to the spline that doesn't disrupt the flow of water. The foam adds stiffness by separating the layers of fiberglass, but this construction tends to be less durable than a straight fiberglass-and-epoxy blade. An aluminum edge provides the most durable tip and significantly affects the blade's longevity. Fiberglass shafts come in varying stiffnesses. The flex in the shaft of this paddle may cause flutter on a strong stroke.

5. Angenent

This wood paddle was handcrafted by Albert Angenent. It has a laminated shaft and blade, with epoxy and fiberglass on the shaft and back of the curved blade, and arborite on the blade's face. An aluminum edge protects the tip. The shaft is a sandwich of ash with a lighter wood in the middle. The fiberglass shaft wrap protects the wood from abrasion on the gunwale. A laminated or solid wood blade may not break with the strongest pull or the heaviest brace, but without something laminated to the blade, the grain of the wood will split easily if the blade strikes a pointed rock or even if it is slapped on the surface of the water. With fiberglass, carbon or veneer on the blade, a wood paddle can be one of the strongest paddles available. Many people appreciate the aesthetics and feel of wood. While wood paddles may not be as light as carbon foam-core paddles, they can be stiff and dependably tough.

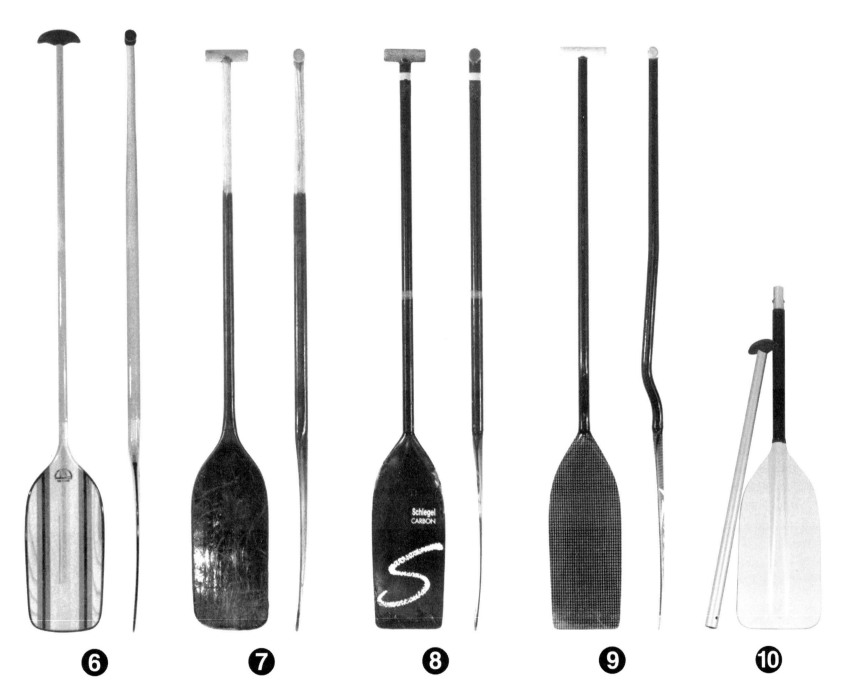

53 Sweet sticks.

6. Grey Owl C-1 Whitewater

This wood paddle has a laminated shaft and blade, with epoxy and fiberglass on the shaft and epoxy and S-glass on the curved blade. A finer weave of fiberglass in the shaft wrap is easy on the hands when the shaft becomes abraded. The durable urethane edge protects the tip and wraps up and around the shoulders of the blade. This is a high-quality inexpensive paddle.

7. Clinch River

This paddle is similar to the previous two wood paddles but is covered with carbon for even more strength and stiffness. However, the cost (because of the carbon) is a disadvantage. The renowned open boater Bailey Johnson crafts these paddles and also makes a fantail-shaped one with less blade area around the shoulder.

8. Schlegal

This paddle is very stiff, and it is one of the lightest paddles on the market. Only people who haven't tried stiff, light paddles or who can't afford them underestimate these two performance criteria. The shaft is carbon, and the blade is carbon with a foam core and an aluminum tip. The edges won't stand up to whacking and chipping on rocks. Paul uses Salamander Rim Guard, which is effective at protecting the edges but also adds weight and turbulence.

9. Robson Ergo Shaft

This paddle is also very stiff and light. The ergonomic bend in the shaft puts less stress on the wrist and therefore gives a more comfortable and more powerful stroke. The slight advantage in reach (perhaps an inch) is insignificant. Once you've tried this type of shaft, it's hard to go back to a straight shaft. Like the Schlegal, the carbon foam-core blade does not stand up well to the abuse of rocky, shallow creeks.

Langman

Joe Langman, a world rodeo finalist, handcrafts a wood paddle that has a carbon-covered blade and shaft and an aluminum tip. The shaft is laminated hardwood in an ergonomic shape. Although slightly heavier, the robust wood laminate is extremely stiff and durable for rocky rivers and creeks.

10. Two-Piece Spare Paddle

This two-piece paddle goes together like a take-apart kayak paddle and has a ferrule (the take-apart connection) and stainless-steel button. It stows out of the way under the float bag in even the shortest playboat. Extra weight and a slight amount of unavoidable play in the connector are its only disadvantages over a one-piece version of the same paddle. You're unlikely to find a paddle like this in a retail store, but most manufacturers have a take-apart connector that you can easily install on a fiberglass or carbon shaft. Make sure to get the connector specified by the manufacturer, as inside shaft diameters may vary.

Clothing for Cold Weather

When we first started paddling, our cold-weather gear–rather, lack of it–definitely hindered our concentration. After all, if you're focusing on how cold you'll be should you flip, you're not concentrating on the line past the rock that might actually flip you. Thermal protection is the biggest consideration in choosing your paddling wardrobe, but freedom of movement, protection from sun, wind and abrasion and, of course, looking good for the cameras also come into play.

With proper cold-weather paddling gear, you'll extend your paddling season, and be more comfortable and safer. Cold water can kill. Being just warm enough may be fine until something goes wrong–when suddenly a falling body temperature can make an innocuous situation life-threatening. It's easy to cool off if you're too warm, but it's hard to warm up when you're too cold. You'll enjoy the river more and even try the odd ender in February if you're not worrying about staying warm. With drysuits, gloves and hoods, you can be as warm as the cross-country skiers you may encounter during your winter paddling outings. By extending your season or paddling year-round, you'll be ready to make the most of the early runoff rivers while others are still flexing stiff muscles and reclaiming rusty skills.

Clothing for Cold Weather

54 Fall/winter/spring

Drysuits

The quickest method of heat loss is conduction through contact with cold water. Latex gaskets at the neck and wrists seal this one-piece Whites drysuit (photo 54, figure 3). Latex provides the best seal, but it can tear if you're rough with it, plus ultraviolet radiation will deteriorate it over time. We like the Discovery suit by Whites because it has integral nylon feet just like the sleepers you had as a kid. These keep your feet dry and warm. Other brands have latex socks; however, the latex is less durable than nylon and increases the cost of the suit. Most suits have a latex cuff at the ankle, but that adds two latex gaskets to the suit and presents the challenge of keeping your feet warm, because they'll be wet. Two-piece drysuits have the advantage of allowing you to use the top separately (not really an advantage for open boaters), but they have the disadvantage of having yet another gasket to seal. Note: a qualification for the term "drysuit." Drysuits are *reasonably* dry—you might get a little water in through the cuffs, and when you're warm and active you'll perspire even in a waterproof breathable drysuit.

Underwear

Drysuits keep out the water but provide no insulation. Fortunately, many synthetic fleece underwear options are available in every thickness, style and color. Avoid cotton for insulation in a potentially wet environment since it absorbs water. One-piece underwear is great because you don't get a cold spot when the top rides up. The more stretch, the better. Fleece tops, designed specifically for paddling, lack cuffs that often get in the way of the drysuit cuffs. A single layer of about 16-ounce sweater thickness for fall, winter and spring (photo 54, figure 1) is a good bet.

Socks

Heat escapes from your extremities quickly, and since your feet are often sitting in water, you must give them special attention. In cold weather, try wearing fleece or wool socks (photo 54, figure 2) under neoprene socks, inside the waterproof attached feet of your drysuit, and a neoprene boot on the outside for further insulation and stiffness in the sole (figure 4).

Mitts and gloves

Your hands are the hardest part of your body to keep warm. They not only need insulation, but also grip and dexterity to properly handle the paddle. Neoprene is recommended, in particular three-millimeter nylon-one-side neoprene mitts (photo 54, figure 7). The neoprene skin on the outside grips the paddle well and the mitts are warmer and less bulky than gloves. If the mitts are glued and blind-stitched, they'll be waterproof until the neoprene abrades, which occurs quite quickly. Precurved nylon-two-side neoprene gloves are popular and more durable (figure 6). A bit of sticky wax on your paddle will solve a slippery grip. Nylon or neoprene pogies are windproof covers that allow your hands direct contact with the paddle. They are fine for cool weather, but for maximum warmth or cold conditions neoprene mitts are the best.

Elbow pads

Elbow pads are an important piece of gear (photo 54, figure 9), especially when you're running shallow, bony creeks and rodeo-paddling. The kind used by in-line skaters, which have hard plastic caps that absorb impact, are a good bet. Some of the worst hits to elbows come from hitting the gunwales while you're flopping around in a rodeo hole.

Clothing for Warm Weather

55 Summer.

Surprisingly, you can get just as cold in the summer as in the winter. How much thermal protection you need will depend on the water temperature, whether you're creeking or freestyle paddling, the length of the run and your metabolism. In the summer, consider wearing the following items.

Paddling tops

Paddling tops come with short or long sleeves and with neck and wrist closures of neoprene and Velcro or latex (photo 55, figure 1). They block wind, water and UV rays but don't have any insulating properties of their own, so for warmth, wear fleece underneath. Drytops with latex cuffs are drier, but open boaters can count on the water getting in through the waist tube. If you need the warmth of the drier, more constricting, drytop, you're better off with a drysuit.

Wetsuits

Neoprene fabric itself is waterproof and provides excellent insulation. Because it doesn't soak up water, it retains the same stretch whether wet or dry. Neoprene is available in different thicknesses and quality, and can have nylon laminated to one (N1S) or both (N2S) sides. Although the nylon layer significantly improves durability, it slightly detracts from the stretch and grip of skin neoprene. There are three common types of seams for neoprene: glued and blind-stitched seams are strong and waterproof but are also the most expensive to manufacture; mauser-taped seams have seam tape on the inside and outside and are extremely strong; and flat-locked seams just use interlocking thread and are smooth and not bulky. Wetsuits are intended to fit snugly enough that water will only seep in, but not so snugly that the suits restrict blood circulation. Even though you are wet, the water next to you remains warm. Farmer John or Jane wetsuits, which are typically three millimeters thick, are popular with paddlers, especially canoeists, because they keep the legs and body core warm but don't restrict movement of the arms and shoulders (photo 55, figure 2). A wetsuit combined with fleece, a long-sleeved paddling top and neoprene boots can be adequate for spring and fall paddling (but not as comfortable or warm as a drysuit). Canoeists find that water seeps in less and more slowly when they wear their paddling tops under their wetsuits.

Short-sleeved tops

The top shown in photo 55, figure 3 has two millimeters of neoprene covering the body core, and Lycra and neoprene sleeves. This combination gives you a little warmth around the core, and protects against the sun and chafing from a rough personal flotation device skin. Neoprene dries more quickly than a nylon outer layer. This is significant because as wet nylon dries, you lose body heat. Similar tops are made from fleece with a waterproof coating (known as fuzzy rubber). Because they have more stretch, they're more comfortable than neoprene, and when dry, they are just as warm. However, the fleece soaks up water when wet and the extra stretch allows water to flow through more easily. For really warm days, you may opt for a Lycra top, which blocks the sun and prevents chafing from your PFD.

Shorts

Shorts are available in neoprene (photo 55, figure 4) or fuzzy rubber. As with the tops, fuzzy rubber is more comfortable, whereas neoprene is warmer. You'll probably want them long enough to cover your thighs and prevent chafing where they come in contact with your thigh straps.

Footwear

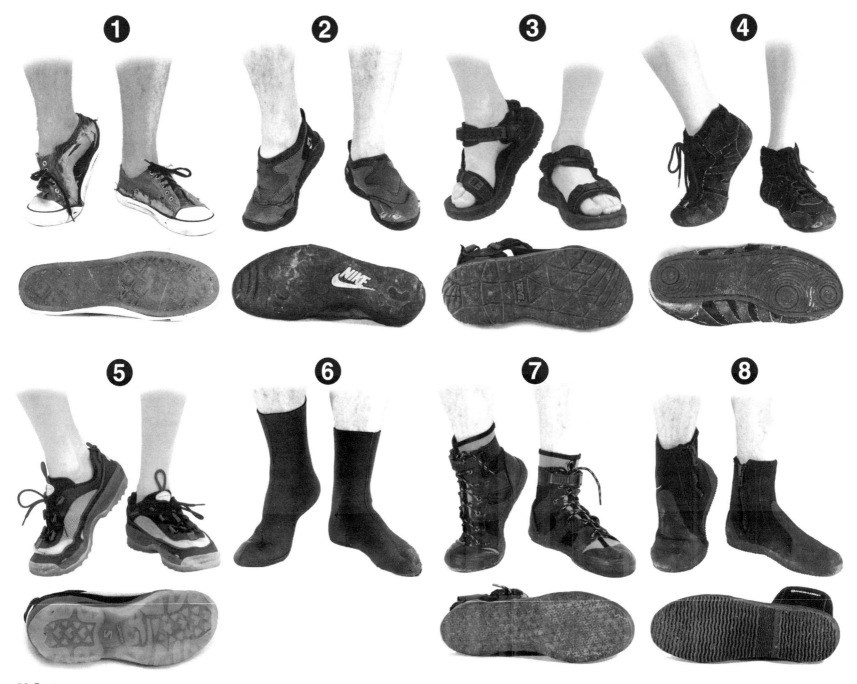

56 Footwear.

Warm, comfortable, lightweight, secure, with the right combination of stiffness and flexibility, are the characteristics we're interested in for our paddling footwear. A stiff sole makes it easy to push against the foot pegs and to scamper around rocks or to portage. If the sole is too stiff and the shoe bulky, you'll have less dexterity in your feet and it'll be harder to bend your toes and get in and out of the boat. Low-cuts are lighter, dry quicker and generally allow more flex. High-cuts provide more protection for ankles among rocks. The recent explosion of the outdoor and water-sport footwear market provides you with multiple options for every condition imaginable. Whatever footwear you choose, make sure it's secure enough to stay on even if you swim.

Summer wear

Canvas running shoes (Figure 1) Who's the goofball with the Super Keds? Paul prides himself on finding the cheapest pair of canvas running shoes possible and wearing them until they're compost. Get with the program. Support the paddle-sport industry and buy the stuff that's 12 times as expensive, black and stretchy, and may even be comfortable.

Aqua sock (Figure 2) Slip-on sandals with a spandex top are lightweight and cool and they dry easily. For me, these have just the right amount of flex and stiffness. Many inexpensive brands have very light, flexible soles but not much of a heel cup. With an inferior heel cup, they may fall off during impromptu swimming lessons.

River sandal (Figure 3) Teva is well known for its many styles of river sandals, but several other brands are also available. River sandals are ideal for river canoe tripping, rafting or hanging around the river and campsite. They allow your feet to breathe and they dry quickly if you're living on the river. The sturdy sole is thick and grips rocks well; however, you sacrifice support and toe protection. Still, some people really like them for whitewater boating. Sandals with buckles instead of Velcro stay on better in the water. The typical floppiness of sandals makes them harder to swim with.

Lightweight River Shoe (Figure 4) Akonas have been my favorite summer river shoe ever since Mark made me throw away my perfectly good running shoes. They have a surprisingly stiff sole for their light weight, good traction and are high-cut for ankle protection. Mine look like I'll get two summers out of them before Mark notices they're wearing out.

River shoe (Figure 5) Salomon's version of the river shoe has the outsole, comfort and support of an outdoor approach shoe. The sole is great on rocks and portages, and just flexible enough for use in a playboat. The cool mesh upper is quick-drying. Neoprene trim makes these shoes very comfortable. They are a treat to walk in, a little heavier to swim in, but, with stiff soles, are great for scrambling on rocks. Wear with a neoprene sock for cool weather or cold water.

Winter wear

Seal Skinz socks These waterproof socks keep your feet dry when your drysuit is not as dry as it used to be.

Neoprene socks (Figure 6) Neoprene socks are essential for cold-water paddling. In the winter, I wear pile socks and neoprene socks inside my drysuit, which has attached feet so my feet are dry, and I wear neoprene booties over top. Although my feet are thermally fragile due to poor circulation, with this combination I'm rarely cold, even with water sloshing in my boat and constantly standing in water to empty.

Lightweight neoprene boot (Figure 7) Salamander's Das Boot has a plastic strap and lace-up support around the ankle. Some people may find the extra support is unnecessary (unless you have week ankles) and incongruous with the light sole.

Neoprene booties (Figure 8) For cold-water paddling, neoprene booties are the standby. They are snug to your foot and the water that does seep in stays there and doesn't flow away with your heat. Zippered boots are convenient to put on. This style has an aggressive tread and rubberized protection over the toe for durability. Most brands are five- to seven-millimeter neoprene with a light sole.

Hoods and Toques

Your head is another extremity that requires thermal protection. A fleece toque is fine unless your head goes underwater, in which case the fleece will keep your head soaking in cold water. The neoprene hoods shown in photo 57 are one to three millimeters thick and provide excellent insulation. Depending on the style and how much of the head they cover, they also seal out the water (for a while). Other options include urethane-coated Lycra hoods, which keep out water but provide no insulation, and hoods of coated fleece, which are stretchy and more comfortable than neoprene but not as effective at preventing water from entering and not as warm as neoprene when they are wet.

It is important to recognize that repeated dunkings in cold water can actually cause problems in your ears. As a defense mechanism, calcium deposits shrink the opening of your ear canal. Initially, this just makes it hard for the water to drain and easier for ear infections to develop. Mark has reached this stage and his doctor has recommended that he rinse his ears with hydrogen peroxide and vinegar after paddling to dry his ears and prevent infections. In fact, I know of some paddlers who've had to have surgery to eliminate the bony buildup. Consequently, some rodeo paddlers wear hoods or ear plugs even in warmer water to prevent this condition. My helmet has a removable foam liner, so I just use a thinner liner in the winter to accommodate my hood.

57 Hoods.

Accessories

Here are a few extras you might consider to completely outfit yourself.

Nose plugs

If you should find yourself hanging around upside down, nose plugs will prevent water from flushing your sinuses and allow you (if necessary) to stay underwater longer and more comfortably. Also, if the water you're paddling in is polluted, nose plugs can prevent infections such as sinusitis. Choose a brand that is snug and streamlined so the current won't catch them.

Visor

The Salamander Beak attaches to your helmet with Velcro. It's removable and doesn't squeeze your brains like a cap under your helmet.

Knife

A knife is an essential piece of safety equipment for all canoeists. Keep it handy, but not protruding where it could snag branches, ropes or restrict your movements. Several suitable knives are available. The Spyderco rescue knife is a good one. You can flick open the blade with one hand. It locks in place and the serrated blade slices through rope quickly. Storing the knife in a pocket with an exposed lanyard makes it accessible and unlikely that you'll lose it while you're using it. If you attach it to your PFD with a large loop, you can quickly remove it. It will also fit in the low-profile Snapper-brand sheath that attaches to your PFD. Check the mechanisms of your folding knife and oil them occasionally. Solid knives in quick-release sheaths are more accessible but are also more likely to get in the way when you pick up your canoe or try to climb back in from deep water. The Gerber knife is short enough to lessen this inconvenience; the tip of the knife is also blunt to reduce the chance of accidents. Most plastic sheaths' securing mechanisms wear out from use. Time will tell how this one lasts.

Wax

Wax gives you a better grip on slippery paddle shafts. Several brands made specifically for paddling are available, or you could use a hard cross-country ski wax for about the same price. (Don't use Klister.)

Sunglasses

Sunglasses can fall off in turbulent holes, get water spots on them and rub against your helmet. However, if you spend a lot of time outdoors, they improve visibility on a sunny day and provide long-term protection for your eyes.

58 Nose plugs.

59 Visor.

Prusik loops and carabiners

These two items are essential in many types of rescues. Two prusiks of five- or six-millimeter nylon rope and several locking carabiners are the minimum. On a wide-open play river like the Ottawa River, a group might have this much gear among them. When traveling solo on unfamiliar creeks and rivers, each member of the party may wish to carry this much gear.

Whistle

Certainly a must-have. It's cheap, light and loud. A whistle or some kind of signaling device is required by law for all small craft (including canoes) in Canada.

Folding saw

A good idea if you are creeking where trees may be in the way. You might need to cut poles, or even cut someone's boat in a serious rescue.

First-aid kit

Store a compact first-aid kit in your boat so you'll always have it, if and when you need it, provided you haven't been separated from your boat.

Duct tape

Having duct tape around is essential when you wear a drysuit. If a latex gasket is going to fail, it'll rip when you are putting the suit on. It would be a shame to miss a day of paddling just because you couldn't repair it. Keep a tiny bit in your first-aid kit and a mammoth roll in your gear bag.

Food

I don't know about you but I paddle terribly when I'm hungry, so I keep an energy bar shoved into a slot cut into my foam saddle. If we actually stop for lunch, a peanut-butter, honey-and-marshmallow sandwich for me, please. I found the recipe in a Calvin and Hobbes comic book–very fortifying.

60 River knives.

Helmets

If you are using thigh straps or if you are running difficult whitewater, you really, really should wear a helmet. Even in Class I water, you can flip and, with thigh straps, you may not fall out of the boat before you go upside down. If you come out of your boat, you may tumble around in the water. In either case, your head may come in contact with rocks. It seems that every sport I like requires a helmet. A friend with similar tastes in sports was lamenting the fact that there wasn't one helmet that he could use for all sports. However, the type of impacts to the head are different in whitewater than hockey, climbing or biking. I do each of those sports often enough to justify the $60 to $100 investment to protect one of my biggest assets (arguably), my brain. In addition, I would be bored wearing the same helmet for every sport. Many people feel secure as long as they have any helmet on, regardless of the quality, fit and protection that it offers. In my first few years of paddling, I didn't hit my head at all. After the first solid contact with a rock, I took my choice of helmets much more seriously. The three components of the helmet are the shell, the lining, and the strap system.

The shell

The shell of a whitewater helmet is made to distribute the force of an impact over a larger area while the foam lining absorbs the shock. Shells are either made from thermoformed plastic or are composite helmets made with thermoset resins, reinforced with Kevlar or fiberglass. Thermoformed plastic helmets are less labor intensive and therefore less expensive. The thermoformed shell will flex and absorb some of the force of an impact. However, if the force is very strong or delivered by a sharp rock to a small area, the force to your head will be greater and more concentrated than with fiber-reinforced, thermoset resin helmets, which are more rigid and distribute the force of an impact over a greater area. In short, the stiffer the material, the larger the area over which the force will be dispersed. Holes in thermoformed helmets make them cooler and lighter and compromise the protection slightly. Holes in thermoset resin helmets are uncommon and would greatly compromise the structural integrity of the helmet. The amount of coverage over the head is important and varies from helmet to helmet. Some helmets cover the ears and more of the back of the head, and these offer more safety to the wearer.

The lining

The energy of an impact is meant to be absorbed by the compression of the lining. Whitewater helmets should have a closed-cell foam lining that will absorb energy and then rebound to its original shape, ready for the next impact. A thicker lining will absorb more energy and put the shell further away from your head to give more protection to your face. Single-impact foams such as those used for bike helmets may actually absorb energy better than whitewater helmets, but that type of helmet is dangerous for whitewater. If you hit your head while tumbling around in a hole or bouncing down a rapid, it is entirely possible that you will receive more than one impact before getting out of that situation. Suspension linings are used in climbing and construction sites where the impact comes straight downward on the top of the head but they offer little protection for impacts from the side, which are the most common type of impacts in whitewater.

The Fit of the Lining   In order to be comfortable, perform the task of absorbing any impact, and keep the helmet on your head, the lining must fit your head. Most helmets are available in different-sized liners or come with foam strips that can be glued in to ensure a snug fit. You may need to change the liner or use a different helmet when you are wearing a hood or hat since they will change the fit of your helmet. A visor on the outside of your helmet is an alternative to wearing a cap underneath your helmet.

The strap system

The straps must be adjustable and pull from several points so that the helmet will stay on your head. The water flow when you're upside down or the impact from a rock can twist or pull your helmet. Try to take your helmet off without undoing the buckles and, if you can, readjust the straps. Make sure the buckles are of good quality and check them regularly for breakage. That small plastic buckle is the only thing keeping that important piece of safety gear on your head.

61 Helmets, a sampling of designs.

1. A Wildwater thermoformed plastic helmet with minicell foam liner. The thin liner means minimal protection for your face since this lightweight helmet does not protrude at the front. There is little coverage for the ears.

2. A Pro-tec thermoformed plastic helmet with closed-cell foam liner. The foam is softer than minicell so the fit is more comfortable for odd-shaped heads. It offers good forehead protection provided the helmet is not pushed back. Good ear coverage but I like to cut out the bars, so that I can get at the blackflies when they get into my ears.

3. This thermoformed plastic helmet by Wildwater is stiffer than their lighter models and offers greater coverage. It has a thick minicell foam liner. The big ear hole is great for pulling it on and for poking at mosquitoes and water in your ears. I added the neoprene sun visor and painted the helmet black. Painting your helmet is a great way to void any warranties on the helmet.

4. This Cascade Designs helmet has a hard thermoformed plastic shell backed by a dense foam liner similar to that of a bicycle helmet. A closed-cell foam liner that wraps around your forehead, ears and back of the head keeps the helmet from bouncing around. Additional thin removable liners finish off the fit. An adjustable strap that tightens at the back of your neck is supposed to keep the helmet from tipping back, thus exposing your forehead. This strap system doesn't work for me when I use the face guard. Your head is likely a different shape so it might be perfect for you.

5. This Primex helmet has a thermoformed ABS plastic shell and closed-cell foam liner. Your ears are very well covered, making it really hard to scratch bugs and pull the helmet on. It has a chin cup, which seems necessary to hold the helmet in place when combined with the mask. A bug bushy beard does not enhance the fit of the chin cup.

6. A fiber-reinforced, thermoset resin lid, outfitted with a minicell liner. Constructed of kevlar and fiberglass, the shell is very stiff, offering excellent impact dispersion. These designs often seem to expose the paddler's forehead, so check the fit and the size of the shell of the particular brand you are buying. These helmets definitely make the coolest fashion statement. Well, except of course for the next helmet.

7. Pseudo forged steel with muskrat liner. Speaking from experience, the horns should be made out of foam rather than wood as pictured here.

Personal Flotation Devices

You'll spend a lot of time in this important piece of safety equipment and it shows up in everyone's photographs. In other words, it's worth taking the time to find a personal flotation device (PFD) that has the safety features you need, is comfortable and looks good. Most important, the PFD should fit and stay on when you're in the water, without restricting your movements. Most PFDs have one or two side-cinch straps; some also have shoulder cinch straps. Straps keep the PFD snug, prevent it from riding up around your ears and allow for extra warmth. Color is a matter of fashion and how visible you want to be. Most countries require all boaters to have a government-approved PFD in their boat. Be aware of your country's regulations. As with any safety equipment, check your gear periodically. Although your 10-year-old PFD may look fine, the foam may have compressed and may have less buoyancy than it once did, or ultraviolet radiation may have deteriorated the fabric. Replacing it is a good excuse to update your wardrobe. We've highlighted a few models here to show several features we really like, but many other models, brands and styles are also available. Decide what features are useful for you in your price range, then head to the store and start trying the PFDs on.

Rescue PFDs and towlines   Many PFDs are now available with a webbing chest belt that has a quick-release buckle. These PFDs can be used with a towline or in river-rescue situations. The belt system, which has a 1.5- or two-inch webbing belt held in place with loops on the chest just below the arms, helps keep the PFD securely on your body. A metal slider should be located just under the quick-release cam buckle. The towline is usually sold as an accessory. One end attaches to the belt in the middle of the back and the other has a carabiner that attaches with some quick-releasing method to the front of the PFD. Many of these PFDs have more than the standard requirement of foam to improve buoyancy in contact rescues. These features can add safety and convenience to your river trips but are incomplete without proper training and regular practice.

Ribbed or paneled foam   In a ribbed-design PFD, two- to three-inch-wide strips of foam are placed in vertical sleeves, leaving about a one-inch gap between the foam ribs. This improves the ventilation and conforms to your body more easily. Because of all the gaps, however, the foam must be thicker and cover a greater area than with a solid foam panel. A ribbed jacket often has foam placed under the arms–where it's effective but can be constricting–or on the shoulders, where it is effective only when your chin gets wet. A panel foam jacket is compact, easier to make snug to your chest and very cozy.

Foam   Stories abound of turbulent holes, eddylines or whirlpools holding people under the surface. In such situations, the more flotation, the greater the force pushing you to the surface, where you can breathe. Because foam is so buoyant, the more foam you have the more buoyancy you'll have. The more foam, however, the bulkier and possibly the more constricting the PFD will be. PVC foams are more durable but less comfortable. Airex foam is more flexible and conforms to your body better but will compress over time and lose its buoyancy. A wetsuit, drysuit and (most significantly) your boat also offer buoyancy.

Zipper or pullover   A zipper makes a PFD easier to get on and off but may come undone when you don't want it to. Like paneled foam, a zipper helps ventilation (even when it's done up) but most zippers create a gap in the foam coverage that results in a more bulky and cluttered design.

Pockets   Pockets are useful for carrying sunscreen, keys, mitts or pounds of lightweight rescue gear. Since not all PFDs were designed by open boaters, ensure that any pockets or knife attachment points aren't located in an awkward or constricting place. Some PFDs are available with add-on rear pockets to hold a throwline in a convenient, accessible place. Mesh panels in pockets and in the lining of the jacket will prevent water from being trapped in the jacket.

62 **Palm Extrem.**

63

64 **Lotus Rio Pro.**

65

Rescue Systems

Palm Extrem River Vest and Cowtail   This rescue PFD, with its large armholes and shoulder adjustment straps (photos 62 and 63), offers excellent mobility. You can also remove extra flotation in the front pocket to enlarge the cargo pocket. The mobility and clean look of this vest are rare in a rescue PFD.

Lotus Rio Pro   The zipper on this rescue PFD is attached to the outside panel so there is no break in the foam coverage of the front (photos 64 and 65). With the secure, quick-release belt, you get the advantages of a zippered, solid-panel design.

Lotus Lola Pro   This rescue PFD is stylish and has contoured panels for comfort (photos 66 and 67). It fits women particularly well. The webbing reinforcement eliminates any chance of the shoulders ripping if you are a pin victim and your rescuer is pulling you by the shoulders of this PFD.

Palm River Tec Fusion   You hardly notice you're wearing this PFD (photos 68 and 69). The front panel is narrow at the bottom and cut away near the shoulders, so your movements aren't impeded at all. Elasticized side panels prevent bulkiness under your arms. Neoprene and webbing shoulder cinches provide security, comfort and adjustability.

Over the years, rescue gear has become more specialized to suit individual situations. This means that, as a paddler, you must determine the kind of equipment you will need for each situation you're likely to encounter.

Before investing in any rescue gear, take a rescue course so you'll know how to choose the equipment you may need, or learn what to choose from more experienced paddlers. A friend once said that as we become more proficient at something, we're able to do more with less. I suspect this explains why novices show up at the river with so much equipment that they're tripping over it, while the experts seem underequipped. However, sometimes experts are lulled into becoming overly nonchalant about rescue gear, possibly because they don't need to be rescued very often. The downside is that when a situation arises, it's likely to be more serious, given the kind of water they paddle.

I tend to fall into the category of usually having too much safety stuff, whereas Mark leans toward too little. On more than one occasion I remember surveying my boat with the first-aid kit, energy bar, water bottle, throw-rope, break-down paddle, tow line, extra fleece and camera. Then I'd look at Mark's boat—one paddler in a nice, light, empty canoe—and realize I

was being scammed. As Mark points out, I carry enough stuff for both of us. The key is to find a combination of equipment that works for you. Several combinations and their applications follow; one may cover the kind of paddling you aspire to.

A PFD with an integral quick-release tow system opens up all kinds of rescue possibilities. A tow belt (photo 70, figure 3) worn around the waist is a slightly less desirable option, as it can cause serious injury if it's not moved up over the PFD during a tethered swimmer rescue. The standard cow tail that comes with a rescue PFD tends to be a bit short for open boaters to tow errant craft. The tow line must be long enough to let the other craft swing clear of your stern; otherwise, steering is pretty tough.

The shorter throw lines in the 30- to 50-foot range are inexpensive, lightweight and quick to restuff. However, their drawback is their shortness. Open boats have more readily accessible storage space than a kayak, so having a bigger, longer throw bag is an option. Besides, 70-foot ropes tightly stuffed into a snug bag make a firmer unit to store and throw. Seventy feet of quarter-inch polypropylene rope is small and light (figure 2), and fits in a bag that you can throw accurately to the full extent of its length. However, it's too stretchy and not strong enough for some rope-and-pulley rescues.

66 Lotus Lola Pro.

67

68 Palm Fusion.

69

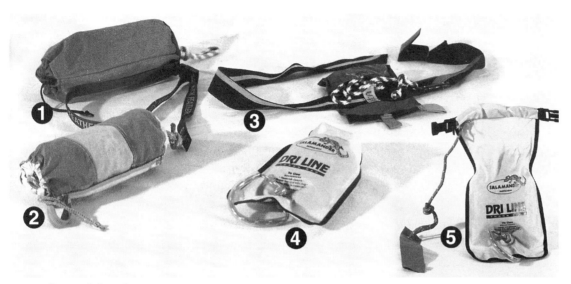

70 Tow lines and throw bags.

Quarter-inch Spectra solves this problem, but it's more expensive than three-eighths-inch polypropylene, which is also strong and, being thicker, is easier to hang on to. Three-eighths-inch polypropylene rope is heavier, making a 70-foot line difficult to toss overhand. As a compromise, I prefer to con Mark into buying 70 feet of the expensive quarter-inch Spectra rope.

How you store your throw bags in your canoe is almost as important as having them in the first place. Regardless of which canoe you paddle–classic or playboat–your objective is the same: to be able to grab your bag quickly, climb out of your boat and heave the throwline from shore. No matter how secure your handhold is on shore, throwing and belaying are almost impossible to do effectively from a boat. Therefore, you must stash the bag so it won't come loose, yet it is readily accessible. I used to use a throw bag secured by a jam cleat on the stern deck of my classic canoe, since we seemed to tow a lot of swamped boats where a canoe-over-canoe rescue wasn't feasible. But as we have evolved toward using more flotation and became more oriented toward playing in rapids, towing is less common. Now I prefer to have the bag clipped in front of me so it's more accessible. This means I can keep a bag with me when I'm paddling bow or stern. Remember: with proper flotation you no longer need to self-rescue your canoe by swimming to shore with a tow line. You simply flip the canoe upright and paddle it to shore with whatever water remains in it. In a classic canoe, it is convenient to clip the throw bag to the airbag tie-in cords and then stuff the bag under those cords. Be aware, however, that with the canoe full of water it may be difficult to free the bag. No system is ever perfect, I guess.

Playboats outfitted with foam saddles offer very accessible storage. Using shock cord, you can secure your throw bag to one end and a water bottle to the other. This system works so well, in fact, that I leave the bag in the boat between river trips, unless I'm taking it out to dry, as we're all supposed to do, or giving it its yearly rinse-off. This habit of leaving it in the boat led to a surprise on the Upper Yough in Maryland one year in March. The Upper Yough is a busy Class 4 run that beckons us south when everything at home is frozen solid. After an entire night of driving, the ice that had accumulated on my boat during our winter surfing forays had melted by the time we arrived at the put-in. As we drifted downstream, we checked our gear. I pulled my throw bag out from behind my saddle, to find that it, however, was still a bag of solid ice. Even soaking it in the river, which was "warmer" than the air, had no effect. We laughed about it, but I'm glad I didn't need to use the bag that day. Maybe that's another good reason to hang up the bag at night to dry. A company named Salamander has eliminated the need to dry out your throw bag; they now make a waterproof bag (photo 70, figures 4 and 5). The other advantage of a dry bag is that you are not lugging around the extra weight of a soggy throw bag.

One last note on rescue gear; in particular, homemade throw bags and harnesses. Remember: one day you may be unfortunate enough to have to trust your life to your gear during a rescue. Having a substandard piece of equipment could result in serious consequences for you or for someone unfamiliar with its idiosyncrasies and weaknesses.

Customizing Your Canoe

Customizing a canoe is the next best thing to going paddling—plus it has some mystical connotations. My wife, Judy, finds the appearance of a canoe in our house to be a more accurate sign of spring than the groundhog's not seeing his shadow. When she steps in the front door and is greeted by the sight of a playboat on the floor surrounded by bits of outfitting foam, she knows winter will last one more month. In fact, now that playboats have become shorter, most folks can partake in this spring ritual, whereas previously you needed a 16-foot-long garage to accommodate a canoe! The beauty of working on your canoe in the house is that you can't actually do anything because of the toxic fumes from the glues you would need to use. This means you can focus all your energy on theorizing and on shaping bits of minicell foam into, well, smaller bits of minicell foam.

Outfitting

I can't recall the exact day that I saw someone stuffing additional flotation under the thwarts of their 16-foot canoe, but I do remember my response—wow, that's really radical! An inner tube tied into your canoe! Times have changed. Now an overinflated truck-tire inner tube is the most basic floatation system I know of for playboating. But since you may have a canoe-tripping background and hope to start playboating by modifying the canoe you already have, let's begin with the basics of flotation. Other equipment such as what kind of helmet you need are covered in the equipment section.

The goal is to displace as much water from inside the canoe as possible so it floats higher and allows you to paddle to shore even if the boat is completely swamped. This reduces the potential for damage, and makes rescues much easier. So, what should you use for flotation? Air springs to mind, followed closely by helium. But helium does not float the canoe higher or make it noticeably lighter—this approach has been tried. Back to air, then. You can use any container that holds air as flotation. Olive jars and plastic barrels work, but they're heavy and really hard to tie tightly into your canoe. Inner tubes are economical, but they, too, are heavy and not the ideal shape. However, a canoe equipped with an inner tube becomes very stable when it is full of water. Think about it. The inner tube actually looks like a raft without a floor. Unfortunately, however, it is just as stable upside down as right side up, so don't even dream of being able to do an Eskimo roll with an inner tube as flotation. Next, turn your attention to keeping yourself in the boat. Minicell knee pads add comfort but before long you'll need a more secure method to hold yourself in position. Thigh straps are the next step in your evolution toward creating a playboat.

Now that you can keep yourself in the canoe even upside down, it's time to upgrade from that old leaky inner tube to airbags. Since you're still in that mammoth 16-foot canoe, you'll need a huge center bag, plus two end bags.

In the solo position without thigh straps you can slide off the bow seat and kneel up against the center thwart for back-ferrying. But if you kneel against the bow seat facing the stern, you won't be able to back-surf at all unless you're willing to deflate your center airbag and restring a lot of tie-in cords. Since opportunities for front-surfing are more common than those for back-surfing, a good bet is to remain at the bow seat facing the stern. Kneeling thwarts located closer to the center of the canoe are another alternative. Unfortunately, this increases the danger of entrapment in a broach, so we don't encourage them for whitewater.

The Royalex Prospector in most of the classic photos can be used for tandem or solo with minimal adjusting, which means it takes about 15 minutes to change from tandem to solo or vice versa for a day's paddling. You could leave it set up for solo all the time, but that would greatly reduce your ability to maneuver when paddling tandem and full of water because the center bag will be folded in half, displacing less water. With thigh straps and fully inflated flotation, you can roll your classic canoe if you flip. However, this skill is really only an asset in deep water. A classic canoe fully outfitted with flotation will still take on a huge load of water. Performing an Eskimo-roll in rocky rapids would be a scary proposition unless you're very confident that your first attempt will be fast and successful.

The solution is to use a smaller canoe. It will be more maneuverable, and because it's designed specifically for tandem or solo, it will have less space for water. Some paddlers purchase a tandem playboat and outfit it with three saddles. This works well for river running since the objective is to stay upright. But playing in whitewater usually translates into paddling around full of water. When you paddle solo, the two extra saddle spaces fill with water, which makes the canoe very unresponsive and heavy to paddle back to shore for your next run on the surfing wave. The compromise in paddling a tandem playboat solo is really a step backward when you face the facts. Playboating begs for specialized designs. And canoes that are hybrid always compromise one end of the spectrum—a tandem or solo playboat.

Outfitting

Trimming your canoe

The installation and fine-tuning of each system are explained in the following section. But before you become immersed in the finicky details, it helps to consider your broad objective—which is to go paddling! Okay, so that's a little too broad. How about this. You want comfort, control and the boat to be trimmed so that it sits evenly in the water with you in it. A canoe trimmed bow up will track well but be resistant to turning; a canoe trimmed bow down will respond quicker to your strokes and therefore not track straight as easily. You really need to fully understand why this is the case before choosing to take advantage of either style of trimming.

Trimming the canoe bow up   Moving the solo paddler's position back makes the boat drier since the bow rises over waves more easily. This means that the bow is less likely to pearl during a front surf. It also makes steering easier on flatwater when you're using a traditional J-stroke.

Trimming the canoe bow down   When you move the pivot point forward by positioning the paddler closer to the bow, you get a very responsive, quick-turning boat that is well suited to river running. A more forward pivot point also assists you in initiating vertical moves.

Mark accidently tested this bow-heavy theory on one of his solo boats. He was trying to do several things at once, and in the confusion he glued his saddle in, almost three inches forward of the center point of the boat. Fortunately, he liked the responsiveness that it gave him for creeking and rodeo paddling. As a general rule, however, trim the boat neutral for general paddling and one or two inches ahead for quicker turns or rodeos. Given all the variables, don't get too worked up about measuring things with a micrometer.

Symmetrical canoes are easy to check by asking a friend to "eyeball" the bow and stem while you kneel in the center of the canoe on the water. The water line should contact the curve of the stem at an equal distance from both ends. Perform this check before you glue in your saddle.

I was once led astray by an asymmetrical tandem boat. We used the technique of putting the canoe in the water to determine our saddle positions. Since the bow and stern had different amounts of rocker and volume, we ended up too far forward in an attempt to make the water line at each end symmetrical. Sensing that something wasn't right, we checked our placement by hanging the canoe on a rope wrapped around the hull at the center. Both our distance from the center point and the imbalance confirmed that we were way off in how we had positioned the saddles.

Our advice: if your canoe is asymmetrical, follow the manufacturer's suggestions. Their instructions can tell you where your belly button should be relative to the center point of the canoe.

71 A full quiver of boats.

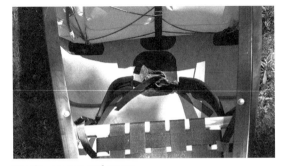

72 Canoe seat and straps.

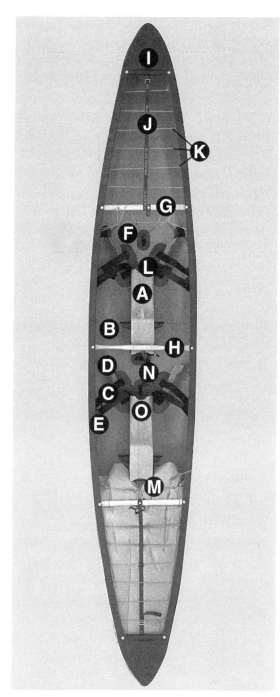

73 Components of a playboat.

Installing the outfitting

Locate the saddle (A) with foot pegs installed (B) on the center line of the canoe so that the center point between the bow and stern is under your stomach when you're kneeling with the saddle. You'll need to suck in your gut a little—or perhaps a lot if you haven't been out canoeing very much. You may also check your placement by hanging your canoe by a rope wrapped around the hull at the center. Climb in, and when the canoe balances, trace the saddle outline on the hull. With the canoe back on solid ground, kneel in the canoe again and locate the thigh straps (C), knee pads (D) and the D-rings on the side of the hull for your straps (E). Trace outlines of everything. Locate your airbag tie-downs (F). Avoid putting one in front of your knee or you'll get rope burn on your skin when you're wearing shorts. To be bombproof, you'll need five airbag tiedowns at the front and four behind your saddle. Place your front thwart close enough that if you lean forward it contacts your chest, not your face (G). It helps if the thwart is positioned directly over the airbag tie-downs. The rear thwart should cross over the back of the saddle (H). This helps to hold the saddle steady and will make the hull more rigid. Front and rear thwarts (I) or decks lessen damage to the ends of the boat during rodeo moves and swims.

Wood gunwales are lighter, drain quickly and are aesthetically pleasing, which is okay if you enjoy sanding, repairing and oiling. However, if you want to paddle your plastic boat in the cold, avoid wood gunwales. Plastic shrinks, whereas wood remains the same at cold temperatures. The difference in contraction rates causes cold cracks to radiate from the screws fastening on the gunwales. The owner's manual will tell you to remove the screws from the last two or three feet of the boat at both ends when the boat is stored in below-freezing temperatures. To be safe, remove the screws back to within two feet of the center and prop the inwale above the gunwale for storage. If this sounds like a make-work project, buy vinyl gunwales instead. Even with aluminum inserts the vinyl gunwales shrink at the same rate as the hull, so you need not worry about freezing. We've paddled Royalex boats with vinyl gunwales in temperatures as cold as −23 degrees Celsius with no visible damage.

A piece of static webbing pulled tight and screwed to the thwarts (J) helps to keep the airbags from billowing up when the boat is full of water. The lash-in cords are either threaded through clips attached under the gunwales or through holes drilled directly through the hull (K). Additional foam on one side of the canoe allows you to lighten your load after rolling up. A water bottle holder (L), throw bag holder (M), camera case tie-down (N) and energy bar slot (O) complete the outfitting.

Whew, sounds like a lot of work, doesn't it? It is— so unless you have really strong opinions on how it all fits together, hire a pro instead. I've outfitted a few boats and it still takes me about 14 hours to do a custom job.

Outfitting–For Your Knees

Foot braces immobilize your lower leg by pushing the knee against the thigh strap, and thereby help you to propel the boat. The hinge joint at your ankle levers the ball of your foot against the foot brace. When you turn your boat, you pull the paddle blade and your opposite knee together. Kayakers and C-1ers do that with arms, torso and thighs, but in an open canoe, your calf and the strong lever at your ankle also contribute. Since your knee is also a hinge joint, ergonomically this force is most efficient if the lower leg is in line with the upper leg. Hip sockets are about nine or ten inches apart, so the balls of your feet should be placed nine or ten inches apart, center to center. Ideally, foot braces should be placed about six inches apart.

Although the objective of foot braces is to keep the knees and thighs tightly secured in the straps, foot braces must nevertheless allow for an instant exit. You need about seven inches between the foot peg of the foot brace and the stern float bag so you can slide your foot back and remove your knees from the thigh straps. The foot brace and thigh straps should be adjusted so that when your muscles are relaxed, you are just in contact with each component of the system. To make these fine adjustments and accommodate different thickness of clothing or different paddlers, you need adjustable foot braces. Tightening your muscles will snug up or "load" the system. For both safety and comfort purposes, the angle of the ankle must be at least 90 degrees to the shin (not to the boat). If the toe is any farther forward, your legs will be snug and loaded while your muscles are relaxed and it will be difficult to exit.

Knee blocks and kneepads

Your knees give you the greatest control over tilt and help to turn the boat. If there is any play in the outfitting for your knees, it will delay the boat's response, your knees may get out of position, or even your stability can suffer. Difficulties with a roll, as we've said, can sometimes be traced to loose or improper outfitting. You can achieve comfort, security and safety by supporting your knees (and thighs) in each direction with a combination of foam padding and a knee-and-thigh-strap system. The lower strap on a double-strap system keeps the knee from lifting and going forward. Thigh straps and knee blocks stop the knee (and thigh) from shifting inward. Foot braces (see next section) prevent the knee from moving backward. The side of the hull (with padding, if required) stops the knee from moving outward.

Knee blocks serve two functions: they are part of a system that locks your knee (and thigh) in place, and they provide comfort and protection from rocks that might hit your boat beneath your knees. For playboats, L-shaped or contoured knee blocks hold the knee on the side as well as provide padding under the knee. *Kneepads* refer to a flat piece of foam that is adequate for tandem classic, where you may want to be able to move your knees to extend your reach across a wide canoe. In playboats, knees should be placed at the chine of the hull (as wide as possible), for stability and for the leverage required to control the boat. If you're short and can't reach the chines with your knees, look for a narrower open boat or check the height of your saddle. Especially in a soft-chined boat or for people with small knees, you may need to add some thickness a few inches up the side of the hull. This will prevent your knee from sliding outward and upward during the roll. On the inside of the knee, you need either the thigh straps or a raised block of foam (two or three inches above the one-inch-thick kneepad) to securely hold the knee because there is a lot of force when you're turning the boat. Install the straps and knee blocks in a V shape, aligned with the inside of your leg and knee.

If you doubt the importance of knee blocks in protecting you from impact, consider this: at least once a year I get painful bruises on one knee or the other despite good thick knee blocks. I recommend a full inch of foam under your knees and up the side of the hull. Without this, I'm sure I would have had several serious injuries. As your boat ages and the hull becomes softer, this is even more important. Minicell foam is the stuff to use. It is a stiff, closed-cell foam, but even it will compress over time and may need to be replaced.

Saddles

Saddles are made of minicell foam. Two three-inch-thick pieces are usually laminated to create a piece six inches thick. From this you cut a seat that is eight to nine and a half inches high. After installing your foot pegs, cut a drain hole in the shape of an upside-down U about five inches wide and almost as deep as the track. The hole allows water to flow from one side of the boat to the other when the boat is rolled; otherwise, you'll be lifting a lot of water when you roll.

Using a belt sander, very lightly sand the front edges of your saddle, being sure to leave a nice wide seat. Also sand away a depression for a water bottle on the front and a throw bag on the back. These items are held in place by one meter of five- or six-millimeter

74 Double equalizing straps.

shock cord run through plastic tubing inserted in the saddle. The tubing keeps thc shock cord from tearing out of the saddle. I usually drill out an energy-bar slot after I glue in the saddle.

Thigh straps

Thigh straps are the most important piece of outfitting for canoeists. Inferior or loose straps contribute to all kinds of common problems for beginner playboaters. Often, you can trace trouble with the open-boat roll to not being able to transfer motion from your hips to the canoe because your knees move in the straps. Insecure tilts are a symptom of not being locked into your outfitting. Without proper thigh straps, you will have trouble staying in the boat while being window-shaded. The bottom line is, if you're paddling a boat that is super-responsive, you need to be able to communicate with it instantaneously.

Let's examine several popular thigh-strap setups.

Double-equalizing Straps   The saddle-and-strap combination shown in photo 74 uses a full-length saddle and regular webbing thigh straps. Each strap is secured at the side of the boat, and then fed through the D-ring on the bottom of the hull and back to a D-ring on the side of the hull. This means the strap crosses your leg in two places, which is better than a single

strap just held together with velcro. This strap system has a quick release on the upper strap for emergency exits. To alleviate the frustration of having straps flopping down while you're trying to climb into your boat, tether them with shock cord to the thwart. The downside of this simple system is that if one of the two floor D-rings goes, your paddling day is pretty much finished.

Double Rigid Straps   The thigh strap setup shown in photo 75 uses four individual straps, each with its own D-ring on the side of the hull. The straps are sewn directly to a vinyl patch on the bottom of the canoe. The side patches are made of reinforced webbing sewn to the vinyl patch; this is lighter than using metal D-rings. The canoe in this photo is outfitted with rigid straps, which is my personal favorite when it comes to thigh straps. These straps maintain their shape using Lexon plastic. This means that entering and exiting your canoe is fast, which is an asset on the river when you don't have a big eddy in which to fiddle with your straps. In playboating you'll have to empty water out of your canoe a lot. So over the course of a long day you'll certainly begin to appreciate a system that's easy to climb into.

Thigh Retainer   The thigh retainer in photo 76, designed by Mowhawk Canoes, uses a combination of foam and straps to create a simple, secure connection

between you and the boat. The thigh retainer is quick to adjust. However, the degree of adjustment is limited. Since all the stress is now placed on two D-rings instead of eight, the D-rings must be really substantial. Some paddlers opt to use two thigh retainers to spread out the stress a little more.

Bulkheads   The bulkhead setup shown in photo 77 is similar to the plastic molded saddle made by Perception. The foam bulkhead provides a tighter fit because it can be individually shaped to you. It has one drawback, however; it does not have an emergency release. Be aware of the danger of being pushed against the stern deck during a broach or stern-first vertical pin. From this position, it's impossible to slip your feet off your foot pegs. Try it. Climb into your canoe on land and ask someone to push you gently back toward the stern. Feels ugly, doesn't it? With properly installed thigh straps, you should be able to reach the quick-release buckle from this pinned position. The bulkhead system also eliminates the storage space that is usually located in front of your saddle.

With all these setups, foot braces of some type and kneepads are essential to provide both paddling comfort and a snug fit. Take some time sanding kneepads to fit. The difference between a good fit and a bad one is comparable to the difference between bucket seats and bench seats in a car.

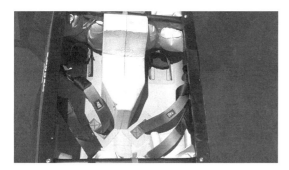

75 Double rigid straps.

76 Thigh retainer.

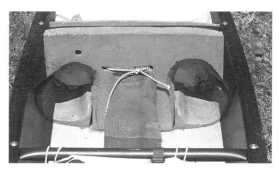

77 Bulkhead.

Outfitting–For Your Feet

Foot pegs

Foot pegs let you keep your knees jammed against the thigh straps. They are usually anchored to the saddle using screws set into a hardwood dowel that extends crossways through the saddle. An alternative is to bolt your foot-peg tracks to a threaded metal rod. Mash the threads on the end of the rod so the nuts are on permanently, or use lock nuts. To avoid having the rod work loose in the minicell foam, use either large washers or drill out a piece of dowel to accept the rod. Install the dowel at least two inches from the back of the saddle for structural integrity. Using 2.5- to 3-inch screws and a dowel is quicker, but make sure that the screws are stainless steel and the dowel is oiled hardwood. If you have trouble with screws pulling out it could be due to using softwood dowel, screws that are too short or a bad rolling technique with loose knee braces. (Excessive knee movement drives your foot against the peg to take up the slack. A smoother roll and more secure straps enable you to lift with your onside knee.)

To determine the height at which you should mount the foot pegs off the floor of the canoe, consider that ideally the ball of your foot should rest on the peg. Kneeling with your toes curled forward or

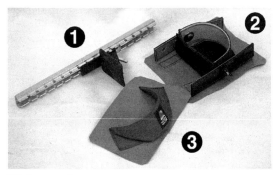

78 For your feet.

pointing straight down won't really affect your placement, height-wise, more than half an inch or so. If the foot pegs are more than two inches off the floor, you may be tempted to wedge your toes under the pegs. Avoid this practice. Why–since this is indeed a comfortable position? Well, one afternoon I was practicing some dryland boofing off a boathouse into a lake. On one particularly flat landing, the impact of hitting the water flexed the hull of the canoe enough to pinch my toes between the boat and the pegs. The results are much the same when the canoe hits a rock amidships near your toes. A more likely situation is that you'll have to wiggle your toes around to wet exit your boat, which could take extra time that you might be a little short on.

Foot pegs come as single-position blocks or adjustable ones. People who like their toes out to the side of the canoe, rather than in close to the center, as with saddle-mounted pegs, prefer the blocks that are glued to the hull rather than attached to the saddle. Some paddlers find that a wider stance is more comfortable and gives a more stable feeling. As well, you might not be able to bend over as far to the side with your feet wide apart. This can negatively affect your roll because you can't keep your head as low as you should while bringing it into the canoe. If you're flexible, of course, don't worry about this. But make sure you can slip your feet off the blocks when your feet are relaxed. This applies to either setup. Building a little slack into the system may allow you to move your feet clear before things become critical. Make sure, too, that, given the amount of force on the blocks during surfing and rolling, you've got the foot pegs seriously attached to your boat. Foot pegs that blow out are not a safety feature you can depend on in the event of being pinned against the stern of your boat.

Yakima foot pegs (photo 78, figure 1)   These foot braces are attached to the side of the saddle (see photo 73), 2.5 or 3 inches from the bottom of the boat to the center of the peg. This should put the ball of your foot on the peg. They can be attached to the saddle if it is long enough or on a separate foam block. My pegs are usually adjusted 4 inches behind the back rest of my saddle. The footrest attaches 7 inches behind the backrest of my saddle to allow for adjustment and bigger paddlers to use my boat. These foot braces are also used in whitewater kayaks and many brands are available. Most are plastic and because of the greater leverage and stress that open boaters put on them, the plastic parts are more likely to flex and pop off the track than the aluminum ones pictured. This system is rigid, and is quickly adjusted in small increments. Your feet can be slid off the side of the pegs and backwards for a safe, quick exit.

Toe blocks

North Water Adjustable Toe Blocks (photo 78, figure 2) Because these toe blocks are attached to the hull with vinyl adhesive, you can put them wherever you want in relation to the saddle. There is then less strain on the glue holding down the saddle. They are adjustable and accommodate a straight-up or bent-forward toe. Since the cup rotates, they also accommodate a C-1 style with the toe pointed backward, but see the comments on leverage in the introduction of foot braces.

North Water Stationary (photo 78, figure 3)   These function similarly to the adjustable toe blocks, but without the adjustment they are not as suitable for playboats. They are ideal for tandem classic use in combination with a seat, kneepads and thigh straps. The thigh straps provide adjustment forward or back.

Outfitting–Anchors

Anchors

Several types of anchors are available to attach all this outfitting to your boat. The most common anchor is either a webbing loop sewn to a vinyl patch or a metal D-ring sewn with webbing to a vinyl patch. These are often collectively referred to as D-rings (photo 80). Some thigh straps are sewn directly to the vinyl patch, which can then be glued with various brands of vinyl adhesive, or Staybond to Royalex boats. Staybond adheres quite well to Royalex but is the only adhesive recommended for R-84 or R-Light hulls. Another type of anchor is a rigid ABS plastic holding down a two-inch metal D-ring for thigh straps (photo 80), or a plastic one-inch D-ring for float-bag tiedowns. Urethane glue is recommended for rigid D-rings, although a new double-sided adhesive tape seems to work well and is easy to apply. Another anchor method is to soak the unbraided ends of nylon webbing or Kevlar rope in epoxy or urethane resin and then apply it directly to the hull, keeping a one- or two-inch section free of resin for the thigh strap or tiedown cord (photo 81). Leave the nylon rope mantle on the Kevlar rope to prevent the Kevlar fibers from fraying.

You might want to add an extra piece on each side in case one tears out on the river. As a last resort, bolt a D-ring directly through the hull (photo 82). Make sure you use big washers on the outside so they don't pull through the hull. The metal bolts and washers do tend to catch on rocks–kind of like the old aluminum-canoe syndrome.

Float bags are typically tied down with cord to either one-inch metal D-rings (stainless steel preferred) or "lightweight D-rings" with only a webbing loop (no metal). Since there isn't a lot of friction, the rope on webbing is fine and you avoid the weight of the metal D-ring. A small vinyl patch is adequate because there isn't a lot of force. However, the forces on thigh straps can be significantly greater. The vinyl patches are larger and consequently the sewing must be well reinforced. For the anchor on the side of the hull, avoid the metal D-rings. The webbing style or resin-soaked rope is lighter and lower profile, and therefore doesn't pull down straps that are designed to remain in position for easy entry (photo 81). A metal D ring is preferred for a double-equalizing thigh strap where there will be friction of moving webbing.

79 Webbing anchor on a vinyl patch.

80 D-ring with adhesive tape.

81 Kevlar rope anchor.

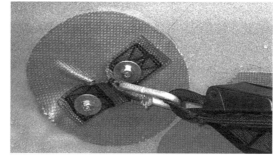

82 Bolts!

Outfitting

83

Tying in float bags   Float bags come in various lengths for the ends (three-dimensional and triangular) or center (rectangular and flat). Length refers to the length of the bag deflated. Measure the length of the space that you will be filling, add three inches for solo or five inches for tandem and get a bag that is at least that long. This will maximize the flotation in the space you've allowed. A little longer is okay, but too long and the bag will be squeezing out between the cross-cords.

Solo boats   If your float bags aren't fully inflated and held in securely, water will get under them and negate some of their benefit. Insufficient or loose tiedowns and an encounter with violent hole can even allow bags to squirt out of the boat. This can be a comical interlude at a rodeo, or a big problem in a long rapid. A standard setup for a moderate playboat paddler has cord placed every five inches and a webbing strap down the middle (see photo 83). A zigzag rope cage between the deck loops or webbing screwed to the bottom of the thwart and three anchors on the hull hold in the ends of the bag. The three corners of the float bags are tied down. You can use a similar setup in a solo classic canoe. Leave about four inches of space between the stern float bag and your foot peg for your foot to move back and release the knees from the thigh straps when you exit the boat.

With a setup like this, I've seen the float bags try to squeeze through and escape between the cords, so the float bags in my boat are held in with cord every three inches, with three webbing or cord straps lengthwise, five anchors holding in the bow and four anchors (plus the saddle) holding in the stern. A slider on the lengthwise webbing with the cross-cord running between it holds the cross-cord in place. Where lengthwise cord intersects the cross-cords, a clove hitch knot serves the same purpose. The cross-cords are attached to the boat either through holes in the hull just below the gunwales or through tie-down loops or sewable D-rings riveted to the underside of vinyl gunwales or screwed to wood trim. Holes bored through the hull do not really damage the structural integrity of the boat and are less likely to break or pull out, but most boats come equipped with loops on the gunwales that are adequate (except that you may want the spacing closer). I use four-millimeter nylon cord, which has very little stretch and enough strength but is small enough to be lightweight and not too expensive. Some people avoid tying the corners of the bag so there is no chance of the bag ripping if it twists in the rope cage. But if you have a good cage and keep the airbags tight, there shouldn't be much movement, plus the corners of most bags are fairly strong. Also, I don't like the little "bat ears" that tend to stick out if the corners aren't tied. Mesh or nylon float-bag covers are also available. If you use these to replace the cords, there may be too much stretch. You can use them in addition to cord to help secure the bags and protect them from abrasion, but they add weight and the bags are tough enough without them.

Tandem boats   The tiedown system for modern tandem-classic paddlers is similar to the solo system. End bags are typically held in place with one small

anchor on the bottom and optionally two on the side. Cross-cords are located every three to five inches and add a longitudinal cord or webbing to complete the security. Center bags are held in place with cross-cords located every three to five inches and one or two lengthwise straps with two or three anchors at each end. The lengthwise straps or cord can be secured with webbing or deck loops under the center thwart or yoke. Tandem center bags are available as one large bag or as two split center bags that occupy the same volume. The advantage of the split center-bag system is that your head will fit between the two bags for portaging. Otherwise your head will be hunched over and very uncomfortable. In the case of split center bags, an additional anchor is required for the two cross-cords in front of the yoke and additional anchors are required to secure the corners of the bag. The tandem setup usually wouldn't have a thwart at the end of the bag. This is adequate, or you could use webbing, which stretches less than rope, to define the end of the bag area and create a tighter rope cage. There isn't quite enough space to effectively put flotation between the two paddlers in a tandem playboat, but I keep considering it. The setup for the ends can be the same as for a solo playboat.

Transporting float bags   Some people remove float bags when they're driving to the river. The ones I have used are sufficiently durable to withstand that stress. If you ensure that they're fully inflated, they won't flap around as much. If you're concerned about leaving your float bags in the boat during the winter, consider that we keep our bags in the boat and use them throughout the winter, and they're frequently outside and covered in ice between our weekly trips in subfreezing temperatures.

Painters

Long painters have no place on a playboat. In fact, throw bags have pretty much replaced painters for all aspects of canoeing. Short painters that are eight feet long are still handy for tying up classic canoes and tandem playboats, since these bigger boats are somewhat cumbersome to manage on steep shorelines. But when the painter is not in use, it must be securely stowed in the canoe.

Decks

Deck removal was all the rage at the 1993 Whitewater Rodeo World Championship on the Ocoee River. The theory behind removing the decks from the bow and stern of a canoe is that when the bow or stern is driven into oncoming water to attempt an ender, the exposed end of the canoe acts like a scoop, causing the canoe to go vertical even if you're off-line a little.

Two years later, the championships were held in Augsburg, Germany. At that competition most of the canoes had been shortened and were sporting outrageously huge decks—the theory now being that with the short canoe getting vertical with ease, the big decks would allow them to rotate faster and easier while vertical; smooth decks wouldn't slow the rotation as much of the open "bucket" as a deckless canoe. Shortly after that competition, rules were introduced regarding the size of the deck relative to the size of the canoe, to avoid having the canoes start to look like big kayaks.

Before you go deckless, there are other factors to consider—structural integrity, dryness, weight and aesthetics. In most whitewater canoes, the deck is molded polyethylene, so aesthetics are not usually a prime concern.

Flotation

During one of my canoe-customizing binges I decided to follow the growing trend of filling the cockpit with extra foam. This displaces water that would otherwise be sloshing around in the boat, making it heavy and unstable. Of course, you're adding to the overall weight of the boat when it is empty of water, because foam is heavier than air. The extra foam glued to the hull greatly reduces the amount of water that remains in the canoe after a roll. I began to experiment with a three-inch thick piece of foam glued to the interior side of the canoe down the length of the cockpit. I noticed that the foam displaced enough water to reduce the depth in the cockpit by about four inches. The additional flotation doesn't hamper your Eskimo roll because the foam is underwater during your hip snap. As you finish your roll, the flotation helps to keep the canoe upright. That's a bonus!

Vinyl adhesives

The vinyl adhesives used to attach vinyl patch D-rings or thigh straps to Royalex don't always come with adequate instructions. Mark where the patch will go and then sand the surface of the hull. Although it may be overkill, I also sand the edges of the vinyl patch (carefully avoiding the threads that attach the D-ring). Clean both surfaces with a solvent that does not leave a residue, such as toluene, methyl-ethyl-ketone (MEK) or alcohol. Acetone is also commonly used, but beware: acetone dissolves Royalex. All of these solvents should be wiped on sparingly so that they evaporate within a few seconds. Apply a thin layer of glue to the patch and the hull and let it dry completely (about 15 minutes). The solvent in the glue will also dissolve Royalex, so if you apply it too thickly or don't allow it to dry completely before attaching the patch,

84 Fully inflated airbags left in the sun.

the solvent doesn't have an opportunity to evaporate and will damage the hull. When the surface is completely dry to the touch, heat both surfaces with a hair dryer. The surface of the glue will become slightly glossy. A heat gun is quicker, but be careful not to overheat the patch, the hull or to melt the nylon threads attaching the webbing. The two surfaces will now bond on contact. Try to lay it down smoothly to avoid air bubbles. Ideally, allow six to eight hours for the adhesive to cure fully. Use the same procedure for Staybond, except that because it is a two-part glue, some people recommend allowing it to cure fully for a few days. To remove D-rings, separate a corner with a knife, grip it with pliers or vice-grips and apply heat. You should be able to slowly peel away the patch. In photo 84, you'll notice that both center D-rings have pulled off. A quick and improper job installing them combined with the pressure of expanding float bags on a hot day caused them to tear off the hull. Take the time to install them properly and they should hold for several years.

Repairs

Abrasion

Because most of the boats used for whitewater are Royalex, this section will focus on repairs to Royalex boats. See Materials in *Path of the Paddle* or any manufacturer's catalogue for a complete description of the attributes of Royalex. In Royalex, the outer (and inner) colored layer is a vinyl skin. Although it doesn't add structural strength, it does protect the ABS plastic layer underneath from harmful UV rays. This vinyl layer abrades easily against sand and rocks and at some point that light-green layer may show through. When you cut through this layer (as you will to repair rips), you'll find that unexposed ABS will cut smoothly, whereas ABS that has been exposed for a year or two is brittle and cracks. The solution is simple: apply vinyl paint. It makes a difference both structurally and cosmetically. Paddle-sports shops sell vinyl spray paint to match the original color of your boat. Apply four or five thin layers and repeat as needed through the season.

Dents

The most common injury that occurs to my boats is dents on the stem (photo 85). Impact resistance is not one of the strengths of Royalex. Impact with a relatively flat area often produces a slight indentation,

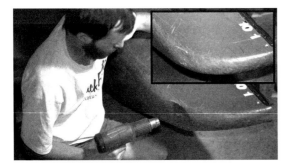

85 Removing dents.

but the Royalex flexes and absorbs the hit. In tightly curved and rigid areas, such as the stem and to a lesser degree the chines, however, a dent is the typical result. My creek boats get dents from running into rocks at the bottom of drops, and, contrary to common sense, the stem is not immune to these impacts. Dents on the stems of my rodeo boats occur more commonly and are caused by impact with the bottom during vertical moves. They can be anywhere from the waterline to the very tip of where the stem meets the deck.

Dents can be removed by slow moderate heat, as you apply pressure on the inside of the hull with a heavy blunt object. After 5 to 10 minutes of heating, the plastic will return to its original shape. Start at the edges to avoid creating sharp kinks. Experience and impatience have led Paul (photo 85) to use a heat gun. It's faster, but you run the risk of overheating the Royalex.

Even after a nice slow job of pushing out a dent, the area will be weaker than before and more prone to denting again with less impact. If the dent is anywhere but the stem, leave it at that. On the stem, however, consider installing an impact-resistance skid plate if the area is likely to receive repeated impact. I usually wait until the ends have been smashed several times before installing the plate, but some people do so as soon as they get the boat. On classic canoes, the impact tends to be concentrated on the stem so that makes sense. If you're lazy or not too rough on your equipment, leave them off your playboat in the name of lightness, since hits are less likely and more spread out on the blunt, more rockered ends. Skid plates are sold in commercially available kits with epoxy or urethane resin and Kevlar felt. Kevlar felt is thick and easy to smooth out around tight corners. Because of these attributes, it provides more impact resistance than

Kevlar cloth, which has more tensile strength, flexibility and lightness and should be used for rips.

Rips

You should repair rips and tears with epoxy or urethane resin and Kevlar cloth. Fiberglass and poorer-quality resins will adhere to Royalex, but due to the forces that will be put on the repaired tear, the tensile strength of Kevlar and the flexibility and impact resistance of epoxy or urethane resin will serve you best. I've repaired hundreds of boats, but my most relevant qualification for giving advice on this comes from cutting a foot out of the middle of my playboats. I put the edges together with a seam of two layers of Kevlar on the inside and two layers on the outside, using epoxy or urethane resin. The edges are abutted. The cut is wobbly enough that resin soaks through into the foam layer of the Royalex. Before starting, I sanded and cleaned the surface. My seam job got a thorough test when I noticed on a trip south that the resin I had used for the outer layer hadn't cured properly and the entire patch had peeled away. I ran the narrows of the Green River, which include several substantial drops and lots of grinding and hitting things (the way I paddled it), with the inside patch holding quite well.

To repair a rip, sand and clean with alcohol the area where you'll apply the patch. If the two edges fit together neatly, make a V-shaped incision just barely into the foam layer so the resin will soak into the foam. On a tear I apply two layers of Kevlar cloth on the inside and two on the outside. The first are two inches wide, and the second, three inches wide. When I put two halves of a canoe together I use a three-inch, then a five-inch, patch inside and out. Apply resin to the tear, put the cloth on, saturate it with resin and let it cure.

You may have to tape the inside and apply the patches on one side at a time. Use only enough resin to saturate the cloth. The strength is in the cloth; more resin means more weight and less flexibility. For a smooth finish without the need to sand, put wax paper on the patch and peel it off when the resin is cured. In cases where a major deformity accompanies the rip or pieces are missing, use Kevlar and a thick marine epoxy resin that is sold by Mad River. You'll need a putty knife instead of a brush, but you can fill in holes and depressions. It works for simple tears as well, but leaves a thicker patch than the more viscous resins.

Gunwales

Vinyl gunwales   Vinyl gunwales require no upkeep, but I like to remove the dents if they are in the zone where my paddle shaft rubs on the gunwale. Using the heat gun (that Mark was harassing me about earlier in this section), I heat up the vinyl, then apply pressure and hold it until the repair cools. Cooling the gunwale with water speeds things up. If the aluminum insert inside the gunwale has been bent, you'll probably need to apply more pressure. First, unbolt the thwarts and set the kinked section of gunwale over a hollow in the ground. Carefully warm the damaged section of gunwale while gently stepping on it. I once used a F-150 pickup truck to straighten the gunwale of an aluminum canoe. It worked great until my third run at it, when the backing board slipped from between the canoe and the tree I was using as a back stop. The dent in the boat probably wouldn't have been so big if the truck hadn't been in four-wheel drive.

Wood gunwales   Oil wood gunwales with tung oil so that they remain supple. Reapplying oil when they appear dry is good maintenance. If they do crack, repair them with epoxy resin. With a completely broken gunwale, splice in a new piece, rather than replacing the whole rail. Use a six-inch scarf joint or taper to spread out the weak spot. Epoxy and screw the gunwale back together.

Drysuit repairs

Drysuit repairs fall into three categories: replacing zippers, replacing gaskets and repairing pin holes in the fabric. The first is best left to the manufacturer; the other two can pretty much be considered regular maintenance by any conscientious drysuit owner. I say "conscientious," since some folks just tolerate leaks until they can afford a new suit. Because drysuits are expensive, increasing the lifespan of your suit is well worth the effort. Here are some practical tips:

- *Apply Seal Saver by Aquaseal to protect latex gaskets from UV rays.*
- *Apply a lubricant such as Max wax by Aquaseal to zippers to ease wear and tear*
- *Wear a wool sock over the nylon or latex socks of a suit to stop sand from abrading your suit.*
- *Before investing in a suit with integral socks, remember that it's easier to repair holes in nylon-integrated socks than it is in latex socks.*
- *Repair any small holes as they appear.*

To repair holes, turn the drysuit inside out; then, using a garden hose, fill the suspected area with water. Find and mark the holes. After the suit has dried, apply Aquaseal to the holes. Decide whether you need to apply it to both the exterior and the interior of the suit. For larger rips, use a piece of urethane-coated nylon or the same material as the drysuit. You can glue it with a vinyl adhesive or Aquaseal. If you use the latter, tape down the edges while the Aquaseal cures; otherwise the edges of the patch will curl up.

Replacing gaskets   To replace a gasket, prepare your suit by cutting away most of the old gasket, but leave about 1.5 inches of the old seal on the suit. This remnant is what the new seal will adhere to. It's very important to find an appropriate-sized object to stuff into your suit to hold open the remains of the old gasket. A volleyball works great on neck seals, while glass jars will fit the wrists or ankles. If your container is too small, wrap it in paper to get the right diameter. Now you're ready to go. Follow the instructions for your brand of adhesive and wear appropriate protective gear–for example, surgical gloves and a gas mask.

If a seal only has a small tear in it, Aquaseal can extend the life of the seal until it's convenient to replace it.

Finally, never lend your drysuit! You can even say I told you not to, so you won't have to worry about hurting your friends' feelings.

Latex cuffs are very fragile, and first-time drysuit users are prone to tearing them because they tug them on.

86 *Replacing a neck gasket.*

87 A canoeing addiction is hereditary.

I now believe that my love of the Chestnut Prospector shape is hereditary–something I have my father, Bill Mason, to thank for. Accepting my fate, I can now spend my energy convincing everyone else how great the canoe is, rather than trying to justify to myself why I prefer to paddle a Prospector.

I readily admit that it isn't the fastest, driest, most stable or most maneuverable canoe. But it has all of these attributes to some degree. So for a canoe that you might take on an extended flatwater trip or use for a little surfing later in the summer, you can't choose a more suitable craft.

Start with the classic canoe that you have, even if it isn't a Prospector. It should have a few key design features if you're aiming to have anything other than

an exasperating surfing experience. The first is rocker. This will allow you to turn quickly and keep the ends of the canoe from submarining. A canoe with a large carrying capacity will be drier, especially if some of that volume is near the ends of the canoe. Tumblehome amidships rather than flare will allow you to reach the water more easily and tilt farther and still stay dry. Take the time to outfit the boat for playing in whitewater. The odds of dumping or sinking are much greater when you're looking for the biggest waves to play in than when you're paddling down the rapids trying to avoid them.

Other practical advice. First, prepare for swimming by dressing for the occasion, including wearing a helmet. Second, equip your canoe with additional

flotation to prevent it from being damaged. A higher-floating canoe also poses less of a hazard to you if you swim. Next, you'll improve the performance of a classic canoe with the addition of knee pads and thigh straps. You've probably experienced that egg-yolk-on-a-Teflon-frying-pan feeling while doing things like eddy turns. Well, when you attempt the first maneuver, unless you have knee pads you'll end up sliding toward the bow.

It's becoming common for people to go directly from walking on dry land to paddling a solo playboat, but many of us did a slow progression from a classic tandem canoe to playing solo in the same canoe before either becoming aware of the new designs or saving the money to buy one. Either way seems to work.

For an extensive review of basic whitewater canoeing strokes, refer to the book or video version of *Path of the Paddle*, written by my late father, Bill Mason, But here's a brief review to ensure that your strokes are as efficient as possible.

Pivot strokes

Draw   This stroke has endless variations as you adapt it to each situation. Ideally, you reach far out to plant the stroke and keep the paddle vertical in the water (photo 88). To do this, your body weight must move out onto your paddle. Use your whole torso to pull your end of the canoe toward your paddle. Finish the stroke with your body centered back in the canoe. If you're pulling with your entire body, you'll naturally find yourself back in the canoe at the end of each stroke. Staying in sync with your partner will keep the canoe from rocking violently. Watch where your end of the canoe is going. Hitting a rock while watching your paddle can produce comical results–for the onlookers, at least.

88 Draw.

89 Pry.

Pry   The main thing to remember with the pry is that the most efficient part of the stroke comes when the paddle is vertical; hence the reason for starting the stroke with the paddle blade actually under the canoe! Keep the stroke short. A general guideline is to keep the paddle within 20 to 25 degrees of vertical. Slicing the paddle under the canoe will cause your upper body to move out over the paddle (photo 89). This is desirable, as you can then use your torso muscles to pull your grip hand back into the boat, creating a strong lever action off the gunwale. This technique is much stronger than if you had used only your arm muscles.

If you're a stern paddler, you should slant the paddle backward at 45 degrees, with the blade close to the stern. This places your stroke farther from the pivot point of the canoe and keeps the blade near the surface, thus avoiding the rocks that seem to inhabit rapids. Since the pry is a very short stroke, make sure the blade actually slaps the hull as you initiate the stroke.

The power of the pry illustrates why tandem classic paddlers should avoid using lightweight carbon-shaft paddles. A more appropriate choice is a fiberglass or reinforced wood shaft. In tandem canoeing, you need a lot more force for a longer time to move the canoe; therefore the stress on the paddle shaft is greater than in solo canoeing.

90 Cross draw.

Cross-draw   This stroke is effective only in the bow. Remember to rotate your torso to face your offside, the side on which you will be doing your cross-draw. Bring your paddle over across the canoe as you rotate your torso, and set the blade in the water a comfortable distance from the canoe (photo 90). This gives you some leeway in case you've misjudged the strength of the current. Your lower arm will be straight. Your grip hand will be low, close to your body. This arm position puts the blade well in front of you without your having to lean forward. If your canoe has forward momentum or you are entering current, just hold this position and let the force of the water on the blade exert a turning action. If there is no current, push out with your grip hand and pull in with your lower arm. For maximum power, untwist your torso a little on each stroke. A variation on the cross-draw is to keep the shaft a little more vertical. Although this is less efficient as a pivot stroke, it does allow you to easily shift to an offside forward stroke.

A good complementary stern stroke for the cross-draw is the **back sweep**. It begins as a pry to initiate the turn, then the paddle blade flattens out, creating a bracing effect. This is desirable given the precarious position of the bow person during the cross-draw.

91 J-stroke.

92

Correction strokes

Normally when you're running rapids, the ability to maintain forward speed isn't usually a critical factor in whether you have a successful run. But once you stop to play in a rapid, you're often paddling against the current. Even in the most advanced rodeo moves, you can often attribute your failure to execute them to poor forward-paddling technique.

Develop a powerful forward stroke by rotating your torso instead of relying on arm power (photo 91). For an in-depth study of forward strokes, see the Tandem Playboat chapter.

J-Stroke   The superior tracking ability of classic canoes means you need less correction than in playboats, so the J stroke is still the best way to correct the canoe's tendency to turn away from the stern paddler's onside. The rudder action of the J-stroke uses the water passing by the canoe. The stroke can be very subtle, yet very effective. In photo 92, note that the paddle is parallel to the hull, with the blade face vertical in the water and the shaft angled well back toward the stern. The thumb on the grip hand points down, indicating that the power face of the paddle is being used for the correction.

To stay in sync with the bow paddler, the stern paddler may need to shorten the power phase of the stroke or occasionally skip a stroke while steering.

93 *High brace (bow), low brace (stern).*

94 *Low brace (bow), high brace (stern).*

Bracing strokes

High/low brace A canoe is most unstable when both paddlers are caught with their paddles out of the water. Bracing strokes stabilize your canoe. Photos 93 and 94 illustrate the usual high/low brace combination. As your paddling skills improve, you'll also be able to incorporate a bracing action into the other strokes. Here's a useful fact to file away in the back of your mind: any pressure on your paddle has a stabilizing effect on your canoe. It's true—try it. Paddle slowly through a wave and apply a long power stroke when you would usually brace. Pretty cool, eh? This allows you to perform a maneuver without interrupting it to brace. Inevitably, of course, a situation arises where you need some serious righting action to avoid a swim. This is when you go for a **high** or a **low** brace. You perform each brace the same, regardless of whether you're using it in the bow or stern.

The high brace now has a simpler purpose and is becoming more effective than it used to be. The new-and-improved (and, I'm sure, calorie-reduced) high brace is used to pull yourself upright when the canoe is tipping to your offside. The key points to remember:

never, ever give up on the brace, and move body weight to the high side!

The low brace is the true miracle brace. It can right the canoe from an almost impossible angle if the other paddler can stay in the boat. There are several important things to remember to avoid shoulder injuries when cranking on the low brace. Set up the stroke by leaving your shaft hand where it usually is during a forward stroke. Place your grip hand, palm up, at your bellybutton and don't let it stray from this spot. Your objective is to lay your paddle out as far from the canoe as possible for better leverage. By leaning out to the side, you can gain extra reach. This transfers your weight from the canoe to the paddle, allowing you to push the high gunwale down while pulling up on the low one with your knees and thigh straps. By leaning out instead of reaching, your lower arm stays bent, protecting your shoulder from nasty and painful injuries. Once you've transferred your weight and begun to right the canoe, duck your head down and forward as you bring your upper body back into the boat. This lowers your center of gravity.

How important is this? Well, try standing on the ground holding a watermelon over your head. Now lean to the side, trying not to fall over. I'll bet that as you started to fall over, you brought the melon down to your chest to regain your balance. I rest my case. This proves that we need to keep our heads low when righting the canoe–and to eat more watermelon to lower our center of gravity.

One additional brace, named the **righting pry**, is covered in the chapter on Solo Playboats because it pertains more to that type of boat.

95 Back paddle.

Most people assume they can do a backpaddle stroke naturally. And someone climbing into a canoe for the first time can in fact make the canoe weave by alternating a forward, er, splash with a back, um, flail. But undoubtedly you want more than just generic flailing.

Your backpaddle stroke needs a vertical paddle throughout and the use of your torso to increase power. Twisting your torso allows you to plant your paddle farther back (see photo 95) and uses larger muscle groups than those in your arms. The technique is the same as for a solid forward power stroke, but reversed.

Several tricks make traveling backward in a canoe easier. Try to look over your shoulder in the direction you're moving. Sounds simple, but you may need some practice to get used to it. Once the canoe starts

to back-surf, the rules change, but this will be covered in the upcoming section on back-surfing.

The trim of the canoe is easily the most important component in maintaining control while paddling backward. The stern, which in this case is the leading end, needs to ride higher than the bow. I admit that this is tough to achieve if the stern paddler is heavier than the bow paddler and is restricted in sliding forward by airbags and thigh straps. If the back-surf potential of the wave is just too sweet to pass up, you may need to make room to move forward by shortening your center bag a little.

The correction strokes for backpaddling are divided into two groups: major correction strokes and minor correction strokes. Major correction strokes control the angle of the canoe but contribute little to its backward motion. Minor correction strokes have a strong backpaddling component with some control over travel direction. The bow person performs minor angle corrections; the stern paddler maintains backward momentum. For major changes in the angle of the canoe, the stern paddler can also help out.

Major corrections

Back Draw   To dramatically turn the stern of the canoe to the bow paddler's offside while backpaddling,

the bow paddler does a **back draw** (photo 96). Because current is passing by the canoe, you can freeze the stroke in the position that your paddle would be in at the end of a dynamic back-draw stroke.

To do this static back-draw stroke, angle the paddle toward the bow, with your grip hand extended out past the gunwale. By pushing the grip hand out farther and pulling the shaft hand in, you can increase the angle of the blade relative to the current passing by. To increase the turning effect, try twisting the blade so it grabs the water more. This will start to resemble a forward stroke and creates a lot of drag, slowing the backward momentum of the canoe, which is a bad thing. Use it as a last resort.

The stern paddler can help out with this major angle correction by doing a **stern cut**. Angle the paddle to the stern, keeping a moderate angle on the blade. This will avoid creating excessive drag.

Cross-Draw   To turn the stern of the canoe toward the bow's onside while moving backward, the bow paddler will need to do a cross-draw while the stern does a back sweep (see photo 97). The bow's cross-draw is a static stroke, relying on the passing water to turn the boat. Pushing the grip hand out will increase the angle of the blade relative to the current, which

96 Back draw.

97 Cross draw.

98 Back sweep.

99 Reverse-J.

results in a faster turn but also more drag. Having efficient, streamlined strokes when back-paddling is especially important, given how difficult it is to generate reverse speed in the first place. After practicing front-surfing, you will realize the importance of speed in catching a wave. How can you increase your backpaddling speed? Well, try controlling the canoe with the following strokes, which emphasize backpaddling over major angle correction.

Minor corrections

The minor correction strokes are exactly the same as the ones you use to back-ferry. Their purpose is to maintain speed as you approach the wave for back-surfing. During minor corrections the stern paddler only paddles backward and doesn't help in the correction.

Backsweep   To turn toward the bow's offside, the bow paddler uses a backsweep (photo 98). Really lean on it to put your weight behind the stroke. Start the stroke more than 90 degrees to the canoe and sweep toward the front, taking the paddle out as the shaft contacts the gunwale.

Reverse-J   To turn toward the bow's onside, the bow paddler uses the reverse J (see photo 99). Keep the paddle vertical through the power phase of the back stroke and pause at the end to let the passing water do the steering. Avoid levering the paddle forcefully off the gunwale, as this will slow the canoe.

Compound back stroke

The compound back stroke is an effective stroke for back-ferrying out to the surfing wave. The benefit of this stroke is that the paddle remains vertical throughout (photo 100). The secret to efficiency with this stroke is to flip the paddle so that you change the power face as it nears your hips (photo 101). Continue pushing the blade toward the bow as you would during a normal backpaddle stroke (photo 102). At this point the bow paddler could do a reverse J to control the direction of the canoe.

100 *Combound back stroke.*

101

102

It's quite possible to roll a big classic canoe, provided you can adequately hold yourself in the boat. It helps to have the airbags fully inflated so they don't float to the high side, since that would make it difficult to finish righting the canoe. A tandem classic canoe, as we discussed in Flotation in the Equipment chapter, will retain a huge quantity of water even when it is well outfitted with airbags. Even if you do roll up, the canoe will be very sluggish; so you need to assess each upside-down situation to determine if the best self-rescue is to roll. If your roll is slow and inconsistent or the rapids are rocky, it may be safer to swim immediately to shore. In a pool after a rapid, a roll can be a practical and fun way to avoid towing your boat and a lot of swimming. The other alternative is to bail out as you upset and then climb back in when the rapids end.

The actual mechanics of rolling a classic canoe are covered in Chapter 4, Solo Classic. Here are some of the differences you need to consider when rolling tandem. You have two options in setting up for a tandem roll. The first is for one person to switch paddling sides so that both paddlers do an onside roll on the same side. The drawback here is that it takes time to switch hands and set up. The alternative is for one person to do an offside roll. Among the people I paddle with, the bow paddler tends to do the offside roll or switching sides. This is only because bow paddlers are often content to paddle on their "weak" side when both paddlers prefer the same side. Since they are on their weak side already, they're actually doing an offside roll to their strong side. Figure out what works best for you and your partner. Timing your roll so the two of you work together is critical. More patient crews use a countdown or knock on the hull to signal each other. However, I'm not usually that calm and rational when I'm underwater. So I just

103 Stern low brace, bow offside.

104

105

pause to set up and go. If my partner wasn't ready the first time, he or she can get in rhythm for the second attempt!

Surfing is something I bet most whitewater tripping canoeists do as a means to an end. You're on the left shore of the river and need to cross to the other side to run a better channel. What is the maneuver of choice? A front ferry. As you ferry across the river, the canoe will catch short rides on each wave you cross. All you need to do is close the angle so that the canoe is parallel to the current and it's surfin' time.

A 16-foot canoe will often span the total length of the wave, meaning you don't have much say in where the canoe rides on the wave. The bigger waves are a different story. The same wave can have opposite effects: it can pull the canoe relentlessly into the trough to bury the bow underwater, or it can seem impossible to stay on. Everything depends on where you are on the wave. To figure that out, you need to be able to recognize the different parts of a surfing wave (see "Anatomy of a surfing wave," page 13).

When it comes to front-surfing, tandem has its advantages. Two paddlers mean more power–or, better yet, more forward power–and canoe angle correction at the same time. Strong tandem teams can actually overcome a downstream current for that brief moment it takes to catch a wave. On the other hand, once a tandem canoe catches a wave, paddlers have their work cut out for them staying dry and upright.

The weight of the bow paddler tends to cause the bow to dive under the oncoming water. And if the paddlers lose their angle they won't get a second chance at recovering a good downstream tilt if they didn't have one initially. Sitting deeper in the current, the canoe will be more responsive to broadside forces and susceptible to flipping upstream.

So tandem front-surfing is a great place to start experiencing the fun of playing in whitewater, but there will be limits to what you can successfully surf. Of course, surfs that end up wet can be lots of fun, too!

Catching a wave for a front-surf

There are three ways to catch a wave for a tandem front-surf: sliding onto it from the side; dropping onto it from upstream; or paddling up and over the crest from downstream.

Approach from the side   The easiest method is to ferry out onto the wave from the side. This approach works especially well if the wave has a shoulder to assist your ferry. The three main elements of maneuvering in whitewater–angle, motion and tilt–still apply. The angle must be narrow as you start into the current and prepare to close the angle, bringing the canoe parallel to the current to catch the wave. As you leave the eddy, forward momentum is important to maximize your chance of catching the wave. You'll need to tilt downstream initially, to stay upright as you cross the eddyline but also to control your angle on the wave. Both paddlers supply forward power, with the stern paddler making the major corrections to the angle. For example, if you were paddling on the downstream side in the stern, you would use a pry to open the angle, or a draw to close the angle. Your bow paddler can assist you in setting the angle before leaving the eddy but then must concentrate solely on supplying forward power to catch the wave. A helpful hint for bow paddlers: look to the side, where the canoe is actually going, to determine how hard to paddle forward; excessive enthusiastic paddling will cause the canoe to plow into the back side of the wave upstream.

Approach from upstream   The second way to catch a surfing wave is to drop onto it from upstream. This is easier in a tandem canoe than a solo canoe, due to the extra forward power available, and is one reason why it's easier to learn tandem first, provided you're paddling with a skilled partner. Still, catching a wave from upstream requires paying close attention to the canoe's angle. The canoe must be parallel to the current as you descend into the trough, with both paddlers applying forward power. Any corrections to the angle must be completed before the canoe begins its descent into the trough preceding the wave. As the canoe crests the wave directly above the one you want to catch, begin paddling forward with an efficient power stroke, using torso rotation. At this point, the stern paddler can still do a J stroke or sweep to fine-tune the angle. The canoe should be angled slightly toward the stern paddler's side to compensate for the fact that it will straighten out during the next few power strokes without correction. As the canoe reaches the trough, increase your stroke rate. Now you'll be using your shoulders and arms to generate power. Any correction strokes at this point will probably blow your attempt. The stern of the canoe will start to lift as it rides up the face of the wave. This is it! Use your arm muscles to crank out an almost continuous forward power in that brief moment before the canoe catches the wave and starts to surf. The importance of paddling upstream against the current long before actually reaching the wave can't be emphasized enough. The less downstream momentum, the better.

Approach from downstream   A less common approach is to paddle upstream over the shoulder of the wave and onto the face. This will work only if the wave is small and near an eddy, or if the wave curls on top. A good foam pile on top of a wave means slower water on the backside of the wave. However, if the foam pile is big enough to create an eddy, you're probably talking about a hole rather than a wave. If the opportunity arises to catch a wave from below, here

106 Tupperware party.

are a few points to remember. Set an angle that won't require any correction until you've attained the foam pile. This may mean that you begin angled to the stern paddler's side to compensate for the canoe's tendency to veer away from that side. Apply efficient forward strokes to obtain as much momentum as possible before leaving the eddy. In other words, really emphasize your torso rotation. As you enter the current, increase your stroke rate so that on the power phase your paddle is moving faster than the downstream current. Maintain a minimal tilt. Your canoe moves faster when it is flat on the water, so only use tilt to avoid having the ends of the canoe catch the current, which would require correction strokes. Paddling upstream over the crest of a wave is a satisfying attainment move that lets you really play the river, so choose your wave carefully and go for it!

Carving turns

Check it out! You've caught your first surfing wave! But your jubilation quickly changes to consternation as the bow of your canoe suddenly disappears into the trough, leaving your bow paddler buried to the chest and too preoccupied with the cold blast of water to be really concerned with the fact that the surf is over.

Or instead of settling into a front surf, the canoe tries to careen across the face of the wave, rocketing you off the far side and ending your ride, albeit in a dryer fashion than in the first scenario. Warning to other paddlers: when you see a 16-foot tandem canoe doing this, *take cover!* An incredible amount of force is at play. A collision could mean kayaks embedded in the side of the canoe, with the resulting bruises or broken bones. The best way to maintain control, stay dry and avoid being despised by all other river folk, is to learn how to carve turns on a wave. The photos on this page illustrates this maneuver on a small wave that would otherwise bury the bow. The carving turns are described relative to the onside or offside of the stern paddler, who will control the angle most of the time.

Turning to the stern's onside   This is the most surefire turn because the stern paddler can use the powerful pry stroke. This stroke alone is a pretty good reason to stick to a paddle with a fiberglass or wooden shaft, rather than a stiffer, more fragile, carbon one.

You do need to have faith in your bow partner throughout this turn, as you're on the upstream side of the canoe doing a pry–something that is usually closely associated with swimming. The secret to staying upright is to establish a downstream tilt early, before initiating the stern pry. In photo 107, the bow paddler is tilting the canoe using a low brace. This gives the stern paddler a solid platform from which to crank on the pry, while helping with the tilt by leaning away from their pry stroke.

As the canoe completes the turn, you will need to center your weight back over the canoe while maintaining the tilt. Initially, the tilt was to stabilize the canoe, but now it plays a more important role in letting the canoe turn. It's much like tilting onto the rounded side of the canoe on flatwater to enhance your pivot turns. The bow paddler's low brace is neither an asset nor a hindrance to the turn, provided he or she doesn't lean on it excessively. Their brace will reduce the boat's forward speed slightly, which may cause the boat to fall off the wave if the wave is small, but otherwise it is strictly a stabilizing stroke.

Turning to the stern's onside with a cross-draw
Previously you were cranking on a stern pry while the bow paddler relaxed on a low brace to provide stability. Having the bow paddler execute a cross-draw is more effective and throws in a fun stroke. The bow cross-draw serves two purposes: it turns the canoe and it slows its descent into the trough. Note the water piling up against the bow in photo 108. This water is pushing the bow across the river, making it very difficult to turn back. Pulling the canoe up the wave and downstream with a cross-draw releases the bow, allowing it to turn back. The bow paddler can control the braking component of the cross-draw by opening or closing the face of the paddle. The stern person can apply more braking action by changing the pry into a back-paddle stroke. Conversely, keeping the stern paddle close to the hull for a gentle pry will allow the canoe to slide down toward the trough.

107 Turning to stern's onside.

108 Bow helping out with a cross draw.

Turning to the stern's offside   This is a very aesthetically pleasing turn because the paddlers are each doing a static draw, letting the current do the work. Once again, it's important to tilt the canoe aggressively downstream as you initiate the turn (photo 109, figure 1). The canoe is carving across the wave toward river left, with the stern paddler on the downstream side. The objective is to change the direction that you're surfing but to stay on the wave. Slow the bow's lateral motion via the bow draw while pulling the stern over behind it with the stern drawn. This initial part of the turn seems easy enough, but the crux is the last couple of degrees that will change the side of the canoe the current is hitting (photo 109, figure 2). The canoe will seem to hesitate. Hang in there, tilt the gunwale right to the water and wait for the response. This is the moment when the stern paddler can push out the grip hand and pull extra hard with the shaft hand on the paddle to "break" the boat

free. The farther back the stern draw happens, the better! Bow paddlers must stay flexible at the waist to allow the canoe to tilt away from their onside. This will feel a little strange initially. The bow draw must happen beside or in front of the paddler's knee versus farther back. Once the canoe starts to turn back, quickly change the tilt to start the next traverse.

Carving across a wave is one of the coolest experiences in paddling. Perhaps that's why, once you've tried surfing, you'll be hooked on playboating forever. Consider yourself warned.

The endless surf

Everyone eventually finds that perfect wave for the endless surf (photo 110). My most memorable tandem surf occurred on the Churchill River near Missinippi, Saskatchewan. My partner on that occasion was Ivor Hedman, not Mark, and we were in a 17-foot Royalex Prospector. We had been on the wave long enough to exhaust all our creativity. Carving, shredding, hand surfing, shudder rudder—we had tried every variation of front surfing. All the fun, though, had worked up a thirst. We were on a river, but drinking water was too simple. Fortunately, some local motor-boat experts were well equipped to come to our rescue. Joining us on the surfing wave in their aluminum boat with a 25-horse outboard, they passed us a can of pop. At about this time we all realized the potential for disaster, so they quickly left us to sip our drink in peace. Due to the steepness of the wave, the really hard part turned out to be passing the can from the bow uphill to the stern. Lacking sufficient gear for an overnight stay on the wave, Ivor and I reluctantly peeled off it to join our now-comatose friends in the eddy.

109 Turning to the stern's offside.

110 The endless surf.

Maneuvers–Back Surfing

Why do it? Back surfing (riding a wave facing downstream) makes your back ferrys significantly more effective, even if you use only the smallest waves. In terms of playing in whitewater, it makes easy moves difficult. You're probably thinking, "That's just great. Another way to rinse my laundry without taking it off." But before you pass judgment on the merits of back surfing, consider these points. When you front surf, most of the steering is up to the stern person; the bow paddler doesn't have much to do. Well, now it's the bow person's turn to run the show. Bow people can rest assured that leaving an eddy backward to catch a surf is very unnerving for the stern person. Sometimes I wish I had a mirror to fully appreciate their facial expression.

Back surfing is, generally, a more technically difficult maneuver than front surfing, so it's a great way to shorten rides if folks are hogging the wave by bottom feeding indefinitely. Personally, I love to try back surfing even on the hard waves just in case I do nail one–it sets the bar a little higher for my friends. If you are into oneupmanship but don't like pressure, be the first to try a back surf on a new wave. It's harder to match someone else's lucky run. (Of course, I am in no way trying to discredit your skill by implying that you'd be lucky to get one.)

So, you've decided to go for the back surf. Well, you have two options for catching the wave: on the fly as you're heading downstream; or back ferrying out to it from an eddy. A footnote here: once you can control your angle leaving the eddy backward, you'll discover this is an easier approach, since you don't have as much downstream momentum to overcome. To avoid starting with a handicap, adjust the trim of your canoe as described in the section on backpaddling. However, leaving an eddy backward is always a daunting proposition, so first let's examine dropping onto the wave.

Catching a wave for a back surf

Use a back-ferry to line yourself up above the stickiest part of the wave (diagram 111, figure A). (If you're not sure where this is, review the anatomy of a wave on page 13) When the stern is in line with the target area on the wave, the stern person should perform a reverse jam or reverse cut to halt the sideways motion of the stern end. This will allow the bow paddler to swing the bow downstream with a back draw or cross-draw (figure B) and line up the canoe parallel to the current. Plan on doing this well upstream of the wave, since these corrective strokes will cause the canoe to gain downstream momentum. Immediately begin back-paddling to overcome this momentum. If the wave is getting smaller, it means you're traveling upstream backward. Ease off! Seriously, though, if you've halted your downstream progress, relax a little and let yourself drop downstream to the trough in front of the wave. Keeping the canoe parallel to the current while applying full reverse power is your goal as you approach the wave (figure C). As the bow starts to lift up the face of the wave (figure D), max out your backpaddling; ignore the angle of the canoe–it's the power that counts now. Leaning back may shift your weight just enough for the canoe to catch the wave. Now reset the angle of the canoe if it was thrown off by all your frantic–I mean, powerful–backpaddling. Once you're surfing and sliding backward into the trough, concentrate on using correction strokes to control the angle of the boat. The stern person may feel a little more comfortable leaning forward and maintaining a slightly downstream-oriented high brace position.

Generally, back-surfs don't seem to be really long-term events, but with a properly trimmed canoe you may be able to work in a little carving on the wave.

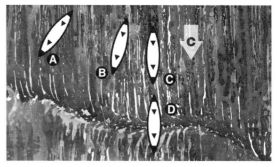

111 Catching a wave from above.

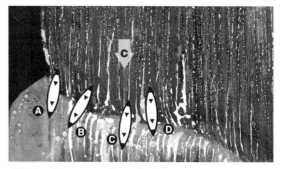

112 Catching a wave from the side.

Catching a wave from the side   The side entry is actually an easier way to catch a wave, provided you can control your approach. Ideally, the shoulder of the wave will reach all the way to the eddy so that you won't have to backpaddle against the current too much. Position the canoe so that there is some room to lose ground as you leave the eddy (diagram 112, figure A). As you back-surf out, open the angle so that the canoe rides up on the shoulder of the wave. This puts the bow person right on the peak of the wave (figure B). This trick of letting the canoe ride up on the diagonal shoulder allows you to slingshot down the face as you close the angle to stabilize the surf (figure C). Without this extra forward momentum, the correction strokes will probably cause you to be blown off the wave. On the other hand, if you ride out to the

wave with your stern firmly planted in the trough, one of two things will happen: plowing into the oncoming current will eventually push you up the wave again, causing you to fall off; or, with the current pushing on the stern, it will be much harder for the bow person to control the angle of the canoe.

Landmarking on a wave

Occasionally, people ask where they're supposed to look when back surfing. As a general rule, if you're the bow paddler, watch the bow wake to determine which side of the canoe the current is pushing on. Also glance from side to side occasionally to check your positioning on the wave.

A back-surf is considered established when the canoe slides down into the trough backward. (Smile—someone is bound to be taking a picture.) If the river is busy, it may be a good idea to have a boat in the eddy, watching upstream to let you know if someone, or something, is coming down. I was taken aback one evening to have a huge, partially submerged log bear down on me while I was doing a little solo surfing. You thought carving turns had no practical use, didn't you? Well, knowing how to do them sure came in handy that day, and allowed me to get out of the way quickly without blowing off the surf—which would, of course, have been terrible.

Staying on the wave

To maintain maximum backward speed, which you may need to catch and stay on a small wave, use a reverse J or a backsweep stroke when you're the bow paddler.

Correction strokes

The correction strokes to control the angle of the canoe are similar to those used when back surfing solo. In the bow, your response time for correcting the angle is much quicker if you stay either onside or offside. The wave itself will usually dictate which side you should choose.

Onside strokes A static back-draw in the bow, with the stern person helping out by doing a stern cut, will turn the canoe away from the bow's onside. Bow paddlers really need to push their grip hand out over the water so the power face of the paddle can catch the current passing by. This is a popular stroke for back-surfing because it provides a solid downstream brace. The stern person's stroke resembles a forward sweep frozen in mid-action. The paddle slanted back toward the stern will provide the most effective stroke. Keep the blade at the surface to avoid its catching on the current. You can't really expect the stern person to turn the boat because he or she would have to pull the stern upstream, against the current. At best the stern person can slow the lateral motion of the stern.

To turn toward the bow's onside while staying onside, try an onside bow pry. Make sure your paddle is slanted toward the bow for the maximum ruddering effect. Leaning away from your stroke will provide some tilt and give you better leverage while prying off the gunwale. Stern paddlers can take a break. Aside from switching sides, they can't do anything constructive except maintain a downstream tilt.

Another option is for both paddlers to do a static forward stroke. Keeping the paddle vertical and varying the pitch of the blade will create a prying or drawing action, combined with a strong braking component, that pulls you up the wave, freeing your upstream end from the current in the trough. This is best suited to a big surfing wave. The downstream motion of the forward strokes prevent the upstream end, the stern, from pearling.

Offside strokes You can choose from three offside strokes. The *cross-draw* turns the canoe toward the bow's onside. It takes place on the downstream side of the canoe, providing a solid stroke for the bow paddler to lean on. It's a powerful stroke because your arms are extended and you're using your stronger torso muscles to pull on the water. The stern person can also try an angled static forward stroke, but the turning effect is minimal.

To turn the canoe in the other direction, to your offside, use an *offside bow pry*. This stroke may take a little getting used to, since it has no bracing action. To get the most out of this stroke, lean away from your paddle and pull in with your grip hand This levers the paddle off the gunwale for a really powerful ruddering action.

Your third option is an *offside static forward stroke*. By varying the pitch of your paddle, you can let it jam against the hull as a pry or change the pitch and it is a draw with a strong braking component. Because it splashes a whole lot, it also looks great in the photos that your friends are shooting of your amazing back-surf!

Unfortunately, I can't tell you definitively to always stay onside or offside; each wave has its own character. Small ridges that seem insignificant can conspire to make one paddling side work and the other not. If the surf isn't working, try a different stroke combination.

Tilting the canoe downstream makes it easier to turn the canoe back toward the center of the wave because it will lift the ends out of the water, making the canoe slightly shorter.

Back surfing is a great way to add new challenge to a wave that has become easy to front-surf. It requires the ability to do strokes automatically as you react to the wave.

Back-Ferry versus Speed and Front-Ferrys

For years, my favorite canoeing maneuver was the back-ferry. The ability to slow down and move the canoe in a direction other than where the current wanted to push me was magic. And it never failed to work. My dad and I could almost back-ferry upstream to ease past a rock or maneuver into a tight channel.

The first time I began to wonder if the back-ferry really was always the maneuver of choice was on the Nahanni River in 1977. My dad and I tried to back-ferry across the vast expanse of water in the Fourth Canyon, just below Virginia Falls. However, the distance was great enough that our back paddling was no match for the strong current, and we were swept into a huge breaking wave. We blasted through, but it wasn't until years later that I became convinced that paddling forward down a river had its place. Again the location was the Nahanni, and this time the water was exceptionally high. A canoeing instructor named Fred Loosemore and I were teaching the park wardens how to run Lafferty's Riffle. Despite its innocuous name, Lafferty's can boast some monster waves and a big eddy on river right with an ugly eddy fence. Fred set up the first boat to back-ferry toward the calm water on river left, starting well upstream in the center of the river. At this point the river was several hundred feet across, with the water pushing slightly right. I decided to stay quiet and see if we really could back-ferry against the current. Bad idea. The first canoe was promptly swept toward the waves, with the crew madly backpaddling. Granted, their angle was a little off, but they were toast anyway. We took off in pursuit before they had even flipped. As we bore down on the now-swimming crew, we saw the park jet boat pick up one swimmer and give chase to the canoe. The other swimmer unintentionally caught the eddy on river right, leaving us no alternative but to enter it ourselves. The swimmer quickly caught the bow of our canoe and by backpaddling frantically we were able to avoid being swept into the eddy fence and whirlpools at the top of the eddy. Fred grabbed the cliff, and one very soggy warden clambered out of the water onto a ledge. He was able to climb out up the cliff, leaving us to fight our way against the eddy to exit out the downstream end. We quickly amended our teaching strategy to include paddling in the direction you want to go as the solution to moving across the river in big water.

The gradient of a rapid will determine the feasibility of a back-ferry. You can overcome current to ferry, but gravity has its own rule, and it's invariable. The more gradient, the faster you'll go down. As the gradient increases you are likely to have fewer standing waves to assist your ferry. The backferry is, however, a cool move. Use it when you can. Just remember that it works best in a moderate gradient and in moving from fast water to slow water, such as back-ferrying to the inside of a corner or into an eddy.

Speed is necessary for aggressive eddy turns, punching holes and dealing with turbulent confused water. It's much easier to maintain speed than to start and stop between moves. Combine this with the huge advantage of speed and control that a front-ferry has over a back-ferry and you'll begin to understand why we choose this combination on rapids that have a substantial gradient.

It's important to remember that there's usually more than one way to accomplish the same feat. The fact that one way is more efficient doesn't necessarily mean it's the only way. To you, the best way might be the easiest, or perhaps the most aesthetic, or perhaps you just like doing back-ferries. That's cool, as long as it works.

Using forward speed to descend a rapid is not as simple as just aiming at your target and going for it. That kind of approach usually results in colliding into what you're trying to avoid. The secret is being able to read the water to determine how far upstream of your target you need to aim. River features, such as eddies and tongues of fast water, all affect your line. Being able to cross various pieces of water that are traveling at different speeds and directions, while still arriving at your destination, requires a balance of speed, angle, anticipation and tilt adjustment. This is the first step in acquiring a technique called *crossing the grain*. Once you become used to powering forward and punching waves and small holes, you'll notice that these smaller river features have less effect on your direction of travel.

Crossing the grain

Crossing the grain means traveling in a different direction from the current. The rule of thumb to allow yourself room to cross the grain of a rapid is to start the rapid on the opposite side from the one you want to finish on. It's similar to setting up for an eddy turn. You need some room to set the angle and then develop momentum. Starting close to your destination–be it an eddy or a tongue between holes–means you'll be unable to set an angle. You'll be forced to paddle forward, and your momentum with the grain of the water will push you toward the obstacle. Your only other option, if you start near the side you want to end on, is that you set a wide angle but restrain yourself from paddling forward until you are almost beside your target. This will work well on rivers with little gradient, but inertia will work against you on rapids with a gradient that increases.

The ability to cross from one side of a rapid to another is the basis for many advanced maneuvers, so catch onto this concept early on and you'll be performing the role of unintentional probe a lot less in your paddling career.

Punching a hole

If a hole is unavoidable, be aggressive. In days gone by, paddlers braced like crazy going into a hole, stalled out and were window-shaded. You need power to punch a hole, and since a power stroke is as good as a brace, use it!

Plant a forward stroke on the green water going down into the hole. The stroke should be late enough that it will drive your bow through the foam pile (photo 113). Plant your next stroke deep into the foam pile. Your paddle will catch the green water going under the foam, helping you pull the canoe out of the hole. Don't ease up while you're still on the foam pile (photo 115). In your waterlogged state, it's best to get off that aerated turbulent water while you can.

Pivot on a hole

There is slower water behind a hole. The bigger the obstacle creating the hole, the bigger the eddy behind it. This means that you can execute an eddy turn behind the boil line of the hole. The pivoting action of the canoe will be slower because the water downstream of the boil line is starting to head downstream. This water does not offer as much contrast in currents as an eddy behind a rock would. However, if you stick your bow in upstream of the boil line, the bow paddler won't even need to do a pivot stroke. Your final objective is to end up behind the hole with more canoe downstream of the boil line than upstream. This is important unless you are up for a little tandem classic open canoe rodeo. I'll take the pictures.

To use the foam pile to assist your turn, approach the hole from upstream on an angle (see photo 116). Gauge your forward speed based on where you would like to end up on the foam pile. The more speed you have, the farther across the hole you'll travel before completing the turn. Where you finish the turn will also be affected by how much canoe sticks into the hole as you drift past. Not enough boat contacting the foam pile will result in your not turning at all and cruising past the hole facing downstream, or turning on the shoulder of the hole and washing downstream. In photo 117, the bow paddler is putting on the brakes to avoid shooting out the far side of the eddy below the hole. In the stern, you can assist the pivoting action. The speed and angle in this case resulted in the boat ending up behind the foam pile on the opposite side of the hole from which the canoe entered. Just what was intended. Really!

113 Punching a hole.

114

115

116 Eddy turn on a hole.

117

118

Pivots

119 Pivoting on top of a wave.

Pivot on top of a wave

The idea is to pivot the canoe on top of a wave when the ends of the boat are out of the water (photo 119). This trick works even better if you're paddling solo. You can achieve maximum pivoting action if you're moving *almost* as slowly as the current. This gives you time to throw in your pivot strokes while you're perched on the peak. Traveling *slower* than the current may cause your boat to be back-surfed–which, although fun, might not be what you had planned. The peak of the wave won't be able to support your weight, meaning that the longer you're balanced on it the more your boat will sink into it, causing water to pour in amidships.

Side Surfing

Convincing me to side-surf a really big hole with you in a tandem classic canoe would be a tough sell. Nothing personal, but our odds of coming out with limbs still attached would be slim. Okay, so I exaggerate a little. But you *can* expect a more violent ride than in a solo canoe. Our combined weight will make the canoe settle deeper into the foam pile during the side-surf. If we don't coordinate our efforts to maintain a down-stream tilt, the green water will grab the upstream chine of the canoe, and we'll window-shade. This can be fun provided the water is deep enough, although you might still pick up a bruise from the gunwales.

Entering the hole   The most direct method of entering the hole is to ferry out above the hole, stop paddling and let the current carry you in. Unfortunately, it's very hard to control the tilt of the canoe when you drop in broadside. Let me set the scene. You are approaching the hole. To avoid window-shading on impact, both of you lean way downstream as the canoe hits the hole. The bow person happens to be on the downstream side, so he or she does a low brace. You're in the stern on the upstream side, so you lean downstream while doing an upstream brace. The boat hits the foam pile and stops, almost throwing you out downstream. You both recover your balance by flattening the boat out and getting your bodies centered over the boat just as the hole pushes your boat into contact with the oncoming green water. No tilt, paddlers sitting upright, chine catches current–need I say more?

   A more controlled approach is to slide in from the side, either by ferrying directly into the hole or by surfing the shoulder and letting the foam pile carry you in (see photo 120).

Flat spins in a hole

Now, this is fun! Flat spins incorporate all the skills necessary for hole riding: entering and exiting the hole, side-surfing and boat control on the foam pile.

The hole in these photos is perfect for a 16-foot tripping canoe. Establish a side-surf (see photo 120); if the hole is grabby, keep the boat moving across the hole. When the bow makes contact with green water passing by the hole, the canoe will begin to pivot (see photo 121). The bow paddler uses a draw stroke to pull the bow downstream. If you examine the photo, you'll notice that the bow paddler's blade is angled for a back-draw. This is to keep the canoe from exiting the end of this hole. In the stern, you are also holding the canoe back with a back-draw, using the power face of your paddle to catch the green water coming into the hole. In small holes like this one, these are the subtleties that make the move work. The bow paddler continues to pull the bow around with a bow draw (see photo 122). The stern of the canoe catches the green water, so you apply power to move the canoe downstream. If you didn't do this the stern would be held by the oncoming current, making it really hard to spin. Once the canoe is on the foam pile, look around to make sure you're not slipping downstream. Back-paddle and slide into the hole backward (photo 123). When the sterns starts catching the current at the shoulder of the hole, it's time to spin (photo 124). In this photo, the bow paddler is bracing offside. By adjusting the pitch of the paddle blade, the bow person can make fine adjustments to the progress of the canoe. In the stern, you can start with a high brace to stabilize, knowing that it will also pull your end downstream. A low brace would let the canoe settle deeper into the hole, making it harder to free an end of the boat. To pull your end of the boat around, use a good draw stroke. Focus on keeping the paddle vertical (photo 125). The bow person is perfectly positioned to keep the bow out of the green water. An offside back-paddle moves the boat out of the hole and a quick offside forward stroke pushes the bow farther in. By varying the pitch and position of the paddle, both these strokes can be accomplished without removing the paddle from the water. Just slice the blade to the new position. The challenge of coordinating both paddlers' strokes and tilts makes a successful flat spin all the more rewarding.

120 Flat spins in a hole.

121

122

123

124

125

126 The Normans (Hair) Rapid, Ottawa River.

In a classic canoe, paddling whitewater solo is easier than tandem in some ways and harder in others. But one trait becomes apparent immediately. As a solo canoeist, if you are not using the proper techniques to make the maneuvers happen, they won't. There is no partner to assist you or to blame. Sloppy strokes will only lead to frustration. These potential drawbacks are balanced by the fact that less weight in the canoe results in a drier ride and a more forgiving craft that doesn't catch currents so quickly. With only one person in the canoe, your chance of someone losing their balance and tipping the boat is reduced by a whopping 50 percent. Finally, the thrill of knowing that you performed a maneuver yourself is worth any extra effort.

It's always worthwhile to spend time refining your strokes in easy rapids. To really concentrate, however, you need to avoid distractions such as noisy whitewater. After a juicy rapid I'll bet you probably can't even recall what strokes you did, let alone how technically efficient

they were. So with efficiency as your goal, spend some time reviewing the forward- and back-paddling strokes. If one of them is new to you, refer to *Path of the Paddle* for a more in-depth explanation.

Skills–Forward Strokes

Over the years my forward stroke has continued to metamorphosize. The subtle changes weren't a conscious decision on my part but were likely the influence of someone else's stroke. When I was canoe tripping in my teens with my dad, my stroke rate was quite high. Then, as I did more teaching, it slowed down, increasing in length. I suppose I was trying to make each individual stroke easier to see. When I started to play in rapids, I discovered torso rotation combined with really short forward strokes. Now, after more than 20 years of whitewater, I hope that my stroke is finally becoming efficient. I should really say strokes, because I now realize there are different forward strokes for different whitewater situations.

Forward stroke without correction

This short powerful stroke is ideal for quickly gaining momentum for a maneuver such as an eddy turn. It has no steering component. Here's how it goes.

The *wind-up*: Rotate your torso so that your onside shoulder is forward, with your lower arm straight. Your grip hand is out in front of your forehead; this allows you to slide the paddle into the water as you would slide a knife into a sheath. It's okay to lean your upper torso forward slightly. Your paddle should be vertical before you start to pull on it.

The *power phase*: Unwind yourself, pulling your hips up to the paddle. The power phase is finished when the paddle reaches your knee.

The *recovery*: The idea is to get your paddle back to the start position as fast as possible before the momentum of the canoe dies.

When you're doing a forward stroke, is the canoe bobbing in the water? If so, emphasize torso rotation rather than upper body lean. Are you finishing the stroke early, beside your knee?

Forward stroke with correction

The J stroke is the most efficient correction stroke for proceeding in a straight line, but it's not the most powerful.

The whitewater pry is a good alternative, since it's a stronger turning stroke. Once the paddle passes your knee, begin to set up for the correction. Flip over the paddle so the blade is slicing through the water in a pry position. Don't pry off the gunwale yet. Let the disturbed water generated by your forward stroke pass by the paddle and then pry with the back face of the blade. You may not even need a dynamic pry; trailing the paddle in a static pry might provide all the correction required.

See Chapter 6 for a more in-depth study of the forward stroke.

The following strokes are the major and minor correction strokes used during a back-ferry, with one modification. You will also use them for back-surfing, so you need to take advantage of the current ripping past the canoe. To simulate this feeling on flatwater, establish some backward momentum before trying the stroke.

Major corrections

Back draw   Place the blade of the paddle well toward the bow, as you would for a bow draw stroke. Let the blade trail briefly in the water. Now try pushing your grip hand out, away from the canoe (photo 127). To turn more sharply, pull your shaft hand in toward the gunwale while you push your grip hand out farther. (No one claimed that this was a comfortable stroke, just an effective one.) Keep your blade vertical in the water so it really bites into the current.

Cross-draw   The cross-draw feels very much like the back draw. You control the angle of the blade by pushing your grip hand out over the water. Your lower arm should stay straight, with your hand acting as a fulcrum for the stroke. You can lean forward to increase the distance of the stroke from the pivot point, giving you better leverage on the canoe.

Minor corrections

The next two strokes supply both backward motion and a turning effect. You use them more to reach the sweet spot of the wave than you do once you are established on it.

Back sweep   Start the paddle 45 degrees from the stern and really lean onto it as you sweep it in an arc toward the bow. The stroke will end naturally as your shaft nears the gunwale in front of you. Take this as a hint and make sure you're balanced in the canoe before you lift your paddle from the water. Admittedly, this stroke feels more powerful than a back-draw, and in a way it is. The problem with a back sweep is that you're fighting the current by trying to push your stern against the green water. With a back draw you're pulling the bow with the current passing your canoe. Working with the current is always easier.

Reverse J   This stroke requires some practice to make doing it worthwhile. Hold your paddle higher than usual at the start of the stroke (see photo 128). This allows your paddle to be more vertical earlier in the stroke. Also, avoid reaching far behind you—all you'll be doing is pushing down on the water. As the paddle passes your body, keep it vertical by pushing it toward the bow with your grip and shaft hand. Once the power phase of the stroke is finished, angle the paddle so that your blade will be extended closer to the bow, farther from the pivot point. Pause until solid green water is hitting the non-power face of the blade.

Compound back

Rotate your upper torso to face the stern so that you can reach well back toward the stern but also keep the paddle vertical (photo 129). Continue the draw stroke until it reaches your hips, then flip the paddle over to change power faces. Push the paddle toward the bow as you would with a regular reverse J stroke.

Positioning yourself for backpaddling

Positioning yourself near the center thwart makes steering easier while moving backward.

Try to build in some versatility when you outfit your classic canoe for solo. By slipping out of your thigh straps, you can slide forward up against the center airbag. Any weight adjustment like this will make backsurfing easier since the stern won't dig in quite as much.

127 Back draw.

128 Reverse J.

129 Compound back stroke.

Skills—Bracing Strokes

A bracing stroke is the key to defying gravity. At least, to an onlooker it appears that that's what you're doing. Many of the other strokes already in your repertoire incorporate a bracing action. But the two pure bracing strokes are the low brace and the high brace. If it wasn't for braces, we'd all be paddling canoes like *Paddle to the Sea*, the little canoe with the lead keel, from the film of the same name. The heavy keel kept Paddle upright through some serious whitewater, although it didn't seem to help with his descent of Niagara Falls.

Low brace

A low brace can be used to stabilize the canoe in turbulent water or to right the canoe in the case of a near flip. The latter technique is really the last part of an open canoe roll; see the next page for an explanation of the roll.

You need to perform a stabilizing brace correctly to avoid needlessly exposing your shoulders to injuries. Roll your grip hand so that the non-power face of your paddle is down. Hold your grip hand at your belly-button; this will keep your shaft arm bent as if you were doing a push-up. (Push-ups are easier to do with bent arms than if your arms are extended way out from your sides and held straight.) With arms bent in a brace position, you are very stable. Your knees, which are in thigh straps, are also pushed against the side of the canoe. Lift your heel on your offside to hook under the seat. You don't want any abrupt surprises from slipping around in the boat. Maintain this position throughout the stroke, which will be short unless the current keeps your paddle on the surface. If the canoe does lurch toward the onside, aggressively right the boat with your knees and hips. The objective is to get your weight centered in the canoe again as quickly as possible.

High brace

The "new" high brace serves a different purpose from the one you may be familiar with. It's now a recovery stroke, used if you're tipping to your offside. Before, it was considered a ready position, capable of righting the canoe in the event of tipping to either side. But choosing between a low brace or a high brace is more effective than relying on an all-purpose brace.

The idea behind the high brace is to get your center of gravity over the gunwale and literally to pull yourself upright (photo 131). Being able to execute an extreme J-lean so that your weight is centered over the balance point of the boat is the key to recovering from such a precarious position.

The **righting pry** is another stroke that prevents flipping to your offside, but it's really more practical for solo playboats, so it will be covered in that chapter.

130 Low brace.

131 High brace.

After many fruitless rolling sessions, the following question will inevitably arise: "Do I really need to be able to roll my classic 16-foot canoe solo?" Look at it this way: rolling practice improves your brace, plus you're now totally comfortable bailing out of your outfitting while upside down.

If you're like Mark and me, the less time spent in the water the better, and rolling up is certainly faster and easier than floundering around as you try to climb back in after a spill. Convinced? Okay. But now a note of caution. If the water is shallow or there are rocks coming up, you're better off far away from your boat. A full-sized classic canoe, even fully outfitted with airbags, is still almost unmaneuverable when it's full of water after you roll up. So don't count on being able to avoid obstacles. If, on the other hand, the rapid empties into a deep pool, then go for the roll.

It takes some solid outfitting to make rolling an option. You need enough airbag volume to float the boat after the roll, and the bags should float it on a fairly even keel—meaning you need some flotation behind you as well as in front. You'll also need thigh straps to hold yourself in while upside down. I can brace my feet against the seat, so I don't use foot pegs. They help you stay in the canoe, but when used with a seat rather than a saddle they make it harder to get out of the boat. So it's really a question of how easily you can get out and how prone you are to feeling claustrophobic.

For the setup, cheat!   We're talking about a seriously big watercraft. It will not respond instantaneously to your hip snap. A high brace that sweeps in an arc from the bow out perpendicular to the canoe will give you plenty of time to position your body near the surface, stretched out away from the boat, and to begin getting the boat rolling in the proper direction (see photo 132).

Initiating the roll   As soon as your body and paddle are perpendicular to the canoe, flip the paddle over to a low-brace position. Don't push on the paddle yet! Let your upper torso float on the surface of the water, with your forehead resting on the paddle shaft. Keep your grip hand between your belly-button and sternum. Right the canoe with a hip snap. Well, it's more like a hip strain and grunt, since the canoe responds quite slowly. Push down on your offside knee and lift up with your onside knee. Think of your lower torso as moving independently of your upper torso. From the cocked start position, pivot your hips until they have traveled to the other extreme, onside knee near your chest. The inertia of such a big boat tends to make you push on the paddle a little early (photo 133). Ideally, it's best to wait until you glimpse the outside of the hull before pushing on the paddle and sweeping your body into the canoe.

Righting the canoe   The bottom of the canoe is almost vertical in photo 134. However, you won't yet be able to see the color of the canoe, so keep your head in the water.

The big finish   Finally the canoe is becoming upright (see photo 135). Now sweep your head into the canoe, keeping it right down on the deck. Swing your head all the way to or past the far gunwale. Sometimes this makes the difference during a sloppy roll or when a wave hits the canoe at an inopportune moment.

This roll is exactly the same as the roll we use for solo playboats, so read the adaptations in that chapter for some other ideas.

132   The set-up.

133   Initiating the roll.

134   Righting the canoe.

135   The big finish.

136 Tim, look out!

Tim, look out!

There is a way out of the situation in this photo. Unfortunately, I hadn't yet discovered it! With the foam pile holding the stern, the current caught the bow of my boat and sent me hurtling across the wave toward Tim Gfeller. Since he was back surfing toward me in his kayak, he was unaware of the 16-foot freight train headed his way. The collision sent me tumbling right out of my canoe. Had I been using thigh straps, they would have acted like a seatbelt and kept me in my craft. Tim caught the impact of my canoe on the back of his PFD. Fortunately, the old Kevlar boat flexed enough to cushion the blow. For the rest of the afternoon I pretty much had the wave to myself. The quickest way to abort a suicide surf like this is to flip upstream. Once your body hits the water, your lateral motion is killed and you and the boat wash downstream off the wave.

Front surfing

This is a really cool maneuver. The first time you catch a wave the water will seem to be just tearing past, and you're not doing a thing! It took many surfs before my senses became dulled to that sensation. Still, the thrill returns with the first front-surf of every new season.

When front surfing, the solo classic canoeist has an advantage over a tandem team because the solo paddler's canoe doesn't sit as deep in the water. This, combined with the solo paddler's ability to more easily shift body weight back, keeps the bow from digging into the oncoming green water. On the other hand, on flatter waves, the weight of a bow person also helps to hold the canoe in the trough, while the stern-heavy solo canoe more often falls off the wave. The solo paddler has the last laugh, however. The extra weight of the bow paddler often causes the tandem boat to submarine or pearl on steeper waves, ending the ride for those folks.

Getting on the wave from the side

Set the angle of the canoe so that it points at your target area of the wave. In this case your target is the trough in front of the wave (see photo 137). Aiming at the wave itself causes the canoe to plow into it and be pushed downstream. It also messes up your angle when all that green water hits your bow. But at this point a bad angle is irrelevant because you can't power over the back of the wave anyway. Blasting enthusiastically into the current upstream of the trough pretty much causes the same results. The bow plows into the backside of the upstream wave or pillow, and the green water pushes the bow off course and downstream. If you scrunch up your face with effort and paddle like crazy, you may be able to overcome the downstream current and catch the wave for a surf–but it won't be pretty.

A better approach is to set the angle of the canoe in the eddy. This will allow you to gain forward momentum before you reach the eddy line. Close the angle as you cross the eddy line before the current catches the bow. Control your angle with correction strokes (photo 138). The momentum you generated will carry you across the eddyline toward the wave. Your optimum positioning on the wave places the balance point of the canoe just upstream of the peak. In this canoe we'll assume that the balance point is between me and the center thwart. The canoe is longer than the face of the wave, so the bow does make contact with the green water. Because I'm side-slipping out, the bulk of the boat remains on the face of the wave.

If the bow were digging in too much, you could tilt the canoe to lift the bow out of the water a bit, which would also make the canoe turn more easily. As an equilibrium is reached between gravity pulling the canoe down the face of the wave and the current pushing it up, you settle into a static front-surf station (photo 139).

Catching the wave from upstream

You'll need to do this maneuver when you're trying to catch waves for a surf or to assist a ferry while descending a rapid. Interestingly, the success of this maneuver hinges again on the basics: the angle of the canoe and forward motion–in that order! All the power in the world won't keep you on a wave if you are rocketing off the end with too much angle. With this in mind, set your angle to the current early–angle, not being parallel to the current–because you need to allow for the fact that your upcoming power strokes will turn you away from your onside.

Pointed upstream, drop down to the wave and paddle forward at a leisurely rate to slow yourself slightly. This allows you to position yourself in line with the best spot on the wave. Set the angle of the canoe, preferably with offside forward strokes because they help to maintain forward speed (see photo 140, figure 1). As you descend toward the trough, paddle forward with quick, strong, aggressive strokes. At this point, the objective is to overcome the downstream momentum you would gain due to gravity and current as you slide down the backside of the preceding pillow (figure 2). By the time you reach the trough, your stroke rate, using mostly your arm and shoulder muscles, needs to be 80 percent of your top speed. Now comes the critical phase. A correction stroke at this point will blow any chance of catching the wave. If you've gauged your angle correctly, these last few strokes on the face of the wave will bring your canoe parallel to the current as you stall your downstream momentum and begin to slide upstream into the trough (figure 3). With the strokes taken on the face of the wave you have to move your paddle blade faster than the current when the blade contacts the water. This forward stroke is like slapping the water and is definitely all arm muscle. You can't keep it up very long, but this high-speed stroke rate will make or break your attempt to catch the wave.

One last trick is to lean forward a bit if your canoe is teetering on the brink of catching the wave. This moves the center of gravity to the upstream side of the peak and allows gravity to pull the boat into the trough. Leaning forward so far that it detracts from your stroke is unproductive, but some subtle body language helps.

137 Catching a wave from the side.

138

139

140 Catching a wave from upstream.

141 Draw.

Carving

The challenge of front surfing will seem insurmountable until you actually catch a surf. Then, after the initial thrill wears off, you'll start to look around. The sensation of sitting on the wave without expending any effort is mesmerizing. Soon you'll get a little cocky and start smiling to the crowd, then maybe throw in a salute to the people with cameras. "Hey, look, no hands!" The canoe just seems to surf by itself. You start wondering, "Now what?" The answer is to start carving back and forth across the wave. It's a more advanced surfing technique used on steep waves and it keeps life exciting.

Turning to your offside   On your first surfing attempt, you'll most likely try to keep the canoe on the wave with a stroke that is a combination stern draw and brace (photo 142). This stroke feels very stable and comforting during this new surfing experience. If the canoe is reasonably parallel to the current, this may be all you need to turn it back toward your offside. But if the wave starts to break a little or your angle across the wave is too wide, then you'll need to refine your stern draw stroke to overcome these forces.

A breaking wave can cause the canoe to become unstable, turning your front-surf into a side-surf. The pry stroke is often strong enough to combat this tendency, but the stern draw stroke does not have the mechanical advantage of the pry, so you can't overpower the wave.

Here's what happens as you surf across the wave and it starts to curl, developing a foam pile on top. This foam pile is moving back upstream. As the side of the stern hits the curl, the stern's lateral motion is stopped. The bow, which is firmly planted in the green water, continues to be pushed across the wave. It's tough to pull the stern through the foam pile fast enough to keep up with the lateral motion of the bow. In other words, the stern is now in a current going upstream while the bow is in a current going downstream. This is

142 Draw and brace combination.

143

just like an eddy turn, except that it is slightly more three-dimensional. Here's how to increase your chances of turning the canoe back across the wave. As you initiate the turn, move the blade farther toward the stern and aggressively pull the stern around. You can really crank the canoe over on its edge because your weight is on your paddle (see photo 143). The key is to make sure your paddle is vertical in the water (see photo 141). If you are cheating your stroke and bracing a bit, with the paddle "skiing" on the water, your energy will be wasted by pushing down on the water.

Tilting the canoe to the outside of the turn is really your only practical option during a stern draw stroke in a solo classic canoe. Leaning back for the stroke combined with the ample width of the hull makes it too difficult to tilt the canoe away from your onside and still pull on your paddle effectively. The good news is that downstream is usually the best direction to be tilting anyway.

We've touted the benefit of achieving a lot of braking action from the pry stroke during a front surf. Compare this with the lack of braking action during the stern draw stroke and you'll quickly agree that an alternative stroke that turns the canoe in the same direction as the draw is needed. This alternative is the cross-draw stroke. At first this may seem contradictory,

but don't forget that being solo, you can reach both behind and in front of the pivot point. The benefit of the cross-draw during a front-surf comes from the braking action of the stroke. This braking action pulls the canoe up the wave, or downstream (photo 145). This relieves the pressure on the bow of the canoe so the stern can swing in behind it, parallel to the current (photo 144). It's important to understand that you need to free the bow of the canoe from the oncoming current; otherwise, you will be fighting the river directly. And we all know who will win that one, right?

Tilt plays a major role in this cross-draw turn, so crank the canoe over as far downstream as possible. If you can engage the rounded center section of the canoe, it will turn even more quickly. It's possible to tilt away from the side your paddle is on because, unlike with the stern draw, you're sitting upright. You can, therefore, apply pressure with one knee and pull up with the other against your thigh strap. This turn looks radical, too, what with the offside stroke, the onside tilt and the water splashing off the paddle. So use it when life is becoming too sedentary out there on the wave.

In case you're wondering about using an inside tilt with the cross-draw, that combination is likely to end in swimming lessons.

144 *Cross draw.*

Offside stern draw

This stroke should actually be subtitled "A Painful But Aesthetically Pleasing Alternative to the Stern Pry." The offside stern draw (photo 147) is a nice transition from a cross-draw turn (photo 146). If you are falling off the wave, it gives you forward momentum that a stern pry cannot provide. It's difficult to pull very hard on the paddle, so be sure you tilt to make the most of your stroke. In this photo, the canoe is almost parallel to the current, yet Mark is just barely able to make it turn back across the wave.

Once the canoe has turned and is heading back across the wave, switch back to your onside and the stern pry. Remaining on the upstream side while doing an offside stern pry and trying to tilt downstream is just a touch impractical.

145 *Cross draw.*

146

147 *Offside stern draw.*

Turning toward your onside   Nothing beats a pry for turning the canoe back toward your onside during a front surf. It has the mechanical advantage of a class-A lever, but you can also use it as a braking stroke to push the canoe up the face of the wave, decreasing the effect of the oncoming current on the bow. As you can see in photo 149, your paddle is on the upstream side of the canoe. Your situation is a little precarious if the wave decides to curl or break, because you'll suddenly find yourself side-surfing on the upstream side of the canoe! Relax, this can be fun, and is explained later in Side Surfing. For now, just be aware that you can tilt the canoe upstream, into the turn (photo 150) or downstream to the outside of the turn (photo 148). Tilting downstream is more stable if the wave breaks; tilting upstream will allow the front section of the canoe to slide sideways down into the trough, helping you to stay on a smaller wave, such as the one in photos 149 to 151.

Let's see how all these details fit together during a pry turn. The canoe is surfing toward river right; it's doing a fine job by itself, so don't mess with it (photo 149). Take this opportunity to look for the best spot to initiate the turn to bring you back across the wave. Begin the pry with the paddle well toward the stern, then add as much braking component as needed

(photo 150). On this wave the bow is buried in the green water, so you need some braking to back the canoe up the face of the wave. The bow never does break loose, but resistance is decreased enough that the stern can catch up and swing downstream (photo 151). At this point, the stroke is becoming a low brace. As the canoe turns toward river left, continue to ease your weight off the paddle while assessing whether you'll need any additional forward power to stay on the wave.

Outside tilt   Tilting to the outside of your turn has a major advantage over tilting to the inside of the turn. An outside tilt uses the chine of the canoe to carve the turn. This also shortens the waterline of the canoe, making it more responsive to your turning stroke. Because the chine is carving, the canoe will be pushed up the face of the wave if you have a wide angle to the current. This can be an asset if you need to move up the wave to free the bow from the current.

If the wave decides to break as you turn, your downstream tilt will be more stable because your upstream chine will not engage the oncoming current. However, if the wave is small or you are already at the peak, the carving effect will push you downstream off the wave. The hardest part of this stroke is to tilt the

148   Turning to your onside with a pry, outside tilt.

canoe away from your paddling side, yet still keep the blade in the water (photo 148). The farther toward the stern you can reach the better, since the more mechanical advantage you have, the less you'll need to push on your paddle. The less you push on your paddle, the less drag you create and the easier it will be to stay on the wave.

149   Turning to your onside with a pry, inside tilt.

150

151

Moving forward to the center thwart to trim the canoe properly makes paddling backward easier. Well, if you expect back surfing even to be possible, you'll need to balance your canoe so that the upstream end of the canoe, the stern, doesn't dig in (the stern of the canoe relative to which end of the canoe you're facing, not which end has a stern seat.)

The advantage of the smaller canoes is that since you kneel at the balance point of the canoe, just leaning forward or backward will adjust the trim to suit your needs.

Catching the wave from the side　There are two ways to begin your approach from the side. If the shoulder of the wave is a bit downstream from the top of the eddy, you could try an eddy turn. This is the easy way to cross the eddy line and end up in the current ready to back-ferry onto the wave. Don't forget to continue the pivot until you have a slight angle out to the wave. This will keep you from being pushed back onto the eddy line.

The second way to exit the eddy is more direct and requires less space, making it the preferred choice if the wave is near the top of the eddy. The same basic principles for eddy turns and front ferries apply, even though you enter the current backward. Choose where you want to cross the eddy line, then set your angle. Develop backward motion that will carry you across the eddy line (diagram 152, figure 1). As you cross the eddy line, concentrate on counteracting the strong turning effect of the opposing eddy and main currents (figure 2). Once the whole canoe is out in the current, you can concentrate on applying more reverse power, as the current will be pushing equally on both ends of the canoe. Tilting as you cross the eddy line will prevent the current from flipping the canoe upstream and make it easier to hold the angle. Leaning forward will keep the stern from digging in and spinning the canoe around. Maintain as much of a back-ferry as you need to move out to the steepest part of the wave (figure 3).

Unless the wave is falling away from you downstream, your canoe must be parallel to the current. As the bow starts to rise up the face, put in some quick back strokes. If the canoe teeters on the brink of the wave, lean back, upstream. Now the canoe starts to slide down the face backward. You are on the brink of catching a back-surf on the biggest tsunami ever!

Catching the wave from upstream　The crux of this maneuver is being able to apply pure backward power, no corrections, as you drop onto the face of the wave. If you end up with your canoe parallel to the current, your chances are as good as catching the wave frontward. To achieve the goal of being in the right spot with the right angle on the canoe, set the canoe a little off parallel to the current, angled toward your onside. Use powerful back-paddling strokes to control your descent. As the bow rises up the face of the wave, increase your stroke rate. A back-sweep will help if the canoe is angled too much to your onside, but if your stroke overpowers your preset angle, you are doomed–using a reverse J that would correct the angle will cause too much drag and will likely blow you off the wave.

Staying on the wave　Once you've caught a back-surf on a wave, the next order of business is orienting yourself to your surroundings and establishing an angle to stay on the sweet spot. Look over your shoulder as you approach the wave from the side. As you reach what you think is the sweet spot, focus on the bow, the downstream end of the canoe. By watching the current trailing off downstream, you can tell which way the canoe is angled and choose the appropriate stroke to keep yourself on the wave.

Your first stroke is usually a back draw or a cross-draw, since these can increase your upstream momentum as well as pivot the canoe. Or, if you need to slow the canoe, you can do a static forward or static offside forward stroke with an angled blade. To add more finesse to the back-surf, you can add an onside pry or an offside pry. Combine these with a draw and a cross-draw respectively and you can now stay on one side of the canoe while carving in either direction. Now, that is aesthetically pleasing!

152　Catching the wave from the side.

Back draw

The back draw will likely feel most comfortable, since it features a consistent pressure on the power face of your paddle and you are onside. The effect is similar to that of a brace. But don't be misled into doing a high brace out to the side; a high brace won't control the angle of the canoe. Likewise, don't fall into the habit of doing a back sweep, because the current going by will push the stern downstream each time you remove your paddle from the water for the next stroke, not to mention the fact that a back sweep tries to push the stern upstream directly against the current (and that's just not going to happen).

When used during back-surfing, the back draw is usually a static stroke. Reach forward and push out with your grip hand to increase the angle of your paddle (photo 154). Tilting will help to free the ends of the canoe from the water so you can turn faster.

Cross-draw

The cross-draw is a more powerful stroke than its counterpart, the back draw, because, with both arms extended, the larger muscles of your torso come into play. Control the canoe by increasing or decreasing the angle of the paddle relative to the current. Photo 153 shows Mark leaving the eddy (A) to catch the wave (B), pulling hard with a wide angle. Ease up as the canoe becomes parallel to the current. This will keep you from being pitched into the water as your canoe suddenly heads back across the wave. It's very difficult to make a sudden swim here look intentional. Your only hope is that the canoe will hit the shoulder of the wave and obediently turn back toward you so you can clamber in.

Static forward stroke

This braking stroke pulls the canoe up the face of the wave. Once the upstream end of the canoe breaks free of the current, it's easy to change its angle. That's when the fun begins! By changing the pitch of your paddle, you can angle the canoe either left or right (see photo 155). The more vertical your paddle in the water, the better it will "grip." Slanting it downstream will move it farther from the pivot point; this makes for a more efficient turning stroke but less braking action. With the paddle firmly planted at the catch phase of a power stroke, try angling the power face away from the canoe. Still keeping the shaft vertical, change the pitch so the power face is toward the canoe. This technique of staying on the wave seems to work better if you keep the canoe's turns quick, not going too far

154 Back draw.

155 Static forward.

153 Catching the wave from the side.

off parallel to the current on each one. The stroke's braking power is such that if you combine it with too much carving action from the canoe, you'll quickly blow off the wave.

The static forward stroke works equally well on your offside (see photo 156). Assume a position as if you were starting an offside forward stroke, then change the pitch on the blade. Power-face toward the canoe or power-face away from the canoe. During the latter, let the shaft push against the side of the hull; it's a lot easier than using arm muscle to hold the paddle away from the canoe.

The combination of a static forward stroke, which reduces speed, and pivot strokes, which add speed, will see you through most back-surfing situations. Now it's time for two strokes that put the finishing touches on your back surfing. The offside pry and onside pry allow you to carve without switching between a back draw and a cross-draw. These strokes are streamlined, so they don't reduce your forward speed and they have a mechanical advantage, meaning less effort on your part. Less effort for better results is always worth shooting for.

Offside pry

The offside pry has the same effect as a back draw, but it allows you to stay on the same side of the canoe as your cross-draw. Reach well forward and keep your grip hand in tight to your body (photo 157). Tilt the canoe downstream not only to enhance the turn, but also to keep your hairdo dry and fully buffed. If the current does catch your upstream chine, you're not in a very good position to brace, to say the least. On smaller waves that just barely hold the canoe I like this offside pry because it can be placed so far away from the pivot point and be quite subtle, meaning less drag. This is my favorite back-surfing stroke, both tandem in the bow position and solo. You can alternate it with a cross-draw so quickly that you are rarely late in reacting to the current.

Pry

This is exactly the same pry stroke that you learned on flatwater. Leaning forward not only extends your reach toward the bow, but also helps to unweight the stern. Control the amount of turning action by pulling your grip hand across in front of you. You may remember how hard it was to tilt a full-sized canoe downstream, away from your cross-draw stroke. Well, good luck tilting away from your onside pry. Just remember, though, every little bit helps.

156 Offside static forward.

157 Offside pry.

158 Upstream brace.

159 High brace.

Side-surfing in a full-sized classic style canoe is probably the easiest maneuver to initiate. It'll give you the most violent ride around and also be the most difficult to end in a manner you would voluntarily choose. Be forewarned: if the hole grabs your upstream gunwale, you'll learn the true meaning of window-shading.

By now you're probably ready to skip side-surfing completely–right? Well, not to paint too bleak a picture, but you do need to realize the forces involved. These forces can flip you uncontrollably, so a helmet is a must. Before starting, familiarize yourself with the section on surfing-hole morphology so you can choose an appropriate hole.

Finally, the moment has arrived; you've scouted out the hole and it looks good. Water flowing over a deeply submerged rock is forming a small hole. The boil line is very close to the face of the hole and there's a good pool downstream to recover your gear if you inadvertently have a yard sale. You notice, as you creep closer, that the hole always seems bigger once you've started in and there's no turning back.

Entering a hole from the side   This is the "softest" way to initiate a side-surf. Sliding in from the side allows you to establish a good tilt as the canoe swings broadside to the hole. If the shoulder angles upstream to the hole, you'll need to paddle forward. If the hole is downstream of where you enter, you need to put on the brakes. On your first approach, letting the canoe front-surf diagonally across the hole is an excellent way to determine how sticky the hole is; it also will help you decide whether you really want to find yourself in there for any extended period.

Dropping into a hole sideways   This is the direct approach. No fancy stuff. Just ferry out above the hole, turn broadside and let the current push you in. Get ready to brace. When you hit the upstream current of the foam pile, you'll be coming to an abrupt stop. This means the transition from drifting to surfing will be very quick, making it tough to establish a tilt. If you tilt the canoe downstream before you hit the hole, the canoe will fill up as it hits the foam pile. In a smaller hole you'll find that tilting excessively causes the chine of the canoe to dig into the green water, pushing you through the hole. On the other hand, if the upstream chine of the canoe makes contact with the green water, it's much more difficult to establish a downstream tilt. It's similar to what happens when you don't tilt before going sideways into a rock in a rapid. Your best bet is to set up a tilt using a low brace. This

low brace will keep you from falling out downstream when the canoe stops abruptly in the hole.

Dropping into a hole angled   There is a way to soften the impact of dropping into a hole. Instead of approaching broadside, try angling your canoe either upstream or downstream. The smaller the hole, the less angle off perpendicular you need. When the end of your canoe hits the hole first, it slices partway through before your canoe is turned sideways. The hole then pushes you back to the trough. This gives you time to adjust your tilt and plan your next step. If the canoe is angled too far downstream, you may inadvertently punch right through the hole.

Hole riding

There are four main methods of keeping yourself upright in the hole, plus some "alternative" techniques, most of which would be impossible to intentionally repeat. If you do ad-lib during a side-surf here's hoping that someone caught it on film for you.

The more conventional methods use one of four braces.

Low brace   Most solo paddlers prefer to side-surf on the downstream side of the canoe.

The ideal body position during a side-surf is a J-lean –your boat is tilted downstream, with your upper body curved back so your head is over the balance point of the canoe. Don't kneel in the center of the canoe. Rather, cheat by shifting your bum over to the downstream side of the boat (which is necessary due to the width of your classic canoe) and lean on a downstream brace. Once you're stable, arc your body back over the boat so you can unweight your paddle. You should be able to remove your paddle from the water completely so you can use it to move the canoe around in the hole.

High brace This stroke used to be my first choice in a hole, but it prevents you from developing a good J lean. Now I use the high brace as more of a righting brace.

Here's what happens. The green water catches the upstream chine of the canoe–and wham! Up comes the downstream gunwale as the canoe tries to window-shade. If you anticipate this, you'll be hiking out over the side of the canoe with your weight on the downstream gunwale (photo 159). Your paddle acts as an anchor to pull the gunwale back down. If the action caught you off-guard, the rising gunwale will have knocked your low brace out of the water. By the time you emerge from the water downstream, you may well be wondering who kicked you in the ribs. Don't take it personally. Doubtless the gunwales didn't smack you out of malice; they were just being enthusiastic about window-shading.

Upstream brace The key to an effective upstream brace is to angle your paddle toward the stern of the canoe so it will be perpendicular to the current (photo 158). The blade is flat on the surface, with the upstream edge slightly lifted to keep it there. This gives you a solid brace to stabilize your tilt. It's possible to tilt

downstream without your paddle in the water at all, but if the hole is bouncy, you'll have trouble maintaining your balance. Occasionally, you'll find yourself leaning upstream with an upstream tilt on the canoe, holding the evil forces at bay with an upstream brace. That's fine, but unless the canoe is turning upstream in a hurry, you'll eventually window-shade big-time. Tilting upstream in a hole is a skill more suited to playboats and will be covered in that chapter.

The upstream low brace is an effective way of moving backward and lifting the stern out of the hole and downstream.

Offside brace The offside brace is an alternative to the upstream brace. Many paddlers often switch hands to be able to execute a low brace in the hole on what then becomes the onside, rather than use a more eloquent offside brace. The crux of the offside brace is maintaining a J-lean. Otherwise you'll be leaning on your paddle and it will sink, causing you to capsize downstream. The advantage of the offside brace is that it can be used as a cross-draw to pull the bow out of the hole or to move the canoe backward. Make use of the fact that the paddle is nearly vertical, by changing the pitch of the blade to maneuver the canoe around in the hole.

How much tilt

Tilting is kind of like eating chocolates–too much will sink you. Tilting a big classic canoe requires that you use body language. Trying to tilt the canoe with only your knees is really tough–although that's what you should strive for to free up your paddle for other activities.

But sometimes leaning on the paddle is the only way to stay upright. The objective is to maintain a solid tilt that doesn't fill up the canoe.

Too much tilt causes the boiling water of the hole to pour in over the downstream gunwale. The canoe will sink, causing it either to be pushed out of the hole or to settle into the hole's stickiest part, where it will be as maneuverable as a stalled truck.

Exiting the hole

Initially, your hole-riding experiences are likely to consist of getting into the hole, smiling briefly at the folks in the eddy and then spending the rest of your time trying to get your canoe out of the hole upright. That's okay. It takes a few rides to become accustomed to all the noise and tumbling water. Once you're used to balancing in the hole without leaning on your paddle, you can then paddle forward or backward across the face of the hole. Use a rocking motion to develop the momentum to carry you out of the end of the hole.

Slightly wetter methods of exiting holes include window-shading and swimming. Window-shading in a hole puts your body down in the green water going under the hole. With yourself acting as a sea anchor you may drag the canoe out downstream. Once you feel the washing-machine effect dissipating, you can roll up in the slack water downstream of the hole.

If you've really had enough and want out *now*, you can bail out when the canoe window-shades, or, for a less violent exit, plant your paddle deep down into the green water under the foam pile. Unhook your legs from your straps and seat, then let the paddle pull you out over the gunwale downstream. If the hole is very retentive you may get recirculated to the trough; this could be a problem if your canoe is still where you left it, tumbling around in the hole.

River Running Skills

Punching holes

You're cruising down the rapids, bobbing and weaving among the rocks, when you notice a hole looming. Deciding to go around it, you pivot the canoe (photo 160). Turning a classic canoe midstream without the aid of an eddy can take a while. Finally, you've got the canoe pointed in the direction you need to go. By this time the hole is too close for comfort, but you have no choice. Go for it. Aah, you're not gonna make it! Bet you wish you'd read the next paragraph before coming out on this cold winter day?

Instead of turning broadside to the hole, try punching right through it. Yes, we know that in this instance you could also back-ferry away from it, but let's pretend this isn't feasible. Back in the midst of the rapid, you are trying to set up to front-ferry to the center of the river (photo 161, canoe at right). Realizing that you won't clear the hole, you turn the canoe downstream. By reaching this decision early, you still have time to develop downstream momentum. Take a good forward stroke to propel the boat (canoe at left) through the hole. A large classic canoe has a couple of things going for it when punching holes: the bow is sharp, allowing it to cut through the foam pile of the hole; and even though the bow is embedded in the foam pile, the rest of the canoe is still being pushed by the downstream current.

If you can hit the hole straight with speed, you stand a good chance of making it through.

160 *Trying to avoid the hole.*

Staying dry

Whether you are paddling a 16-foot classic canoe or a nine-foot rodeo boat, the one feature that distinguishes these boats from all other whitewater craft is that they take on water. Although the lines you choose on a rapid will reflect your goal of staying dry, sometimes waves are unavoidable, so here's a trick that keeps those small waves from slopping into the canoe. Normally when you hit a wave sideways, you tilt downstream (photo 162). This lets the wave break right into the canoe. However, a quick tilt upstream and the wave is deflected away by the bottom and side of the hull (photo 163). You can use an upstream low brace, as shown in 163; or, if you're paddling on the downstream side, you can use a high brace. If the wave is high or there's a substantial foam pile at the top and you have approached it sideways, you may end up side-surfing

162 Downstream tilt, wet.

163 Upstream tilt, dry.

briefly. Oops! You'll likely pivot off the wave still dry. Then why not hit the wave head-on, so you don't get surfed? Well, a classic boat tends to span the waves, causing the bow to plow through and under the waves.

The optimum angle of approach to a breaking wave is about forty-five degrees with forward momentum. The forward speed shortens the length of time you rely on your brace. The upstream tilt should be made with just a wrench of your knees, followed by re-establishment of a downstream tilt.

161 Punching the hole.

Crossing the grain

If you've ever paddled the Ottawa River, you've likely been introduced to Phil's Hole. In fact, some of you may have come to know Phil's intimately after dropping in for a visit.

Phil's is the big hole located right smack in the middle of the very first rapid. The rapid is named McKoy's and it always gets the old adrenaline going. This rapid consists of two slightly overlapping holes—Satler's on the left and Phil's extending from the center to the right shore (illustration 164). After Phil's comes some fast water that allows time for a quick recovery—hopefully before the current takes you around the corner into the meat of the Horseshoe Hole. If you are unfortunate enough to be swimming into Horseshoe, some bruises are a real possibility. Finally, you'll pass over or under Babyface, a great breaking surfing wave. I trust you get the idea that in a classic canoe staying upright and dry is a much valued option. And there are several sneak routes, but you may as well scare yourself a little by going near Phil's, right?

When we first began running the Ottawa in classic canoes, we emphasized only momentum. (We're talking some serious speed here, folks.) About 200 feet upstream, we'd start to paddle like mad. By doing this we achieved three things. First, we were winded by the time we actually hit Phil's. Second, we had so much downstream momentum that we blasted through Phil's, whether we were right on the tongue or not. And third, we couldn't change our direction of travel very much. (Of course, we didn't realize this until we were traveling downstream at warp ten before trying to turn between Satler's and Phil's holes!)

During the process of shooting photos for this book, I once again found myself at the top of McKoy's in a big classic canoe. Again I chose to cross between the holes, figuring that I now knew more than I had on my earlier attempts. Several kayaks and a solo playboat were in front of me, lining up to do the same thing. Their plan was to paddle downstream, starting as close as possible to Satler's, the hole on river left. This meant

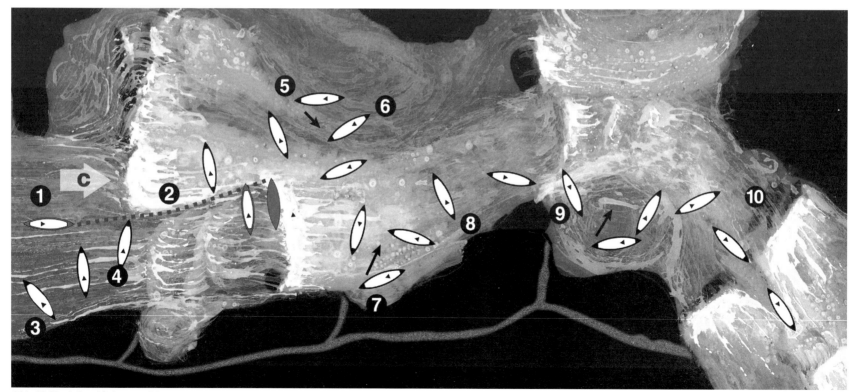

164 McKoy's Rapid, Ottawa River.

they couldn't set an angle until after passing Satler's on their left. The first kayaker tried it. He paddled hard downstream, turned as he passed Satler's and swung into Phil's sideways. Oops. The next couple of kayaks did exactly the same thing. Instead of AMT (angle, motion, tilt), they were doing MAT (establishing motion, then setting an angle and tilting), tilting big time as they side-surfed Phil's.

By the time the solo playboat (figure 1) went, I had it figured out. He started out in the middle (dotted line) to pass close to Satler's. He had to paddle forward to gain steerage, and was cruising at approximately 4 km/hr in a current that was traveling at least 12 km/hr. He turned as he passed Satler's and squeezed in two forward strokes before dropping into Phil's. He was moving downstream at 15 km/hr and laterally at 1 km/hr. That was not enough to move sideways past the second hole.

It was time to test the crossing-the-grain stuff. I started at the downstream end of the staging eddy against the river right shore (figure 3), and let the canoe peel out until 90 degrees to the current. Then I drifted downstream (figure 4). A forward stroke started me toward Satler's, and as I neared it I poured on the power. To my amazement, I broke across the reactionary waves with one stroke, and the next stroke took me past Phil's. Cool! My direction of travel was probably something like 9 km/hr downstream and 4 km/hr across the river. This technique of crossing the grain works even better if you can use a wave to surf you across the river. Take that as a subtle hint if you are at McKoy's in a solo playboat. The only real drawback is that if you mess up the approach or break a paddle, you're above where you really don't want to be.

Once you successfully cut between the two major holes, let momentum carry you into the slow water on river left (figure 5). Start the front ferry back to river

right nice and high (figure 6). Keep a wide angle so the boils below the hole don't stop your ferry. The eddy at figure 7 would be an ideal place to set up safety with a throwbag for the next boat down. For the next stage of the rapid, you'll need to do a wide peel-out (figure 8), then develop some speed to punch into the next eddy (figure 9). Now it's time for the wahoo ride down the center through Horseshoe Hole. Don't relax yet—the hole on river right is nicknamed The Pit and the hole to river left is a premier world-class rodeo hole. Not many folks attempt cartwheels in a classic canoe, so plan on hitting the tongue. The trick is to leave the eddy very low and paddle across the boils until you are lined up on the tongue (figure 10). Now crank it up and go for air as you blast through the waves.

One additional note: although I've just described in detail how to run McKoy's Rapid, don't in any way, shape or form hold me responsible for how your run goes. I've taken some artistic liberties with the diagram.

In *Path of the Paddle*, my dad recognized the hazard of going with the grain of the current; namely, that you will almost invariably be swept into river features that you had vowed to avoid. The solution he presented so evangelistically was the back-ferry. Indeed, a good back-ferry can perform miracles to keep you on line. Unfortunately, back-ferrying across a large diagonal wave is almost impossible. He came to this conclusion, albeit underwater, in Wilberforce Canyon on the Hood River in the Northwest Territories. The truth is, it wasn't until much later that we agreed that a back-ferry is not always the solution in big water. The trick is to punch diagonal waves perpendicularly. We will discuss this in more detail later.

To hit diagonal waves with enough momentum to carry you through or over them requires that you take a run at them. So start as far away from them as you can. Then, taking into account that you will be moving

downstream sideways, paddle across the river toward them. This, as we've learned, is called *crossing the grain*. You can also use this technique to avoid rocks or holes. You may ask, isn't this just the same as arriving at a rapid and deciding to go for it, paddling pellmell downstream? No. The key is to set your angle before gaining momentum. Once the angle is set, the forward momentum equals steerage. Small waves and eddies will not affect the direction of the canoe as much, since the canoe slices through them, spending less time in each feature.

165 Incorrect approach.

166 A correct approach.

The prime reason to run a rapid under speed is to avoid being swept along with the current. The two issues of crossing the grain and punching diagonal waves are illustrated in two photo collages: 165 demonstrates an "alternative," which results in the paddler being swept out of control through the wave train; 166 illustrates the correct approach. Here's why one person made it to the "safe" eddy on river right, while the other hapless soul did not.

Look at the starting position of the canoe in 165. The paddler wants to hit the eddy on river right at the bottom. He concludes that the closer he starts to river right, the better his chances of ending up in the eddy. Since he started on river right, he has to aim the canoe downstream to avoid running into the hole on river right above the eddy. He has some speed approaching the diagonal wave, but he is at best perhaps 45 degrees to the wave. As soon as the bow contacts the curler, it is thrown left. The paddler must brace to avoid flipping upstream. The diagonal curling wave surfs the canoe out into the center, turning it toward the opposite shore. Now the canoeist is wallowing through the wave train, just bracing to stay upright. The fact that he missed the intended eddy is likely not his main concern at this moment.

Contrast that with the far river-left start position of the paddler shown in 166. He has established his angle before even entering the rapid. This means he can concentrate on generating forward speed. Arriving at the diagonal wave, he prepares to plant his paddle on the wave to punch through. Successfully breaking through the diagonal curler results in some seriously fun air time. A low brace is the ticket here. The momentum of the canoe carries it into the eddy. Wahoo!

Boofing

Our first boofing experience went like this. Mark and I, Curtis Berryman, and a couple of other paddlers found ourselves with a little energy and adrenaline to spare at the takeout on the Petit Nation River in Quebec. Before long, we were loitering on the bridge, looking down at the river. "Hey, the water is pretty deep here," Mark observed as he leaned over the guard rail. I had a brilliant idea: "Why don't we push a canoe off the bridge to see what happens?" "Yeah! And I'll get in it!" exclaimed Curtis, gleeful about having first dibs on the ride. Mark and I exchanged glances. "Ah, okay," we replied in unison.

With the plan set, we turned to the technical details. We'd have to put the canoe on the roof of my car to clear the guard rail. Not a problem, since the car was borrowed; besides, the roofracks had a sheet of plywood bolted to them that would provide us with a place to stand as we launched the canoe out into space. We parked the car against the guard rail and proceeded to make last-minute preparations. With Curtis kneeling in the boat, we pulled the huge tractor-tire inner tube back to his knees and tied it in place. He tightened his helmet. We discussed how Mark and I would push the canoe off the roof as fast as possible and shove the stern down to keep the boat horizontal to avoid its penciling in. We weren't concerned about landing too flat, since we figured the 10 feet of boat already hanging over the rail would counterbalance Curtis's weight.

The passing cars weren't paying any attention to us, which we took as a positive sign that our activity wasn't too far off normal activity on the bridge. With a camera ready to record this historic event, we heaved on the canoe. As the tail neared the edge of the roofrack, however, Mark and I knew our calculations were off a "little." The boat was already at a 45-degree slant and it hadn't cleared the car yet. We gave it a good shove. As it left the car, Mark and I glanced at

each other, both thinking the same thing—"Uh, oh". We watched as Curtis did an excellent air brace, leaning way back, preparing to pencil in and go deep. Maybe this would work after all—the boat hit the water—then again, maybe not.

Evidently, there's a whole lot more volume in the end of a canoe than in a kayak. The canoe plowed into the water vertically but stopped dead. Curtis was flung forward. He planted his face in the inner tube, which acted like an airbag in a car, except it was bouncier. Curtis bounced right off the tube back onto his seat, then crumpled into a sitting position in the canoe as it settled into the water. From this semi-prone position he blinked up at us with a dazed expression. Being the safety-conscious paddlers that we are, we were equipped with a throw bag, and we pulled him back to shore from the roof of the car.

This experience taught us several valuable things, almost all of which we probably could have learned safely in a physics class, although not as quickly or dramatically. First, big canoes do not pencil into the water very far; we figure the Explorer penetrated the surface approximately three feet. Second, it's important to locate the thwarts in your canoe so that they do not line up with your face when you lie forward on the canoe. Third, Curtis was the most durable person we've ever known. (He later confirmed this by tumbling 300 meters down a mountainside and surviving without any broken bones.) Finally, people in cars stop to gawk only *after* a crash.

Yes, there's a limit to what you can do in a big canoe. At some point, if you still want to push your whitewater skills higher, it's time to move into a shorter playboat.

167

168

169 A steep learning curve.

5 TANDEM PLAYBOAT

170 A tandem playboat front surf.

Initially, I considered it to be a step backward to spend time in a tandem playboat rather than in my little solo boat. Now, before all you diehard tandem paddlers start sputtering in rage, let me explain my reasoning.

In the early 1980s, I discovered how much fun playing in rapids could be. Dad and I began with side-surfing and front-surfing in 16- to 17-foot tripping canoes. Playing around in the rapids was generally perceived by all involved as a way of intentionally going swimming, since invariably that's what happened. Just

seeing the contortions that people went through to stay in the canoe and keep it upright made it all worthwhile, though. This was long before even knee pads became common—at least for us. Sliding around in the canoe on that wet slick Royalex was just part of the fun.

Eventually, we discovered high-tech. Someone thought of tying in inner tubes for flotation. About this time it was becoming apparent that swimming happened a lot less if you were solo in the canoe while surfing.

This phase lasted until about 1987, when we noticed the first solo playboat in our area. Man, it was short–14 feet!–so short that it took a while to convince me that it was a step forward from my beat-up Mad River Explorer, which was 16 feet long. If you included the tractor tire flotation, the additional hockey-stick thwarts, the two-by-twos holding the bottom in place, Styrofoam flotation for the ends of the canoe and the gobs of excess resin holding the hull together, you were looking at a 100-pound-plus canoe.

171 Refining front-surfing technique.

Still, it took a while before I could make the little canoe do what I could easily do in the big canoe. Now I paddle an open canoe that is under nine feet long, weighing in at less than 45 pounds. It's super-responsive, and, with a little body English I can even bury the bow on flat-water!

So when Mark and I decided to include a chapter in this book on tandem playboating, I recalled the days of old when "tandem" meant a heavy, relatively unresponsive craft. However, two minutes on our local surfing wave in a tandem playboat changed my opinion about the new designs. The new tandem playboats are dry and easy to roll! A bonus is that you have twice the power of a solo paddler in a craft that may only be two feet longer than an average solo playboat.

Since the saddles are usually located so close to each other near the center of the canoe, communicating during the action is really helpful. And for couples, a mid-surf smooch is a definite possibility.

The real bonus, though, is that partners can learn from each other fast and efficiently, since feedback is instantaneous. This instantaneous feedback is helpful if it is correct as opposed to being composed mainly of expletives. It's fun being on either end of the stick, honing skills during a mind-bending fast surf with Mark (photo 170) or helping my wife, Judy, refine her front-surfing technique (photo 171). Learning to do something new is a large part of canoeing's appeal. After all, that's why we continue to progress to harder rapids. So yes, I do find tandem playboating to be a lot of fun. I may never be able to perform all the moves tandem that I can do solo, but now I don't view tandem as a step backward–more a step sideways, onto a different path if you will.

Skills—Strokes

See the Tandem Classic chapter for the basic strokes you'll need to maneuver a tandem canoe. The minor adaptations required to make your strokes effective results from the more responsive behavior of the boat and the new positions in the canoe for both you and your partner, since both of you are now located closer to the canoe's pivot point.

A responsive tandem playboat will likely be narrower than your classic canoe, with plenty of rocker and a harder chine. These three features play a major role in how a canoe responds to your strokes. The narrow width allows you to kneel centered in the canoe, yet still be able to tilt the boat using a J-lean. A J-lean keeps your upper body over the balance point of the boat, rather than your having to lean out over the gunwale of a wider canoe. The rocker allows you to easily pivot the canoe from your positions in the mid-sections of the boat. Last, the harder chine provides an additional tool to use when turning.

A turn using an inside tilt is the most stable, but it's not the fastest. So what, you say. Since when does it matter how long it takes to run through a rapid? Good point. The advantage of using outside tilt is that it assists in turning the boat more quickly so that you can maneuver down the rapid more precisely and catch eddies at the spur of the moment. That is certainly an advantage on any river.

How does it work? Well, instead of sliding around a corner, you engage the outside chine of the canoe to carve through the turn. This is particularly useful for turning the canoe in midstream. You may also use it to enter eddies, although the outside chine will really catch any oncoming current or rocks, so in shallow rapids I usually use a traditional inside tilt. As you become accustomed to the outside tilt, you'll find it very useful in keeping the boat tracking in a reasonably straight line. Tilting the boat while doing a correction stroke results in less drag, since in this position the boat is more receptive to a change in course. At first the boat will seem like a living thing with a bad attitude. But don't worry: with practice, you'll master it and then we'll be talkin' some serious fun.

Outside tilt, bow duffek

The key to doing a tilt to the outside of the turn (photo 173) is a good J-lean. The bow paddler doing the draw must use his or her knees to tilt the canoe while keeping the upper body centered over the boat. Leaning way out to plant a draw far from the hull will counteract the stern paddler's efforts to tilt, frustrating everyone. The actual stroke should happen close to the hull so that the paddle is as perpendicular as possible. Continuous pressure on your paddle during a duffek stroke will keep you from falling out of the

175 Outside tilt, cross draw.

canoe. As you finish the turn and let the tilt off, turn your duffek stroke into a forward power stroke.

Notice that the stern paddler also uses her lower body to tilt the canoe, while remaining centered over the balance point (photo 173). This means she can continue to paddle since her body weight is in the canoe. The benefit of being balanced in the canoe is that the tilt won't wobble, which is important since you're trying to carve through the water.

Outside tilt, cross draw

To the bow paddler, an outside tilt while doing a cross-draw (photo 172) feels remarkably like an outside tilt with a draw. So it should, since paddle placement is almost identical. A cautionary word: since neither paddler is in a position to low brace if things go badly, the likelihood of flipping on an eddyline is increased a "little."

172 Outside tilt, duffek, for a faster turn.

173

174

Forward stroke with correction

A tandem playboat is designed to be maneuverable. The downside to this, however, is that tracking and hull speed are compromised. To overcome these deficits, you'll need to focus on the mechanics of the stern person's correction strokes.

With this stroke you have two options: using a quick pry to stay in sync with the bow paddler, in which case the forward stroke tends to be shorter than usual; or maintaining the angle correction as long as necessary and skipping a forward stroke to stay in sync with the bow paddler.

Note that a subtle trailing pry slows the canoe less than an aggressive pry that creates drag. Why are we promoting the pry for a steering stroke when people used to call it the "goon stroke"? It's still called that when used on flat-water in a classic canoe, but for whitewater playboating the pry has benefits over the J stroke. The whitewater pry, as it's now called, is less likely to catch the current and push the gunwale down. It's very effective as a turning stroke and you can quickly turn it into a low brace if necessary. Since your grip hand is not rolled over as during a J stroke, you can exert or withstand considerably more pressure on the paddle blade and your body position will be more centered in the boat rather than favoring your onside.

When you learn to pivot the canoe towards your onside using an outside tilt, you can incorporate it into your forward correction stroke. Tilt the canoe to the outside of the turn while you do your corrective pry stroke. Using the chine of the canoe to turn makes the canoe carve through the water. In fact, it will carve so well you'll overcorrect unless you flatten out the tilt once you've got the canoe pointed in the right direction.

Forward stroke

There's no such thing as too much practice when it comes to a forward stroke. So refer to the photos accompanying this text and then get out there and pay your dues. Start your practice session by sufficiently slowing your stroke so that your body can learn what each phase should feel like. Pay particular attention to how it feels to "wind up" prior to the "catch." Try to make the torso rotation initiate as low as your hips (see photo 176). The objective is not to just wiggle your shoulders. Unwind your torso like a spring to generate power (photo 179). Keep the paddle vertical to minimize the turning effects of the forward stroke. Also keep the stroke short; the "power phase" should be complete by the time the paddle reaches your knees. If your paddle is too long or your shaft hand too high up the shaft, it will be hard to keep your stroke vertical and short. Try holding your shaft hand just above the gunwale. This will cure all sorts of ailments and generally restore good health.

176 The catch.

177 Forward stroke with correction.

178

179

180 Both paddlers onside to roll.

"Bombproof" roll

Being able to Eskimo-roll has unquestionable merit. Unfortunately, however, the skill is sometimes elusive. You may bang off several rolls in a row one day and then the next day you just can't seem to get it. If this sounds familiar, you'll love tandem rolls–provided, of course, that in learning you're paired up with someone who has a bombproof roll.

First, you can quickly gain a feel for the motion of the canoe during a roll. The paddler with the stronger roll can supply most of the power to right the boat while you just go through the motions of rolling. That should be enough to make the attempt successful, provided you aren't actually countering the roll. If this still isn't working, the second option is for one person to bail out, let the other paddler roll up, and then clamber back in. Recovery is pretty quick.

I used this technique one day on the Ottawa River with Eric, a friend who's a little bigger than me. I mention Eric's size because this size difference actually added a bit of excitement to the run. We were trying to cross between two large holes. I blew our angle and we ended up careering into the shoulder of notorious Phil's Hole. The boat did a violent 180-degree flat spin when it hit the wall of water, depositing us on top of the foam pile. From there we slowly started sliding in for what would have been my first tandem cartwheel. Fortunately, Eric lost his balance and fell over, taking the canoe with him. I just caught his expression as he disappeared under water; his eyes were as big as saucers–not surprisingly, as he claimed to have flipped rarely before he paddled with me. Anyway, the downstream current caught our bodies and pushed us downstream out of the hole. I rolled up and Eric climbed in. He just managed to flop across the gunwales, before losing his balance and taking us over again. I rolled back up. We floated through some waves

I must confess–I'm in favor of any technique that makes rolling an open canoe easier. Having one paddler switch sides so you're both doing an onside roll is the easiest way to roll your tandem boat. It's simple for the bow paddler to quickly change his or her grip on the paddle when the canoe tips to the stern's onside (photo 180). I don't have any real reason for suggesting that the bow paddler make the switch other than the fact that the more experienced paddler usually gravitates to the stern position, and likely has the stronger onside roll. In line with this, if the canoe tips to the bow paddler's side, then both paddlers go right underneath the boat to roll up on the stern paddler's side. The other options are for the stern person to switch sides and roll up on the side tipped to, or for the stern person to do an offside roll. We haven't had much success with the stern offside roll, however, so good luck on that one.

Let's assume that you've agreed to roll up on the stern's onside (in these photos, the right-hand side of the canoe). It's useful to agree upon which side to roll

up on before flipping, since any discussion during the roll is just incoherent sputtering! Regardless of which side you fall over on, use a sweeping high brace to orient or cheat the canoe in the direction it's going to roll. Then flip the paddle over into a low-brace position. Rotate your shoulders to face your paddle and let your body float on the water with your face against the paddle shaft and the blade at the surface (photo 180). The trick then is to almost completely right the canoe using only your hips. This allows your upper body to remain floating at the surface. From here you can slide your body into the canoe, bending at the waist and keeping your head right down on the airbags. The momentum of your head swinging across to the far side of the canoe ensures that the craft stays upright. It's crucial that you right the canoe with your lower body. Any pressure that you apply to your paddle will cause the paddle to sink. Then, even if you do right the canoe, your paddle will be too deep to offer any resistance to help your upper body swing into the canoe.

Hog's Back Falls, Rideau River, Ontario

Crystal, Moose River, New York

Back Bacon, Rideau River, Ontario

Wa-ki-ki, Ottawa River, Ontario

Beaver Creek, Ontario

Top Youghiogheny, Maryland

Hog's Back Falls, Ontario

Upper Youghiogheny, Maryland

Trick or Treat, Quyon River, Quebec

The Lorne, Ottawa River, Ontario

Fowlerville Falls, Moose River, New York

Above and Below: Sureform, Moose River, New York

Baby Falls, Upper Tellico River, Tennessee

Section 2, Inn River, Switzerland

Matilla, the sneak route, Moose River, New York

Fowlerville Falls, Moose River, New York

The Wave, Champlain Bridge, Ontario

Agers Falls, Moose River, New York

Full James, Waikato River, New Zealand

Centre Slot, Ottawa River, Ontario

Muria Falls, Muria River, South Island, New Zealand

Butterfly, Ottawa River, Ontario

Hog's Back Falls, Rideau River, Ontario

and into a big swirly eddy, where he tried to get in once more. He made it onto his saddle this time before we flipped again. This led us to proclaim that our Dagger Caption is a little tippy when full of water. True or not, that's our excuse. We likely could have mastered the recovery if we had practiced on flatwater or if Eric had not outweighed me. Eventually, we floundered over to shore in a somewhat undignified manner. But after all was said and done, it was still better for me to be free to roll up and paddle the canoe solo than to have both of us swimming.

One fact that became apparent to both Judy and me while we were doing the underwater photo shoots for this book is that the person with the stronger roll should initiate the roll. The other paddler should wait until the canoe begins to move before starting the hip snap. If the person with the weaker roll begins first, he or she will be out of position when the canoe actually starts to roll, and will fall back into the water, pulling the canoe over with them. This was the trouble that Judy and I encountered initially. Once Judy let me start the roll, we had no problem.

Offside roll

A bow paddler choosing to do an offside roll can use either an offside low brace (photo 182-186) or an offside high brace (photo 181). The positioning of your body and paddle, relative to the surface, is the same as for an onside roll. Note that the paddlers in these photos extend their paddles above the surface so they can feel air. See photos 182 and 185. This ensures that their blades will be at the surface when they do finally

181 Bow offside high brace.

put some pressure on them to finish the roll. The critical part is keeping your head low as you bring your body into the canoe (photo 183). Keep your rolling momentum going by swinging your head right across to the far gunwale (photo 184).

182 Stern low, bow offside.

183

184

185 An underwater view of the bow offside roll.

186

Tandem playboats really excel at front surfing and give the novice playboater an ideal introduction to surfing. The bow paddler provides forward power, while the stern concentrates on controlling the angle of the boat. This means that a less experienced paddler can enjoy the thrill of front surfing and develop a feel for how to catch the wave successfully. You'll have a much more positive experience than if you try to front-surf in a solo boat, because it's difficult to maintain momentum and steer at the same time.

Throughout this book you'll see a variety of play spots that we have used to illustrate a skill. The areas vary in size from small friendly waves for beginners to big gnarly waves for case-hardened experts. The wave pictured on this page falls into the latter category, but the skills required to surf it are the same as for a smaller wave. On this particular occasion, I teamed up with Jeff Richards, one of the premier open boaters in the eastern United States, to surf this wave, aptly named Wa-Ki-Ki, on the Ottawa River.

Catching the wave from the side Approaching a wave from the side is the easiest way to catch it for a surf. Set an angle so that the canoe is aiming at the *precise* spot where you want to leave the eddy. Yes, the precise spot. You need to read the wave to determine where to slide out onto it. This, plus the angle at which you leave the eddy, is the crux of your surfing attempt. To review this, examine illustration 9, anatomy of a surfing wave.

With the angle set, you can make adjustments as you hit the eddy line. Paddle forward to develop momentum and keep the power on as you cross the eddy line (photo 187), until the canoe starts to slide down the face of the wave (photo 188). Then ease up on the power so that you don't drive your bow into the back side of the preceding upstream wave. Avoid doing this for two reasons: one, it tends to push you back up and over the wave and downstream; two, the bow will likely be forced off to the side by the oncoming water, particularly on a big wave. With the bow firmly planted, you have no options. You are out of there!

Okay, back to Wa-Ki-Ki. Once you've established yourself on the wave, the trick is to stay there. Sometimes a simple bottom-feeding front-surf suffices. At other times, you need to carve across the face of the wave, either to compensate for diagonal ridges on the wave or to keep your bow from burying in the green water. In photo 189, we've been cutting across the face toward river right and are just beginning to turn back toward the center. Jeff is doing a pry in the stern while we both tilt to the outside of the turn. Notice how the bow is hitting the near shoulder of the wave. This position, combined with our tilt, will really help to turn us back on the wave. Photo 190 captured us attempting to turn back the other way. We've surfed across the wave to river left, tilted to the outside of the turn and are doing some relevant strokes to turn back to river right. This time a diagonal ridge of water is trying to push us off the wave. You can see it striking the bow of the canoe, making life a little more difficult. The solution is to tilt more and wait until we pass the diagonal ridge of water before turning back. Of course, with the water screaming by this fast, you'll be in a different time zone before you realize what's happening.

187 Catching the wave from the side.

188

189

190

Catching the wave from above This more difficult method of catching a wave is sometimes your only option if no convenient eddy exists beside the wave. The difficulty lies in overcoming your downstream momentum. Luckily for you, a tandem playboat has a better chance at this than a solo canoe because of that extra paddler to supply forward power. (Just for future reference, the wave pictured here is a really big wave! You may wish to start on something a little smaller, but the technique for catching it is the same. The face of this wave is very steep, but it has no curl on the top, making it a front-surfing dream if you can catch it.)

Drop down from upstream with the canoe angled slightly toward the stern paddler's side (photo 191). This slight angle compensates for the canoe's tendency to turn away from the stern paddler's side. Why not just steer? Because any correction strokes at all will create drag and pull the canoe downstream off the wave.

Start crankin' on the paddle as you slide down the backside of the previous wave or pillow. Waiting until you feel the stern start to rise up the face of the wave before putting on the power, is too late. You'll need to have slowed the canoe almost to a standstill by the time you reach the trough. As your stern rises, pick up the pace of your strokes. Judy, in the bow, focuses on supplying power (photo 192), while I take a peek at our location on the wave. It's now or never. Your stroke rate should be so fast that you're using only your arms, rather than your torso, to generate power. There is no paddle "plant," as the paddle must be moving faster than the passing current when the blade hits the water. Leaning forward at this critical moment also helps

(photo 193). It pushes the bow down so the canoe will slide down the face as it slides towards the trough. The stern person should adjust the canoe's angle so it's parallel to the current for a bottom-feeding front-surf, or set an angle to stay out of the trough. As shown in this photo (photo 194), the bow person will probably be a microsecond slower to realize that he or she has caught the wave and ease up on that forward stroke. Communication helps so that the bow person knows where you want to go and can respond accordingly.

191 Catching a wave from upstream.

192

193

194

Carving

A massive wave like the one shown in photo 194 is a spring phenomenon near the Champlain Bridge in Ottawa. The first time Judy and I caught it we cheered–then promptly slid down its face, buried our bow and were blasted off toward Quebec.

Catching the wave is only the first part of a good front-surf. Equally challenging is staying on it. One technique is to remain parallel to the current and let the boat settle into the trough. We refer to this as "bottom feeding." It's a slightly derogatory term, but it really is appropriate for those front-surfs that could last for hours with little effort from the paddlers.

An alternative to bottom feeding is carving. In the case of the Champlain Bridge wave, it was our only choice, since the wave was too steep to surf straight on. Besides, carving is way more fun than should be legal.

Once you've set an angle that lets the canoe race diagonally across the face of the wave, maintaining it is relatively easy. The tough part is turning back in the other direction before blowing off the end of the wave.

Turning to the stern's onside In photo 195 the canoe has just begun to traverse the wave. The bow person has finished a draw stroke and is staying in a high-brace position in case more angle is needed. The stern paddler uses a subtle pry stroke that trails in the water like a rudder to keep the canoe from turning broadside. Establishing a good tilt (photo 196) keeps the canoe from tipping upstream and begins a carving turn. The bow paddler's low brace does not contribute to the turning action but allows both paddlers to tilt aggressively to the outside of the turn. Using the current ripping past, the stern paddler does a static pry. You need to continue to help the bow paddler tilt while executing your stern pry. Try not to push down on the gunwale while prying. Placing your pry stroke

195 *Turning to the stern's onside.*

196

197

well toward the stern ensures that you can't push the upstream gunwale down. As the boat becomes parallel to the current (photo 197), it starts to slide down the face of the wave. Cross this transition zone quickly so that you don't slide into the trough and bury your bow. The stern paddler can exert quite a bit of braking action by prying out farther from the hull. This will help to hold the canoe high up on the wave.

The bow person has an alternative to the low brace–the cross-draw. The canoe will turn faster with a cross-draw, but neither of you is doing a bracing stroke so you're living life a little closer to the edge.

The photo collage (198) shows a turn on a small wave using a cross-draw and tilt to the outside of the turn. The canoe is carving across the wave from river left toward river right. As the boat surfs across the wave, you maintain an angle with a stern pry. Since the wave is small, the bow paddler provides some forward power so you don't fall off the backside of the wave (figure 1). Previously, I mentioned that not very much bracing goes on while the bow person is doing a cross-draw and the stern person a pry. Well, the camera caught me. In figure 2, I've just finished my pry and I am in a righting high-brace position. (Not that I

thought we were going to flip or anything–really.) Notice that the bow's cross-draw has helped to pull the canoe up the wave, which has freed the bow of the oncoming current. This allows the boat to quickly spin on top of the wave to carve back in the other direction (figure 3). At this point the bow paddler eases off the cross-draw and goes to her onside in case forward power is needed. In the stern you use a draw placed well toward the end of the canoe to control the angle. Notice that a downstream tilt is already established.

198 *Turning to the stern's onside with a bow cross-draw.*

Turning to the stern's offside This turn is major fun! You can heel the canoe right over onto its side because both paddlers are doing draw strokes–which, you will recall, incorporate a bracing action. In fact, since the draw isn't as powerful as the pry, you'll need to crank the canoe on edge to obtain results.

Let's look at the vertical photo progression first. In the stern you need to begin to establish a tilt to the outside of the turn. The bow person uses a static draw stroke while the stern stays on a static stern draw (photo 199). If, when doing this move, you still have trouble turning the canoe, it's time to crank the gunwale right to the water and move your grip hand out over the water so your stern draw is pulling as hard as possible. The bow paddler must remain upright (photo 200) because leaning out to pull on the paddle would flatten out the tilt. This turn was difficult because the bow was firmly planted in the green water by photo 200, so the current was working against us. One solution would have been to tilt more, sooner.

On to photo collage 201 for a different view of this turn toward the stern's offside. Here the canoe is surfing across the wave from river right to river left. Since the wave is small and steep, the bow is buried in the oncoming green water despite an extreme tilt (figure 1). The fact that this playboat possesses ample rocker is really the only thing keeping it from surfing right off the end of the wave. Of course, no amount of rocker will help without efficient turning strokes. The bow paddler needs to hold her duffek stationary, letting the current do the work, and allow the canoe to tilt to the outside of the turn–not always a comfortable feeling, I will admit. The stern paddler must transfer his weight to the paddle for the stern draw to be effective. Finally, the canoe's lateral momentum slows (figure 2) while we continue the pivoting strokes to complete the turn.

Note that you'll still be using the same stroke you started with–meaning, do not pull your paddle to the canoe to increase power. Instead, change the angle of the blade in the water. For example, if you're in the bow, you can open your power face to the current for more turning action. If you're in the stern, you can increase the force on your paddle by moving your top hand out farther from the canoe, while pulling your shaft hand in a little (figure 2). This increases the angle of your paddle to the current while still keeping the blade vertical in the water. Now we're talking an efficient surfing stroke. One last thing to remember about surfing strokes–well, about all strokes, actually. The more vertical your paddle, the more efficient the stroke. Flattening out the blade will look spectacular, as it skips on the water, but that's really just a brace, not an effective turning stroke.

Once the canoe starts to surf back to river right, relax and catch your breath in preparation for the next turn. Carving is addictive, but if you're still shredding it up when the fireflies come out, take the hint and go home–although I wonder how many fireflies you'd need to safely surf at night.

199 *Turning to stern's offside.*

200

201 *Carving up the waves with a pair of draws.*

Using the Foam Pile

As an experienced paddler, you've likely already tried to front-surf a breaking wave. Isn't it frustrating how the foam pile seems to grab the stern and hold it while the bow continues moving laterally across the wave? You usually run into this situation when you are bottom-feeding on the wave–that is, surfing down in the trough. This means your bow is engaged in the oncoming current, while your stern is buried in the face of the wave. This is fine, provided your angle to the current is narrow and the wave doesn't break. But if the wave is breaking and has a foam pile, you need a different approach.

Try surfing the wave in the trough and, as you near the breaking part of the wave, increase your angle toward it. The objective is to let the downstream current push you up the face of the wave. The canoe needs to be angled enough so that the front half of the canoe will hit the foam pile (photo 202). Tilting your canoe upstream as you cross the wave will accomplish two things: one, if you tilt upstream while increasing your angle, the upstream chine of the canoe will dig in, pushing you farther up the face of the wave; and two, when you contact the foam pile, the bottom of the canoe will be sitting flat on the face of the wave, allowing the bow to bounce off the curl and slide back down the face. Why isn't the chine digging in at that point? Well, the slope of the face of the wave becomes steeper as you near the crest. If instead you tilt downstream as you hit the curl, your downstream chine will dig in and the current will push you off the wave. That's a bad thing. As the canoe bounces off the curl and pivots to face upstream, quickly right the canoe before your bow contacts the oncoming green water (photo 203). You really, really want to avoid sliding down into the green water while still angled toward the hole and leaning upstream. If you do slide in this way, be consoled by the fact that you'll window-shade so fast your brain won't have time to worry about it until next Tuesday.

In another scenario, from the position in photo 203 you could go either left or right. While balanced on the foam pile, the ends of the canoe will be free of the water. This allows you to quickly set an angle in either direction. A narrow angle to river left will take you down into the trough for a warp-speed surf across the hole. A wider angle to river left might take you across the top of the foam pile or, if there is enough backwash, push you sideways down into the meat of the trough for a really juicy side-surf.

On the other hand, if you angle to river right you could surf back onto the green part of the wave. In this instance, however, we had headed out to the wave with the intention of trying for an ender. Mark was in the bow; since he outweighs me, we thought this might help to drive the bow down. (I'm not sure how he builds all that heavy muscle sitting at a computer, but I'm expecting to build bulging muscles from writing this book. To date, I must confess that the results are a little disappointing. Anyhow, back to the wave.)

We banked off the foam pile and lined up the canoe parallel to the current. Then I steered the canoe as we dropped into the trough. Leaning forward aggressively as the bow hits the green water helps to initiate the ender. Unfortunately, I was so busy steering I didn't shift my weight forward, so the bow didn't catch as much current as it could have. Although we both agreed that the large volume bow of the Caption makes it a very obstinate boat to ender, doubtless it will ender if you find a hole big enough. But I, for one, do not relish the prospect of being in a tandem boat in a hole that big in the first place!

As with any attempt to go vertical, there is the drawback that the end of the canoe is likely to hit bottom. The difference with a tandem playboat is that being a bigger boat, it will experience considerably more force on the hull when it does hit bottom. Expect a generous dent.

202 *Using the foam pile.*

203

204

Back Surfing

205 Backsurfing is life in the fast lane.

One good reason for trying to back-surf on a wave is to keep pushing your skill level without having to run harder and harder rapids. The point is, if you're achieving a front-surf on a wave with ease, then it's time to spice life up with a back-surf. I often feel compelled to try a back-surf even when I think it isn't possible. I guess I enjoy the challenge, plus when you do happen to nail a back-surf on a tough wave, then you have set the bar a little higher for yourself and your paddling friends. The bottom line for me is, if it hasn't been done before, what have I got to lose? I am, of course, assuming there are no serious consequences if I fail. I hate serious consequences.

Enough of the why. Let's get down to the how. Do your homework and review the tandem backpaddling strokes in the chapter on Tandem Classic.

One of the main differences between a classic canoe and a tandem playboat is the effect that body language has while surfing. Leaning forward or backward can make or break a front- or back-surf. Since paddlers kneel near the center of the boat, which is the balance point of the canoe, they can push the stern down by leaning back. This lets the boat slide backward down the face of the wave. This sliding action down the face won't be dramatic. After all, the tandem playboat is pretty long, so the stern will probably already be near the trough, while the bow will extend downstream past the wave. The important thing to remember is that the balance point of the canoe must be on the face of the wave.

It took Mark and me a while to realize this. We were trying to back-surf a small steep wave but kept falling off downstream. Mark, who is used to paddling solo, was utilizing his body position as a reference point, keeping himself, positioned in the stern, on the face of the wave. This left me pretty much

downstream of the crest, wondering why I was the only one backpaddling like crazy to get back on the wave. Fortunately, both of us are inclined to figure out why a maneuver isn't working rather than to get steamed up by assuming that it's the partner's fault. Of course, in this case it *was* my partner's fault. Mark redeemed himself by noticing a flaw in the angle I was giving the canoe on the approach to the wave.

Catching the wave from the side   This must be the most difficult way to enter the current. But provided you can control the angle of the canoe, it can be a really sweet method of initiating a back-surf.

Begin with enough momentum to carry you across the eddy line. Crossing the eddy line with authority will lessen the time that the ends of the canoe are in opposing currents. Besides, I'm pretty sure a canoe can smell fear. Watch over your shoulder until you enter the current. In a fast current such as the one shown in photo 206, it's easier to maintain your balance while looking downstream. As the canoe crosses onto the wave, decide whether you need reverse power to stay on it, or a braking action to avoid burying your stern in the green water. In photo 206, it's the latter. The stern person is doing a stern cut, which will help to keep the canoe straight. The bow person is doing a static forward stroke, which can be angled one way or the other to control the canoe's angle and speed. Once the boat is established on the wave (photo 207), use pivoting strokes to stay on the sweet spot.

Catching the wave from upstream   This approach allows you more time to set your boat's angle for the wave. But don't be fooled! The angle of the boat is no less critical if you hope to catch a surf. The following steps are the same whether you're catching a wave one-foot high or a mammoth kahuna like this one.

Approach the wave with as little downstream momentum as possible. As you begin your descent down the back side of the preceding wave, set an angle toward the bow paddler's side. The bow paddler is using a reverse J to accomplish this in photo 208. Now it's time to start backpaddling harder. A last-minute back-sweep by the bow paddler fine-tunes the angle of the canoe (photo 209). The goal is to have the boat parallel to the current as it rises up the face (photo 210). GO, GO, GO! Increase your stroke rate as the canoe rises up the face. Remember: as the canoe slows down, the current will be going by correspondingly faster. As the canoe rises up the wave, lean back to try to make it slide back down into the trough.

206

207 Pivoting strokes maintain position.

208 Catching the wave from upstream.

209 Backpaddling and reducing angle.

210

Strokes

The strokes for back-surfing tandem playboats are similar to those for solo classic or tandem classic backsurfing, and are covered in depth in Chapters 3 and 4. Here are the key points.

Onside strokes   The onside correction strokes are the back draw, bow pry and static forward stroke. To capitalize on the benefits of the **back draw**, really push out with your grip hand. Keep the elbow of your shaft-hand arm in close to your body. Your arm muscles have better leverage when they aren't fully extended. In the **bow pry** (photo 212), keep your shaft hand above the gunwale, not resting on it. In the bow, lean away from your pry stroke so you have better leverage to pull the grip hand in toward the center line of the canoe. Leaning your upper body also prevents you from counteracting your stern partner's attempts at maintaining a downstream tilt. The **static forward** stroke is the catch phase of a forward stroke (photo 211). With the paddle vertical and your arms extended, vary the pitch of the paddle. This will cause it to push against the hull like a pry or pull like a draw. The benefit of the stroke is that it has a strong braking effect that pulls you up the wave, making it easier to turn the boat and enabling you to quickly make subtle steering adjustments.

Offside strokes   The **cross-draw** and **offside bow pry** are a combination that is hard to beat. You can alternate between the two in the blink of an eye, and both are powerful pivot stokes. To do the cross-draw, rotate your torso to face your offside. Push out with your grip hand so your paddle bites into the water

211 *Static forward stroke.*

212 *Bow pry.*

213 *Bow cross draw.*

rather than skimming it (photo 213). With the offside bow pry, rest the shaft on the hull of the boat and lean toward the other side, away from your paddle, so you can pull your grip hand in toward the center line of

the boat. You do the offside static forward (a third possibility) exactly as you would an onside static forward. Leaning forward a bit will move your stroke farther from the pivot point.

Hole Surfing

Side-surfing

A side-surf is pretty much the easiest playboating maneuver to initiate. You're probably thinking, So why isn't it the first maneuver to learn? Well, I did say easiest to initiate. Conversely, it is the most difficult to control without becoming really wet. I'm referring to the sinus-plugging, water-in-the-ears variety of wetness here, folks. We will assume that our goal is to get in the hole, side-surf a little, maybe crank in a 360 and get out while still relatively dry.

There are two likely ways to initiate a side-surf. One is to drop into the hole from upstream; the other is to approach it from the side.

To soften the impact of dropping into a hole from upstream, approach it on an angle. It doesn't matter whether your boat is pointed upstream or downstream. The idea is that the boat will cut partly through the foam pile before being turned sideways. This gives you a moment to establish a solid downstream tilt before you're pushed down into the trough by the backwash. The alternative is to catch an eddy beside the hole and then front-ferry into it from the side. This is the softest way to start a side-surf. Ferry right into the hole, letting your bow make contact with the oncoming green water. At this point, the opposing currents of the green water and the hole will quickly turn your boat sideways (see photo 214). The downstream paddler is in the best position to brace, but both paddlers contribute to the tilt of the boat. The goal is to tilt just far enough downstream that the upstream chine is not grabbed by the green water. Too much downstream tilt will let the foam pile fill up the boat. The tilt is looking pretty good in photo 214. The stern person has a good J-lean; the bow paddler is cranking on a backpaddle stroke to move the boat backward to the sweet spot of the hole. Okay, so sometimes you just can't keep the water out of the boat. But then, if you really wanted to do that, you could paddle a C2, right? Besides, a boat full of water can produce a pretty funky ride in a hole. See photo 215 for what amounts to a pseudo-mystery move out of the hole. As the boat fills up, it sinks deeper into the trough; it hits the green water passing under the foam pile, catches the current and is pushed downstream. The weight in the boat keeps it from floating immediately to the surface. In this instance, the bow mysteried out more than the stern.

You may find that at times the stroke you are doing just doesn't seem effective, or the side you're paddling on leaves few options for helping out with the maneuver. Experiment. That's what I assume Mark is doing behind my back in photo 216. When you come up with a new use for a stroke, such as Mark's stern cross draw, spend some time determining if it is actually effective given the pivot point, current and such. Just because it feels like it works does not necessarily mean it's the best choice. Think back to the forward stroke and how vigorously you can pull with your arms. Remember how ineffective that is? In the case of the stern cross-draw, the stroke does provide additional bracing on the downstream side of the boat, but it's not the optimum stroke for maneuvering the boat from the stern position.

214 Side surf.

215 A funky ride.

216 What is your stern partner doing?

Flat Spins in the Hole

It's time to crank up the fun dial and try some flat spins in a hole. The goal is to spin your canoe horizontally 360 degrees while in the hole. Ideally, the hole won't be too trashy–meaning bouncy. A trashy hole will quickly fill your open canoe with water, making it about as maneuverable as a raft.

The first step is to decide the direction in which the hole wants to spin the canoe and how to get there dry. Often, you can just slide in at the corner of a hole and start side-surfing immediately. But this particular hole will push you across and out the other side because of the way the right shoulder angles toward the center of the river. A more aesthetic entry is to ride out to the meat of the hole on top of the foam pile (photo 217). When the canoe hits the stickier part of the hole, the foam pile will stop the bow, while the current pushes the stern downstream (photo 218). The

key is to keep the canoe high, with the bow out of the green water until it points in the direction you want to go (photo 219).

Assist this maneuver with pivot strokes. In photo 218, I'm in the bow doing a draw while Mark does a sweep. As we gain momentum sliding down into the hole (photo 219), I move my draw back for some braking action and Mark does the same. Once you're established in the hole (photo 220), some patience is required. Read the currents. With practice you can determine where the end of the canoe will catch the downstream current and spin. I have my paddle ready to do a draw stroke as soon as the bow starts to lift. The stern isn't going anywhere, as it's in the strongest part of the hole, with the most backwash. Mark has his paddle in an upstream brace position in case we start to flip upstream. The bow lifts and the canoe spins.

Mark stays on a forward sweep stroke to assist in the pivoting action and to keep our stern from dropping back into the green water too soon (photo 221). In the bow, I continue to hold my back-draw stroke to ensure that we're angled to river right as we slide into the trough backward. An additional benefit of holding the back draw is that it pulls the bow toward the stickiest part of the hole. This is where we want the bow to be for the next spin. As we slide into the trough, I switch to a static forward stroke to avoid shooting down and out the river-right side of the hole. Mark is doing the same thing with his static sweep. He's using a sweep rather than a pure forward stroke to provide a little lift to the stern to encourage the current to catch it as the current washes out of the hole.

Whew, lots of stuff to remember. Fortunately, you need to remember only half of it! Isn't tandem fun!

217 Flat spin in a hole.

218

219

220

221

222

223 Top Youghiogheny River, Maryland.

Sometimes the hardest part about teaching or explaining a technique is noticing how and why you do it yourself. To offer helpful insight into tandem playboat river skills, we needed to test our skills a little. Paddling our Dagger Caption in Class 2 or 3 water didn't seem any different from paddling a solo boat. This wasn't the case in the Class 4 rapids of the Top Youghiogheny, particularly since the river was running at a natural flow of 2'4" on the Sang Run gauge. At this level the Top Yough is pushy, with some big holes starting to form.

Realizing that you need to think of the boat as a tandem canoe first and a playboat second is the first step in being able to catch the eddies.

The rocker of the boat can easily deceive you. The bow of a highly rockered tandem playboat does not catch the still water of an eddy in the same way that a classic canoe does. You need to drive more of the boat into the eddy, especially when both saddles are located near the center of the boat.

Tandem playboats are a blast to front-ferry. They have the speed of a tandem boat but won't pearl like a classic canoe. Their extra length and weight also help when your only option is to punch the hole. This, in

fact, leads me to the next issue: communication. Yes, it's a good thing, and ideally, it will happen in several different ways. Scout from either the boat or shore to agree on the line, and then iron out the details of a particular move from the eddies. During the run, react to your partner's initiative and go with it. It's better to be successful on a second-choice line than to debate the issue and be on neither line. The line you go with likely won't be a disaster just because it wasn't your line—unless, of course, your line was *the* line.

When boat scouting from an eddy, be aware that initially the bow paddler will be concentrating on keeping the bow behind the rock. By the time he or she can twist around to scout, the stern person will be finished reading the rapid and ready to go.

At the end of our experiment on the Top Yough, we agreed that, in general, paddlers who are equally skilled will find a solo playboat a little easier than a tandem boat to run the same rapids. But on any given move the tandem boat may be at an advantage or disadvantage; it depends entirely on the situation.

Boofing seems simple: paddle off the lip of the falls and arrive at the bottom. Fair enough. After all, gravity ensures that you land at the bottom of the falls. What you want is to have some input into *how* you land.

There are three phases to a good boof off a drop: the approach, the launch and the landing. The first two dictate the quality of the third. Approach refers to everything you do to arrive at the lip—where, hopefully, you'll remember phase two. The success of the boof directly reflects how much planning and effort you put into the approach. (The slang for this ratio is "Charc in equals charc out." The phrase is borrowed from Jim Snyder, and it means something like "the cake is the sum of the ingredients." See the boofing section in the Solo Playboating chapter for more on this charc stuff.) A good approach has three attributes: staying upright, maintaining your forward speed and keeping your eyes open.

Now that you've arrived at the lip, it's time for phase two: the launch via the boof stroke. It's funny how such an advanced maneuver harkens back to the three components of the basic maneuvers: angle, motion and tilt. The angle of the canoe relative to the lip helps to determine where you will land and at what attitude—bow up, bow down or heads down. The motion of the canoe at the lip is the crux of a boof. The canoe needs to be accelerating. This is accomplished with a *boof stroke*, a powerful stroke planted right at the lip of the drop, with the blade of the paddle actually placed on the face of the falls. Both paddlers must take their boof strokes at the same time. As they do the stroke, they thrust with their hips to launch the boat out into space. The idea is for the stern to clear the lip before the bow begins to drop. Once airborne you may need to adjust the tilt of the boat to avoid flipping on impact—uh, I mean landing. Tilting the boat as you land will make the chine of the

Boofing

bow dig in, causing the boat to veer, which will throw you into the suds. Tilt is a lot easier to control if you keep your eyes open throughout the boof.

Straight off the lip The top three photos show a 14-foot tandem playboat executing a less-than-perfect boof straight off a drop. By straight I mean 90 degrees to the lip. Both paddlers are doing a boof stroke in photo 224. (However, I confess my stroke in the bow is not quite on the face of the drop—not that it would have helped a whole lot anyway.) Because the boat is going off the lip straight and not at a great speed, the bow drops long before the stern leaves the lip (photo 225). This results in the nasal flush shown in photo 226. The only thing you can do in this situation is brace as the canoe comes back to the surface.

Angling off the lip You can leave the lip at an angle. The advantage is that the bow and stern leave the lip closer in time. It also means that the stern paddler's boof stroke will be more in sync with the bow person's (photo 227) on this particular drop. Note that the paddle blades are planted right at the lip. Halfway through the stroke the bow has left the lip. Thrusting the boat out clears the stern so that the boat free-falls relatively flat (photo 228). Both paddlers lean toward the falls to counteract the tendency of the boat to roll off the lip. They correct the tilt with their knees on the way down and the result is a really flat landing—boof! (And you wondered where the name came from!) Landing flat is important because it keeps the boat dry and maneuverable for the rest of the rapid.

224 Boofing straight.

225

226

227 Boofing angled.

228

229

Who paddles left?

Or, if you're both lefties, who paddles right? Everyone doubtlessly has convincing arguments to support their preference of sides, but let's be a little more specific. Is there a good or a bad side to be on when boofing? Yes. Especially if you're leaving the lip at an angle. Examine photo 230. Mark and I have approached the lip at an angle from right to left. I'm in the bow paddling on the right, while Mark, in the stern, is paddling on the left. I've long since finished my boof stroke, yet Mark is just barely reaching the lip. This is because I clear the lip sooner on my side of the boat, due to the boat's angle, and so I must begin my stroke sooner. The net result is a poor launch. There can be no concerted effort to thrust the boat out into space to clear the stern. The lip holds up the stern as the bow drops. Think vertical splashdown, folks. Either change the angle of the boat—which may not be feasible, in this drop—or switch paddling sides.

The goal in a tandem boof, of course, is to coordinate the boof strokes. This is much more possible if the saddles are closer together. As well, having the saddles closer to the canoe's balance point delays that moment when the bow paddler's weight starts to push the bow down. You can also gain some advantage by having the heavier paddler in the stern; as well, his or her boof stroke will likely be stronger.

230

231

Dry land practice

Before actually running a steep drop with water, I like to iron out the bugs with a little dry-land practice. Mark and I had launched off this boathouse roof many times with our solo playboats; it's sort of like a circus ride—all thrill, no skill. But it did acclimatize me to the feeling of floating through space in my boat. (Okay, it was more like plummeting, but doesn't "floating" have a nicer ring to it?)

Anyway, one day it occurred to us, in a flash of brilliance, to launch off the boathouse roof in our tandem Dagger Caption. Clambering into my saddle in

the bow, which was overhanging the water, did cause me some uncertainty. But, nothing ventured nothing gained. So, ignoring the creases developing in the center of the boat, off we went. We did a good boof stroke off the wall, leaned back, dropped straight down! But it was fun! After several more attempts we decided we'd learned everything available from this site so we could quit. Oh, yes, the strange longitudinal crease developing on the side of the hull had some influence on our calling a halt to the experiment.

After debriefing, we determined that the longitudinal crease came from the stern hitting the wall of the boathouse when the bow contacted the water. The force trying to bend the boat in half must have been tremendous. The discovery that the impact of hitting the water was quite similar to that of being in a solo boat reassured us. The bow of the tandem playboat has more volume than a solo boat so the boat stops a little quicker, causing the paddlers to be flung forward at the same instant; so they aren't likely to bump heads. Keep in mind that we dropped approximately 12 feet. Higher drops certainly increase the disaster factor, which we later discovered.

Airtime

Some paddlers run increasingly higher drops to maximize their "airtime." If you're tempted to test what you've learned on a higher falls, focus on these two words: *attitude* and *tilt*.

Attitude is the angle of the canoe from end to end, either bow down or bow up. Bow down means the canoe is close to vertical. Bow up equals a more horizontal attitude. So, a canoe falling at 30 to 40 degrees is, relatively, bow up. The objective is to land the canoe flat because that will keep the boat driest and make the loudest *boof* noise. But, as height increases, a flat landing can lead to spinal injuries. Having stated this warning, realize that you'd need a perfect launching spot to ever hope to land a tandem playboat flat. Perhaps a flat boof will be more feasible in the future when tandem playboats are designed shorter.

Tilt, as always, refers to which side of the boat is up or down. The objective in a boof is to land the boat with the gunwales level, or no tilt. Having just said no tilt, we now have to refine the objective a little. Strive for *optimum tilt*, which is when the bottom of the boat is perpendicular to your line of travel. Here are two examples: The boat leaves the falls parallel to the current. Simple—the boat needs no tilt. Keep it flat. If, however, the boat leaves the falls at an angle to the current, tilt the boat upstream. When you land, your weight will be centered over the hull, and the chine won't dig in. Not doing this allows the chine to dig in, catapulting you into the water.

Pretend for a moment that you're downhill skiing. If you go straight down the hill, your skis are flat on the snow—no tilt. If you suddenly turn your skis to stop, you must tilt them on edge, mostly to bite into the snow but also to avoid having your downhill edge catch, dig in and pitch you head-first down the hill. Hitting the stationary pool of water below a drop with your canoe angled but sitting flat has much the same effect.

Attitude and tilt are fun to play with on small six-foot drops, where paying little attention to either does not produce catastrophic results. On higher falls,

232 *Ice makes an effective undercut.*

however, both of these factors play a much greater role in the outcome of the boof.

An airborne canoe is a highly responsive craft. Tilts initiated before leaving the lip, or any attitude "adjustments" caused by bumping a rock at the lip or failing to accelerate away from the lip, are highly exaggerated by the height of the drop. No doubt a mathematical formula exists to calculate the effect of forces imparted to the canoe multiplied by the height. But let's keep it simple: lack of control over your attitude and tilt will result in bad things!

Mark and I had honed our tandem boofing on the small drop featured in the photos on page 110. We confidently headed out to 18' Hog's Back Falls in Ottawa. After a couple of warm-up runs in our solo boats, we teamed up to give the tandem Caption a try. Truth be known, we weren't paying undue attention to the drop itself. Rather, the Class Three runout through the short canyon had our attention. This runout was complete with undercut ice and a small falls dumping in at the end. (Being a professional cartoonist is a drawback for a paddler because I can imagine all kinds of potential disasters in full living color, complete with captioned sound effects–WHAM! KER-SPLASH! KA-BLOOIE! This plays havoc with your concentration.) Sitting in the eddy, we agreed, if we tip we roll up on the right, no matter what. With this positive decision ringing in our ears, we launched off the lip.

We did roll up on the right. Sitting in the eddy at the base of the falls, we theorized that we had left the lip crossing the tongue of descending water, and this had caused the boat to tilt slightly. With no leverage to correct the list, the canoe continued to tip until we hit the water, making us flip upon landing. We decided to sleep on the experience for a few days, before attempting a vertical drop again. Besides, the runout through the canyon proved to be even more eventful.

We hit some ice, flipped and I swam. We both received a shower in the falls at the bottom, although Mark was still in the boat waiting for a chance to roll up, so he missed the full impact of the spout.

A week or so later we gave it another shot. We discussed extensively how to avoid penciling in and how to prevent the boat from tilting. The water approaching the lip was very slow, so our plan was to angle to my side, the left, which would allow our boof strokes to be in sync and to swing the stern clear of the lip sooner. By paying attention to our tilt, we could adjust it with our hips to land in control. This would give us a flat dry landing and make the run out of the canyon easier.

As I planted my boof stroke, I knew that things were going to be bad. Our strokes were not in sync. This meant that Mark was about to boof with a 155-pound dead weight in the bow. Not that the dead weight was inactive–I was looking for the pull cord on my parachute! The lack of acceleration at the lip allowed the bow to drop too early. About then the forces of evil really kicked in. Since we were leaving the lip angled left, the canoe wanted to tilt to the right, which it did. And since our torsos were centered in the boat, we had no way to flick the boat back to an upright position. Apparently, while you fall through space the canoe continues with whatever motion was imparted to it before it left the water. We rolled up on the right. The upshot is, some drops you should paddle off straight. This may not produce the flattest boof, but it does improve the chance of controlling the boat's tilt.

233

6 SOLO PLAYBOAT

234 Wahoo!

Introduction

Paul and I spent years paddling flatwater and then whitewater in classic canoes before we ever tried a whitewater playboat. Actually, we both had paddled many miles before they were invented. Now solo playboats are my craft of choice. You'll note that the maneuvers described in this section are more numerous and allow you to paddle more difficult water. That is not just because Paul and I spend more time in playboats. You can run harder stuff, and take advantage of more subtleties in the river's currents with a solo playboat than with any other canoe. If you've flipped to this chapter by accident, read on. The knowledge you'll gain by paddling a solo playboat or (I hope) even reading this chapter will greatly improve your whitewater skills whether you're entering a rodeo, running a steep creek

or descending an easy rapid on a wilderness trip. I still like paddling classic canoes but I feel I learn more paddling the latest design of solo playboat.

I recall a riverside debate I had about 10 years ago at a whitewater instructor school. We were considering the fact that we had spent years in classic canoes learning to front-surf while in front of us a young buck who had started his paddling career in a solo playboat two years earlier was ripping on the wave. My friend contended that although this relative neophyte could handle these "newfangled" playboats as well as us, he wasn't as good a paddler since he hadn't learned "the hard way." I agreed that we had more river-reading experience but I contended that heaps of experience in big boats on Class II water was

worth only a fraction of the experience of playboating on Class III or harder water. This young buck proved my point by paddling a classic canoe as well as anyone in the course. So if you've been paddling classic canoes and want to steepen the learning curve and have some fun, get your hands on a solo playboat or better yet a recently designed solo playboat.

Skills–Strokes

A foundation of good stroke technique is essential if you want to improve and enjoy solo playboating or even contemplate some of the more advanced moves. We will go into quite a bit of detail to help you make these strokes as efficient and powerful as possible.

Pivot strokes

In this section we'll discuss how to pivot the canoe abruptly while the boat is moving forward. In addition to what you are doing with the paddle, we will also consider how the tilt of the boat is used to improve the turning ability of the boat. The tilt is controlled by the knees so make sure your outfitting is snug. Put your weight on one knee and lift up with the other to make sure there is no play in your setup.

Draw-inside tilt   This draw stroke uses the passing

water or current, since the boat is moving forward, to pull the bow toward your onside. Plant the blade toward the bow, with the power face open and held that way. Hold the leading blade edge out so the paddle is catching water (photo 235). Tilting the boat shortens the water line length and makes the boat turn more easily (photo 236). Keep the paddle planted securely in the water throughout the stroke to provide a solid brace with which to confidently tilt the boat. As the boat slows (photo 237), complete the draw to the bow and do a power stroke. This will maintain your forward momentum. That's always a good thing–ask any slalom racer.

Draw-outside tilt   The draw stroke remains the same as in the draw-inside tilt, but now it's time to make the boat earn its keep. When you engage the outside front edge of the boat, the resistance of the

chine digging into the water forces the canoe to turn. The response is more immediate because you're presenting a sharper edge in solid undisturbed water. When you use an inside tilt, however, the water striking the inside chine has first met the sloping bottom of the hull. (See the diagrams on eddy turns, page 136 for more details.) Initiate the turn by transferring your weight to your knee on the outside of the turn. This will be your offside knee, since you're doing a draw (photo 238). I find that rotating my upper torso to face my stroke helps me shift my weight. You're supposed to be rotating your torso anyway; if you're not, pay special attention to the next paragraph on the duffek stroke. Maintain a stable tilt throughout the turn because a consistent tilt will create a smooth carving action. As you complete the turn (photo 240), complete the draw to the boat.

235 Draw, inside tilt.

236

237

238 Draw, outside tilt.

239

240

Pivot Strokes

Then, finish with a forward stroke as you reduce the tilt. This is my favorite method of changing direction midstream in a rapid. You can also use it to enter or exit an eddy.

Duffek   The duffek stroke incorporates a bracing action into a draw turn. The tilt you use can be to the inside or outside of the turn. The boat pivots around the paddle plant (photo 241). Note how your torso is twisted so that you're facing your paddle, which is out 90 degrees from the boat. Plant the paddle with the power face of the blade perpendicular to the current you're going into and adjust the blade angle so it stays perpendicular. Winding up your torso provides the power to pull the blade and your opposite knee together. This will leave your blade in a position to do a forward stroke at the end of the duffek (photo 243). The stroke works particularly well when you're trying to catch micro-eddies.

Cross-draw   The bane of every paddler learning solo playboating is the cross-draw. The stroke itself is easy to perform, but feeling confident about staying upright while executing it is another story. Having to exit from an eddy into a strong current will give most paddlers pause for thought.

I've reached a level where I'm comfortable with the cross-draw no matter how formidable the eddyline. But add some consequences downstream if I blow it and, well, suddenly chicken feathers start sprouting from my drysuit. I may have performed an eddy exit just like it dozens of times, perhaps into even stronger current. It still feels unnerving! Eventually, however, I get a grip on my anxiety, bear down and successfully end up where I want to be.

You can do a cross-draw stroke with two different tilts: tilt to the inside of the turn and tilt to the outside of the turn.

A **cross-draw–inside tilt** should be familiar. You use it to pivot the boat on both flatwater and whitewater. In a whitewater situation, a cross-draw allows you to plant your paddle on the downstream side of the boat, helping to stabilize your downstream tilt during a maneuver such as an eddy turn. The secret to a solid tilt during the turn is to let the current do the work. To refine your stroke without the distractions of whitewater, simulate the current by paddling forward before doing your cross-draw. Twist your torso around to face your stroke. Keeping your grip hand high near your ear means the blade will be in the water near your body. This allows you to incorporate some bracing action into the stroke. The face of the paddle is open to catch more water.

You tilt a solo playboat by pushing down with one knee while you pull up on the thigh straps with the other. Your lower torso moves independently of your upper torso. This keeps your body centered over the boat. If you lean your upper torso to tilt the boat, your paddle will sink, forcing you to push yourself back in to take another stroke, meanwhile losing the tilt. As your momentum slows, ease up on the pressure on your paddle. This will allow it to remain at an optimal angle out away from the hull. As with the draw, you can plant the cross-draw and hold it to carve around the turn or use the more aggressive style of the duffek. In this variation you plant the blade perpendicular to the current and pull toward the opposite knee throughout the stroke. Move the top hand forward so the paddle finishes in a vertical position, ready for a cross-forward stroke.

241 Duffek.

242

243

Cross-draw–outside tilt–now, this is cool! Once you master this turn, you'll be doing it everywhere all the time. That's okay. The novelty will wear off and then you can save it for the right moment–either when you need it or when you're trying to impress someone.

The cross-draw stroke itself remains unchanged, except that the canoe's hull will be closer to the paddle. This is due to the J-lean (248). To practice this stroke, develop some forward momentum to simulate current, initiate the turn with a sweep, then bring your paddle across by rotating your upper torso so you're facing your offside, then plant your paddle (photo 247). Weight the front outside edge of the boat by leaning forward slightly and putting your weight onto your knee opposite your cross-draw

stroke. This will cause the chine to carve through the water. Once the hull is carving, you can increase the tilt (photo 248) without any surprises–provided, of course, that your boat doesn't hit any currents or hidden rocks. Note the bow wake in photo 246. The chine of the boat is carving through the water to such an extent that the water is piling up and pushing the boat into the turn.

Using an outside tilt in midstream of a rapid allows you to quickly and efficiently set an angle toward your destination, provided you already have some forward momentum. Since the chine of the canoe is digging in, the canoe has a strong tendency to come to a stop. This is particularly useful when you're trying to catch a micro-eddy that otherwise wouldn't provide much current differential to turn the boat.

244 Cross draw, outside tilt.

245

246

247 Cross draw, outside tilt.

248

249

Steering Strokes

In this section we will discuss how to control the direction of travel while maintaining forward momentum.

Forward stroke and forward sweep

The forward stroke and forward sweep turn the boat away from your paddling side and towards your offside. The forward stroke is used when only a slight turning is desired. A stroke that is vertical, close to the hull and parallel to the center of the boat will maximize forward propulsion. The forward sweep is used for stronger offside turning effect while still providing forward propulsion. It is easiest to steer the end of the canoe that is trailing in the turbulence caused by your passage through the water. Don't try to awkwardly push the bow. Rather, start your stroke with the blade out wide and a little forward of 90 degrees to the canoe and sweep it all the way to the stern. Pull the paddle in to the stern hard! The last bit of the stroke is where you achieve the greatest turning action toward your offside.

Corrective strokes

Corrective strokes are steering strokes and techniques that turn the canoe towards your onside while providing forward propulsion. Each has advantages that are suited to different situations.

The **J-stroke** is the most relaxed correction stroke and therefore works well with a cruising forward stroke. In a playboat, however, the stroke is shorter and at a faster pace than what you may be used to when paddling tandem or solo in a traditional canoe. Because of the slower hull speed of the playboats, a long stroke causes the forward momentum to die between strokes. A shorter stroke and a quick recovery will maintain hull speed, as slow as that may be. To review the mechanics of the J-stroke, see page 56.

The second correction stroke is the **whitewater pry**. It has the benefit of being a more powerful correction stroke than the J, and is easier to execute in narrow, tippy playboats. Since you don't rotate your wrist outward as in the J, the reach to keep your paddle perpendicular is easier, and you can keep your upper body centered more easily over the boat. For this reason it is preferred over the J-stroke for front-ferrying with your paddle on the upstream side while using a downstream tilt. (See page 95 for a review of the whitewater pry.) But it will still slow you down—as I learned the hard way one day in full view of a television crew.

Mark, Phil Green and I had agreed to paddle the Des Chenes Rapids near Ottawa for a media event. We were supposed to perform some moves near the top of the rapid, scout it and make it look easy as we ran it. The line near shore wasn't difficult, but an old hydro dam straddled three-quarters of the channel, offering a variety of ugly places in which to not go. This feature and the availability of better play spots in the area account for the rapid's lack of popularity among local boaters.

To warm up, we paddled and surfed to an island on the far side of the channel. It seemed like a good idea at the time. With a signal from the television crews that they were rolling, we began the 300-foot ferry toward the camera crew. Some smooth waves made ferrying easier because you could catch a short ride before falling off the backside of the wave. Each time I fell off a wave, I reset my ferry angle with a hard pry and resumed paddling. With each pry, I was able to glimpse the dam. It was closer, and so was the rapid. The eddy where the camera crews and photographers were filming, however, did not seem to be getting closer. I was already paddling at 80 percent of my top speed, so it was going to be close—too close. Twenty

feet from the eddy I opted to turn downstream and beach my canoe on a shallow slab of rock beside the eddy. At least then I would seem to be getting out to scout. Great plan. I was able to scout from the rock for about five seconds before the fast-flowing water pushed me off, back into the current. Saving face was not an option now, since I had to concentrate on saving my skin. I had seen this chute once before and dimly remembered that it was really just one hole beside the old dam.

Thinking that there might be a tongue beside the shore, I lined up there for the hole. Fortunately, there was. Phew! Meanwhile, Mark and Phil were scrambling down the shore to see if I was okay, all the while trying to appear nonchalant for the media. Unfortunately, the six o'clock news coverage was extensive and accurate. I learned a good lesson: don't base your route on what might look good for the cameras. But more important, if I had used the offside forward stroke to control my angle, I wouldn't have had to use pry strokes and lost so much ground during the ferry.

250 Smile, you're on TV.

The **offside forward stroke** uses the same three components as the forward power stroke: the catch (photo 251); the power phase (photo 252); and the recovery to the next stroke (photo 253). Because the offside stroke is shorter than its onside counterpart, it is even more important that you do the catch–planting the paddle–smoothly. Plant your paddle with a minimum of splash. Rotate the shoulder of your shaft hand forward. Don't lean your body forward as if hinged at the hips. This may actually cause your boat to bob, killing forward speed. With your lower back upright, reach forward with your shoulders and upper back. Now, with your lower arm extended and the same shoulder rotated forward, begin the power phase of the stroke (photo 255). Use your torso and shoulders to pull your lower arm back. Your arm

muscles have a very poor mechanical advantage at this point, so your lower arm will bend very little until you start the recovery (photo 256). As the paddle reaches the end of its power phase, near your knee, try thrusting forward with your offside hip to get an extra boost as you reach the full extent of your torso rotation. (When I say your offside hip, I am referring to the side that your cross forward stroke is on. Even though your paddle may change sides during a stroke, your onside remains the same, unless you also change your grip on the paddle.) The effectiveness of the stroke decreases and recovery becomes difficult if the paddle travels too far past your body. Rotate your grip hand so that your thumb points forward, and slice the blade forward for the next stroke.

Although I consider this a correction stroke, the

emphasis of this stroke is on forward speed, so keeping the blade close to the center line of the canoe will give the most power. I should have been using it during my long onside ferry at the Des Chenes Rapids because it would have opened the angle of the boat toward my onside while maintaining forward momentum. For more angle correction, consider the offside forward sweep; or, to turn in the opposite direction, toward your offside, try starting with a cross-draw that becomes an offside forward stroke.

251 *Offside forward stroke.*

252

253

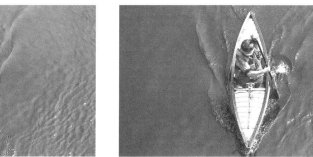

254 *Offside forward stroke.*

255

256

119

I first started experimenting with the offside forward stroke in a very old misshapen Mad River Explorer. I discovered that an offside forward stroke in a 35-inch-wide canoe is excruciating to perform as well as pretty ineffective for forward power and directional control. It wasn't until I moved into the more narrow playboats that I started to see the merit of the stroke. Now, with a rockered 10-foot playboat, the offside forward stroke is indispensable. In fact, to gain any kind of speed at all I use a combination of power onside and offside forward strokes. An offside forward stroke combined with an onside forward stroke is called the *Perk*, after southern racer Randy Perkins.

Mark and I stumbled across a slalom race on the Mulberry Fork in Alabama during one of our road trips. Of course we quickly signed up, eager to meet other open boaters and to see where we fit in to the boating world skillwise. For us it was the introduction into a community of hot paddlers, including Dale Johnson, Jeff Richards, Bailey and Lynn Johnson, Eric Baker, Phil Photi and Frankie Hubbard. We watched Frankie do some bizarre offside sweepy kind of draw thing as he tore down the slalom course. We've since refined the term for this stroke to **offside forward sweep**, or **offside sweep** for short.

The benefit of this stroke is that it provides both forward momentum and a strong turning effect. The drawback is that it puts your body in an awkward position, with poor leverage on the paddle, and it's difficult to brace from this contorted position. The sweeping action begins right at the catch phase. The

paddle is angled so that the power face is perpendicular to the direction it will travel. Your lower arm pushes the blade out on an arc from the bow as your grip hand comes across in front of your body to increase the sweep motion. This sweep is marginally longer than a regular offside forward stroke. For more emphasis on angle control, continue the stroke until it describes almost 180 degrees. This stroke is primarily used for offside front-ferries. It is surprisingly effective at holding an aggressive angle in strong current. You initiate recovery by turning your blade parallel to the current. Your grip hand thumb should now be pointing forward. Slice the blade forward to start your next stroke.

The final correction stroke is actually a technique, called **Paddling Against the Arc**. Undoubtedly, you've experienced that aggravating phenomenon of a canoe that starts to turn to your offside (away from your paddling side), builds up more and more turning momentum and finally skids around to a stop. If you counteract the turning momentum with strong corrective strokes, it just kills the forward momentum. This responsive turning ability of the short, rockered playboat makes the canoe feel alive–or possessed, depending on your frame of mind. You can use turning momentum toward your onside to replace the need for corrective strokes; this will allow you to do consecutive powerful forward strokes.

Initiate some turning momentum toward your onside. You can do this from a moving or stationary position. Many combinations work, but perhaps the quickest way is to start with an offside forward

stroke (photo 257, figure 1), followed by a C-stroke (a J-stroke with a draw added to the beginning of the stroke) on your onside (figure 2). These strokes also work if you are already moving. The offside forward, the onside draw or the C-stroke are preferred, since they actually initiate the turning momentum in the bow, whereas the J-stroke initiates the turn in the stern and if you don't have sufficient speed or the pry of the J is overdone, you develop a skid, which slows you down rather than creating an arcing path toward your onside. You may need to emphasize the draw until you've developed some forward momentum.

If you've started enough of a turn, a full forward stroke without correction will almost straighten the boat and move it aggressively forward (figure 3). During the recovery you should notice the turning momentum. If you stopped paddling, the canoe would arc toward your onside. The turning momentum is greater the faster your boat is traveling, so go light on your first few forward strokes until you're up to speed. The key is to have enough of an arc or turning momentum that your strongest forward stroke will achieve an equilibrium between the canoe wanting to arc and your paddling against the arc (figure 4). The path of the canoe will be almost straight, with a slight arc toward the onside. To stop the onside arc, overpower the turning momentum with a sweep and turn the boat to the offside.

When you have the feel of this technique, try experimenting with tilt. The boat turns more when tilted, so if you want to increase the turning

momentum, increase the tilt either to your onside or offside. On hard-chined boats, the offside tilt is more effective since you're presenting a more vertical edge in harder, undisturbed water, but the onside tilt is an easier reach for a good vertical forward stroke or C-stroke. If your forward stroke overpowers the onside turning momentum and you start to turn to your offside, regain the onside turning momentum with an offside stroke or a C-stroke. If you're still overpowering the arc, make sure that you're not sweeping and that your forward stroke is vertical and parallel to the boat; ease up on the forward stroke until you've accelerated fully; tilt to increase the onside turning momentum or add a slight draw at the beginning of the forward stroke.

This technique is indispensable in a variety of situations, such as dropping onto a surfing wave, gaining momentum to cross an eddy line, paddling in shallow water where it is difficult to use a corrective stroke, punching holes and gaining speed to boof. Practice on flatwater so that distractions such as an approaching falls with lots of mist won't leave you floundering at the lip.

You can also use this technique on the offside. An onside forward stroke sets up the offside arc. Use the offside forward stroke and a vertical cross-draw at the beginning for minor corrections. You would use offside forward strokes with an offside arc if you're approaching an offside turn. By having that turning momentum already, you maintain more forward momentum through the turn and your paddle is already in position for a cross-draw.

257 Paddling against the arc.

121

Forward Strokes

An efficient forward stroke is important regardless of whether you're paddling solo or tandem. I haven't harped on this point until now because in the bigger canoes you can manage to get by with poor forward stroke technique. With the more responsive playboats, however, bad habits are exaggerated.

In the video *Take the Wild Ride,* Scott Shipley (1995 World Cup champion) explains, "Rodeo moves are easy–they just take practice. It's the forward stroke that's hard." This struck me as a very astute comment. Almost every time I see someone having trouble with a maneuver in a solo playboat, I can trace it to a poor forward stroke. An inefficient forward stroke won't move the boat forward terribly fast, but that isn't the real problem. A poor forward stroke requires lots of correction strokes to keep the canoe straight. This is what causes you to miss maneuvers such as front surfing, which requires forward speed.

Even when I'm boating regularly, I still like to get out on a lake or use those flatwater stretches to practice my forward stroke. The first step is to learn what the stroke looks and feels like. Examine the sequence of photos on this and the next page.

Some people have a paddling style that makes a lasting impression. I vividly recall two. One was a newcomer who was taking a first lesson. He would have made a paddlewheel steamer proud as his paddle scribed a perfect circle beside the canoe, touching the water briefly at the bottom of the arc. Then there was Dale Johnson. Dale's strokes, particularly his forward stroke, were a lesson in concentration. He paddled extremely focused, with his chin locked on his chest and his eyes glued on his next objective. He rotated his whole torso to bring the bigger muscles of his back into play. I've been using his forward stroke as a model of good form and concentration ever since.

Power forward stroke with correction

The power forward stroke with correction is the best choice for gaining speed over a short distance. This would be important leaving an eddy, punching a hole or approaching a boof. Not that you shouldn't ever use the J-stroke again, but in a solo boat use it only for minor corrections. The pry is better for major corrections, or if you're on the upstream side.

The key to the power forward stroke with correction is rotating your onside shoulder forward. Do this by twisting at the waist. Avoid leaning forward

258 Forward stroke with correction.

259

260

261 Forward stroke with correction.

262

263

as if you were hinged at the hips. Your lower back should rotate, but stay upright to keep balanced over your knees to prevent the boat from bobbing. Reach forward with your upper back and shoulders so your back is arched forward to extend your reach and take advantage of the power in your back. Your top arm should be straight to extend the reach and so the paddle shaft is close to vertical. If your paddle length is correct, your head will tuck below your top arm.

The strongest part of this stroke is the beginning, so every little extra bit of reach helps. For the catch phase, plant your paddle firmly in the water before starting to pull on it. If you hear a *kerplunk* and see a splash, you're pulling too soon, which will cause your paddle to cavitate. This sounds bad and it is—your paddle won't have a hunk of water to pull on. With your paddle planted, pull yourself forward by using the large muscles of your upper back and unwinding your torso. As the paddle nears your knee, your lower elbow will bend, signaling that it's time to start the correction phase of the stroke. When the paddle passes your body, flip the paddle over so that it's in position to do a pry, power face against the boat. The thumb on your grip hand will point up. Pause for a second to let the disturbed water pass. The paddle shaft should be vertical and resting on the gunwale right in front of your

hip. Pull your top hand in quickly to accomplish the pry. To recover, lift the paddle up and out of the water with both your elbow and your top hand. Whip the paddle forward for the next stroke as quickly as possible. This move differs from the relaxed cruising stroke, where you drop your top hand and lift the blade to the side.

When practicing this stroke, I use a trick to remind me to rotate my torso. I tuck my chin into my chest so that I've locked my head into my torso rotation. This causes me to look to my offside at the catch phase and my onside for the recovery. It feels (and appears) slightly robotic, but it provides you with a reference point to check torso rotation. Try to get a rhythm going.

This stroke is worth practicing often to refine your technique. If your lower side torso muscles get sore, then you're on the right track. I didn't even know I had muscles in that area, let alone what they were for, until I started to concentrate on this stroke. There may be other as-yet-undiscovered parts of the body we can use to improve our paddling power. Hey, maybe our appendix has something to do with paddling.

Power forward stroke without correction
The power forward stroke without correction uses the lower arm as well as torso rotation to provide a very fast, short, intense stroke. It is an ideal stroke to use

with the paddling against the arc technique. Because your arm muscles will tire quickly, its use is limited to situations that require bursts of power, such as catching a wave for a front-surf in fast current.

The positioning of your body for this stroke is the same as for the power stroke with correction: onside shoulder rotated forward; lower arm straight and reaching forward; upper grip arm also extended, so that the paddle is vertical in the water. The stroke consists of pulling back the paddle fast with your torso and onside shoulder, 12 to 18 inches only! If you're traveling against the current, as when attaining or catching a surf, you'll need to pull back the paddle that much faster; so speed up the "catch" phase as if you were slapping the water. A lightweight stiff paddle really shines here. The moment you start to pull on your paddle is when you generate the most power, and it is lost if the paddle flexes. When the power forward without correction is performed well, the canoe won't stall between strokes, as it would with the slower correction stroke.

This stroke has no steering component other than perhaps a very slight diagonal draw. The lack of corrective steering in the stroke means that you must set your canoe at an angle you can paddle against, so that the canoe ends up pointing in the correct direction right at the crux of the move.

264 Forward stroke without correction.

265

266

Backpaddling

Having good backpaddling strokes is the foundation for back-ferrying and back-surfing. It will pay benefits when you're spinning or doing any moves initiated at the stern. Backpaddling is a little more difficult than paddling forward because you can't see where you're going. In most back strokes, you don't have the mechanical leverage that you do in forward strokes, plus you tend to practice back strokes rarely. Once you've mastered backpaddling strokes, try them in whitewater. If a front surf is too easy, try a back-surf. It's even fun to try backpaddling down a rapid, including doing backward eddy turns. More than once I've ended up going down a rapid backward and used a backward eddy turn to get out of the current or at least turn around and look cool doing it. If you're trying to figure out a move backward, think about how you would do it forward, then visualize the paddle doing the same thing with your body position reversed.

Back stroke

For backward propulsion, let's begin with a simple back stroke. The paddle should start close to the gunwale, the shaft should be vertical throughout the stroke and the paddle should travel in a line parallel to the keel of the boat. The stroke uses the back face of the blade and it should start between the hip and knee and finish with the body reaching forward, the way it would for the catch of the forward stroke. As your arms straighten to reach to this position, rotate your torso and push your bottom shoulder forward. In terms of power and mechanical advantage, the beginning of the stroke is less effective than the end. At the end of the stroke weight is shifted to the bow. When applied in whitewater, this may be an advantage if you don't want the leading end of the boat to pearl, or it may be a disadvantage if you are trying to catch a wave. This stroke turns the boat toward the offside.

Compound back stroke

The compound back stroke is a little more awkward and slower, but the catch is more powerful and you can shift your weight to the stern or leading end of the boat. You use both the power face and the back face of the blade for this stroke. Rotate your body and reach to the stern of the boat. The paddle should be vertical and both of your arms should be fairly straight. You can angle the blade or path of the paddle to add a stern draw effect, which will start the boat turning to your stern onside. Using the power face of the blade, pull toward your hip. When the paddle gets to your hip, quickly twist the paddle 180 degrees so the back face of the blade is now propelling the boat backward.

Photos 267 and 268 show this stroke just before and just after the blade-face transition. Complete the stroke with the basic back stroke, or the back J-stroke for a turning effect to the onside. With a stern draw at the beginning of the stroke, you will turn toward your onside. The stroke is a good one to use to start backward motion or backward onside turning motion.

Major corrections

Turning towards the offside–back draw The back draw has a very strong turning effect and adds some backward propulsion. Reach forward and start the draw level with your knees and instead of pulling straight to the boat, open the blade face and pull toward the bow. You should be pulling your shaft hand and opposite knee together. The paddle takes the same path as the end of the back sweep, but the shaft is more vertical and the stroke is very effective right up to the boat (photo 269). Your upper arm will be nearly straight and will push across your body. Your arm does not have a lot of strength in that direction, but since you're applying the force away from the pivot point, you don't need much strength to make this a very powerful stroke. Because you are leaning forward slightly at the end of the stroke, the leading end of the boat is unweighted, making the turning effect even greater.

267 Compound back stroke.

268

269 Back draw.

Turning toward the onside–cross-draw/back cross-draw

Turning toward the onside–cross-draw/ back cross-draw The cross-draw has a very strong turning effect, with some backward propulsion included. Keep your arms almost straight and rotate your torso until the blade is on your offside. With your grip hand low and the blade forward, use the power face to scoop water toward the bow until the blade reaches the boat. Keep your arms fairly straight through the stroke and use the rotating torso to provide power. Pull your shaft hand toward the knee on the onside. Lift the blade out of the water for the recovery. The last foot or two has a very strong turning effect. For more backward propulsion, keep your grip hand higher, rotate the blade open so that the power face of the blade is facing forward toward the bow. Shovel the water forward to provide back propulsion, then drop your top hand and

270 Leaving the eddy.

pull the water toward the bow (photo 270). This is called the back cross-draw to differentiate it from the cross-draw. The paddle moves through the same position as the back draw, but your arms have better leverage to pull on it. Quite often just one cross-draw will be all the correction you need. If you're back-ferrying, you might find yourself alternating between the back stroke and cross-draw. That is a perfectly reasonable approach, but you could also try either to open the angle slightly, with a back cross-draw, or close the angle and stick with the back J stroke. Between the back J stroke and the cross-draw or back cross-draw, you should favor the one that puts you on the downstream side.

Minor corrections

Toward the offside–back-sweep A back stroke will turn the boat to your offside just as a forward stroke will. For a little more offside turning effect, use the back-sweep. Drop your top hand and reach out as wide as necessary with your blade. The wider the stroke, the greater turning effect it will have. Rotate your torso through the stroke, tilt the boat for a greater turning effect and keep the blade vertical in the water. Since you're sitting on the pivot point of the boat, any part of a wide arcing stroke will turn the boat, but if you reach towards the stern to start the

blade close to the hull, the shifting of your body weight pushes the stern down, creating more resistance to turning. Start the stroke at four o'clock–or eight o'clock (photo 271)–and continue until the paddle is at 1–or 11 o'clock when the gunwale gets in the way of the stroke (photo 272). The back-sweep stroke combines turning effect to the offside with propulsion, just as the front sweep does for forward paddling.

Towards the onside–reverse J-stroke The reverse J-stroke will turn the boat toward your onside and is used to keep the boat going straight or to turn toward the onside. The J or pry is added to the end of a back stroke or compound back stroke (photo 274). When the paddle shaft gets past your knee, quickly rotate the paddle so that the back of the blade is facing out and the shaft is vertical and touching the hull or gunwale. As with the forward J-stroke, hesitate a second until the disturbed water has passed, then apply as much pressure as you need either to counteract the turning effect of the back stroke and keep the boat going straight or to make the boat turn toward your onside. Not prying outward but, rather, applying pressure and letting the passing water do the work is more streamlined and efficient. The reverse J is quick to put in if you need to make subtle adjustments during a back stroke.

271 Back sweep.

272

273 Reverse-J.

274

Bracing Strokes

As paddling technique has evolved, it has shifted away from using a brace as a "ready" position. Now the brace is more often used as a response to an abrupt motion of the canoe. But before you float off down the rapids with your paddle held high in the air, read on to find out what has replaced the old ready-for-action brace.

The emphasis should really be on doing something proactive with your paddle. This usually means a forward stroke–the pressure on your blade as you pull on the paddle offers a very firm anchor to stabilize the boat. Save your actual brace for recovering from impact with a wave, current or rock.

As you scan photos 277 and 278, you're likely muttering, "There's no way he didn't flip right after that picture." I can truthfully say I didn't. However, I do admit that it took a couple of attempts to catch the shot of the righting pry (photo 276), and I did get a dunking then.

Righting pry For those of us with a wilderness-canoe-tripping background, the righting pry is not a natural reaction to tipping to your offside. Come to think of it, I'm not sure what background would make this weird brace seem natural. But, natural or not, this brace does work.

Think back to when you were learning to do an efficient flatwater pry. The emphasis was on the beginning of the stroke because when you pried the paddle off the gunwale, it began to lift water as it neared the end of the stroke. This in turn pushed the gunwale down. Got the picture? This lifting action is the force we are bringing into play to save our hides.

As the boat tips toward your offside, aggressively slice your paddle into the water and pry off the chine of the hull (see photo 276). It may take more than one stroke to level the boat. The effectiveness of this brace is increased if current is going by the boat (see photo 275). Angling the leading edge of the blade down will provide some serious leverage to right the boat. Doing a righting pry successfully is sort of like cheating reality, and it's legal!

275 *Righting pry in action. Wa-ki-ki, Ottawa River, Ontario.*

276 *Righting pry.*

High brace   This is one of two alternatives to the righting pry. It saves you, hopefully, from tipping to your offside. Keep the paddle vertical so it catches the water, enabling you to pull your boat to an upright position. I say "boat," because your body should still be centered over the balance point of the canoe (photo 277). The key is to flick your boat back underneath you with your lower torso. Outfitting that lets you slop around in the boat just won't cut it here, folks.

An effective brace not covered here is the offside high brace. The reason is, it is usually used during an offside surf. (See text on page 133.)

Weight shift   The action in photo 278 looks like an air brace, but it's not, really. Counteract the lurch of the canoe by throwing your weight out the other side.

This isn't as effective as a high brace or righting pry. Consider it a last-ditch effort to stay upright when you're caught off-guard. It has worked for me.

Low brace   This is the workhorse of the braces. Most paddlers will favor a tilt to their onside because they know they can salvage almost any tipping motion to their onside with a low brace. When strong river currents are involved, the force you exert on your paddle can be tremendous. The possibility of injury is very real, so eliminate your bad form right here and now.

The boat tips to your onside, and you react by transferring your weight to the paddle (photo 279). Some key points to check are your shaft arm, which must be bent and over the top of the paddle. This will

happen only if you keep your grip hand in close to your belly-button. Your grip hand must be palm-up. With your weight placed momentarily on your paddle, you can then right the canoe with a hip flick just as you do during an open canoe roll. The next job is to get yourself back in the boat. Drop your head as low as you can and then swing it in over the gunwale and across the airbags (photo 280). Slide your paddle into the canoe as your upper torso slides across to the other side of the boat (photo 281). Bringing your paddle into the boat keeps your lower arm bent, thus protecting it from all kinds of bad stuff. Notice that you should swing your head all the way to the far gunwale before lifting it. This will be one fluid motion that saves the day and keeps you from a dunking.

One other low brace, which is rarely used, is the offside low brace. Best spend your time elsewhere.

277 High brace.

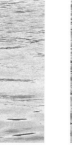

279 Low brace.

280

281

282

Self-Rescue

The very first move to try after you acquire your new boat is a wet exit. With someone spotting for you, tip over and swim out of your boat. Escaping is easier if you slip your feet off the foot pegs first. Don't worry about practicing the wet exit too much—you'll have lots of chances when working on your roll! Until you learn how to roll your boat, you'll spend much time trying to clamber back in, so here are a few hints to make a deep-water re-entry easier.

Buy a really big, wide boat! Just kidding. But it *is* much harder to climb into a short, narrow boat—once you're sprawled on top, the boat is so top-heavy you end up somersaulting right back into the water. Check that all the paraphernalia attached to your PFD won't catch on the gunwale at a critical moment. I've often had this happen and vow to adjust the junk on my PFD accordingly, soon.

Re-entry

Set up by kicking your feet to bring your lower body up to the surface perpendicular to the boat. Note which end is the bow. Don't laugh—I've ended up in the boat backward. Not a big deal in a classic canoe with seats, but a total drag in a solo playboat with a saddle. Now vigorously kick to propel yourself up onto the boat (photo 284). Maintain a low center of gravity by keeping your head down. Swing your knees in board and slide them into your straps. (This should be easy, since you're using a system that keeps your straps in place even when you're not in the boat, right?) Once you're back in the boat, you'll remember your paddle and start looking around for it. Avoid this problem by holding it in the hand that reaches across the boat when you're preparing to climb in.

Re-entering an upside-down boat

Providing you have a reliable roll and outfitting that is easy to get into, this is a handy trick. Try it only if you find yourself in a lake after a rapid with no one nearby to help you back into your boat. You're probably wondering what the heck you'd be doing out of your boat if you have a reliable roll. Well, sometimes after being worked in a hole, bailing out is an attractive option.

283 Deep water re-entry.

284

285

Emptying Your Canoe

Bailer versus no bailer

When I started playboating in 1988, my boat was 14 feet long and had a huge space in front of the saddle for bailing or splashing water out with a paddle. My next boat was 12 feet long, with barely enough room for a bailer. The boat shrank again—11 feet, then down to 10 feet, at which point trying to bail in such a tiny space just didn't make sense. It was far faster to simply hop out onshore and empty the boat. Consequently, I became convinced that leaving space for bailing had absolutely no merit. After all, no bailing space meant less room for water, and therefore a more maneuverable boat even when full. After several years of harassing all my paddling friends to fill their boats with flotation, I'm afraid I must qualify my point of view.

The Whitewater Rodeo circuit has exposed me to paddlers from all over the world, all of whom have adapted their outfitting to suit their home turf. Some boat on primarily pool-drop rivers, while others have continuous rivers in their backyards. Boaters who spend time on rivers with continuous rapids offering few eddies where they can get out to empty have a bailing space in their boat. The bottom line is, it's a regional thing. One other factor to consider is whether you prefer playing or river running. With the latter, you generally stay drier and need to bail occasionally. If your goal is to get vertical on every wave or hole you

can find, your boat will be full of water on every run, making bailing a very slow and tiring alternative.

For a dryer ride, take standing waves at a slight angle and tilt slightly upstream at the peaks of breaking waves, or dive into eddies to avoid the waves altogether. Plan your line to include emptying spots. When you finish a rapid, empty quickly and then relax. You'll be ready if you have to do a rescue.

Flip it

The best place to empty your boat is in 6 to 18 inches of water over a smooth bottom. If the bottom isn't rocky, you can safely leap from your boat and land on both feet. If you have a hard-chined boat, flip the boat right over, as shown in photo 286. Rest the gunwales on your thigh, then lift the other side by the chine and flip the boat upright by pulling up on the chine (photo 287). Jump in and you're ready to go in less than 15 seconds. If you choose a shallower spot, you have to reach down farther to pick up your boat. If the water is deeper, it will be harder to get back in the boat. If you have a soft-chined boat and can't grab the hull, keep the boat upright and lift the far gunwale. Push the lower gunwale out with your knee.

Tipping onshore

Another quick method for emptying your boat uses a

shallow rock. You need a sloping rock that is above the surface of the water and tapers into the water. Paddle up onto the rock and tilt over onto the dry part of the rock. You may need to really throw your weight, but with this method you don't even have to get out of the boat. Although this may not seem like an important creek-boating skill, if you spend a lot of time emptying your boat, you might not see the kayaker demonstrating that intricate line on the next rapid.

Paddling with water in your boat

So you've tried to stay dry but you were forced through a hole at the top of a long rapid. No worries. Just change your strategy and hope your airbags are well filled. When paddling with a boat full of water, maintain your forward momentum. If you're just floating at the same speed as the current, you may get pushed into rocks and you won't be able to get out of the current into an eddy. If no accessible eddies are nearby, stay parallel to the current so that you won't hit any rocks sideways. Once you've picked an eddy and got your boat moving toward it, you can make surprising speed crossing the grain of the current. Start your turns earlier and choose a route with a little more space than usual. Only experience will teach you the limitations of paddling with your boat full of water, so in safe spots filling up your boat and seeing what moves you can make won't hurt.

286 Flipping the boat.

287

288 Tipping on shore.

Rolling

289 Motivation.

Motivation

An incentive such as the less-than-balmy weather and, no doubt, water temperature in photo 289 certainly motivated me enough to make a roll successful. The amount of motivation each of us requires to roll up will vary. You can't always expect to have the great paddling conditions pictured. The mantra I use is "If you bail out, it only gets worse." Whenever I swim, Mark helpfully rubs in that saying.

I can still recall the exact time that my roll moved from a party trick to a useful tool. On that occasion I didn't even flip. Years ago, in my first playboat, I was scouting a boily, turbulent rapid on the Ottawa that precedes an even bigger rapid that I definitely didn't want to swim. "Angle right, punch the hole and if I flip, roll and paddle down the right side," I told myself. I laughed out loud as I realized that for the first time,

flipping wouldn't mean the end of the run. With newfound confidence, I focused on the rapid and ran it without flipping.

In rodeo or freestyle moves you'll be spending a lot of time upside down, so a quick, instinctive roll is necessary and even part of many linked rodeo moves.

The open-canoe roll is not a muscle move, but it does require proper technique. Good form alleviates strain on all kinds of muscles you didn't know you had until after a pool session.

Onside roll

For the onside roll, you will be coming up on your onside; that is, the side you do a forward stroke on, regardless of the side you flip to or the side you normally paddle on. A good exercise when you're learning to roll is to have a friend stand in the water and hold your hands. Put your head and upper body in the water. Twist and bend at the torso and arch your back so your upper body is at the surface of the water and your shoulders squarely face the bottom of the pool or lake. Using your hips and knees and lower back, drive the boat as far upright as possible, while keeping your upper body in the water in the same position. You end up with your hips and torso bent the other way and your lower back hunched, while your shoulders remain square to the bottom of the lake. This is the all-

important hip snap—the first phase of the roll. Right the boat by bending at the torso and lower back, rather than pushing down with your arms and upper body. You can even try this using a PFD. If you push too hard with your arms, you'll simply sink the PFD. In photos 301 to 304, Andrew Westwood demonstrates excellent hip-snap technique as he does a hand roll in flatwater.

Now try the same movement holding on to the paddle. Fall to your onside, with your paddle in a low-brace position. Your forehead should rest on the shaft of the paddle, your grip hand around your belly button; your torso is bent and your back arched so your upper body is at the surface of the water and your torso twisted so your shoulders are squarely facing the bottom of the pool or lake, as shown in the underwater photo 293. You can have a partner support your paddle at the surface for the first few tries while you get oriented. This photo clearly illustrates that the paddle blade is at the surface of the water—and that I need a new watch strap. Do the hip snap with your knees, torso and lower back while putting as little pressure on the paddle as possible. During practice, keep your head tucked onto the paddle shaft and look toward your stomach. When you can see the side of the hull and can tell what color the canoe is (photo 294), you can finish the roll with the second phase, which involves getting your upper

290 Onside roll.

291

292

body out of the water. You need to delay the second phase, as late as possible without interrupting the momentum of the hip snap. Once you start the second phase, you should continue pushing with your knees, hips and back until the boat is upright and flat. As mentioned previously, your head weighs about the same as a watermelon. From the position shown in photo 294, if you lift the watermelon straight up out of the water, its weight will flip the canoe over again. You'll just have enough time to get a breath before flopping back down to where you started. So instead of lifting your head, as the boat becomes as upright as possible, untwist your torso and bring your head around to the boat. When it reaches the boat, lift your head just out of the water (photo 295) and sweep your nose across the float bag until you are past the center line and the boat is upright (photo 296). As you're sweeping your head around, you can be pushing the paddle downward and inward so your grip hand ends up near the offside gunwale.

Tipping to your offside

If you flip to your offside, you need to go all the way under the boat. Then start with the high-brace setup. As you are falling over, rotate your torso and extend the paddle blade forward, along the side of the boat. Go with the momentum by pushing your head

forward and downward. Think of reaching for the surface on the other side of the boat with your head and hands. The forward lean will reduce your resistance and minimize exposure of your head to the riverbed. Some hard-chined or high-ended boats will resist turning all the way upside down. Going with the momentum will help, but you may have to use an underwater scoop stroke to pull the boat over and your body around to the setup position shown in photo 293. Your torso is bent and your hands and upper body are as close to the surface as possible; the paddle is parallel to the boat. With the outside edge of the blade raised, sweep the paddle on the surface until it is perpendicular to the boat. Now twist your torso so your shoulders face the bottom of the lake, and flip the paddle blade over into a low brace. You are now in the low-brace setup already described. When you learn this setup, it helps to have someone in the water holding and guiding the paddle to the proper position. Visualizing the position is hard because you need to think three-dimensionally, and the horizon changes in relation to the boat's position. Occasionally, you may need to use this setup if you get flipped to your onside while doing an offside stroke.

Now that you've got a reliable roll in flatwater, try it in whitewater. It takes a bit of time to get over the

293 Setting up.

distractions of noisy rapids. Where a rapid flows into a deep pool, practice flipping to your onside, then offside. Should you roll up on the upstream or downstream side? *It doesn't matter.* Roll up on your onside; after you've flipped you'll instantly be going the same speed as the current, so it will be just as easy on either side. The only exception to this is rolling while you're still in the hole, which we'll discuss in the offside roll.

The best roll is a quick roll. Once you've mastered the basics, try to speed things up. The less time you spend underwater, the less you're exposed to the possibility of bad things happening. When your hip snap is very strong, you can cut the last part of the roll short. Continue driving the boat upright once you start the brace phase, but you can stop bracing and start paddling again as soon as the boat is flat.

294 Back deck roll.

295

296

Back deck roll

The back deck roll is often used when you're facing upstream. This occurs while you're front-surfing or if your bow is engaged before, during or after a vertical move. Instead of leaning forward with the blade at the bow, when you know you're going to flip, throw your upper body back and under the stern of the boat (see photo 297). With your back against the float bag (see photo 298), reach under the boat to the surface at the stern of your onside. Sweep the high brace around to 90 degrees and flip the blade over to the low-brace setup or if you are in a hole roll up on the high brace. Even though you stay close to the back deck when you're underwater, your face may be exposed to the riverbed. While side-surfing, you can do this roll as long as you have ample water depth. Flip to the

upstream, stern side, and catch the green water with your blade. You'll go around really fast and roll up on the high brace. You can also use this roll if you want to get up higher on the foam pile to set up for a bow move. If you do the roll when your bow is underwater during an ender, the stern will be out of the water (see photo 300). Flip over, throw your upper body under the stern and keep your head dry. Lift the leading edge of the blade and skim it along the surface to help support your upper body. (This move is also called a bow screw-up.)

Offside roll in a hole

The two situations in which you'll need to roll up to your offside are paddling tandem with someone who insists on rolling up on his or her side, or rolling in a hole. In a hole you can roll up only on the downstream side, which might sometimes be to your offside. In tandem you can rely on your partner, who is rolling onside, to do most of the work. In a hole the current will do most of the work. You have three viable choices for rolling up on your offside: you can switch hands and use an onside roll; you can use an offside high brace; or you can do a one-hand roll.

Switching hands You can switch the paddle to the other side and use the normal onside roll. The advantage? It is a strong, dependable roll even if the current

297 Back deck roll.   ***298***   ***299***   ***300***

301 Hand roll.   ***302***   ***303***   ***304***

doesn't help you up. The disadvantage? It leaves you unstable and vulnerable once you are upright while you switch back.

Offside high brace   A lot of flexibility helps for this roll. As you fall over to your offside, reach out and forward in an offside brace. Arch your back to keep the blade near the surface of the water and do a strong hip snap. The awkward part of this roll is trying to get your head low and across the boat. As you can see from photo 305, the lower arm is in the way. In a hole, the current holds the blade at the surface and makes this move a lot easier. The advantages? It's quick, you're ready for a stroke as soon as you come up and it develops a good offside brace. The disadvantages? It requires awkward twisting and leverage is poor if your paddle doesn't get help from the current.

One-hand roll   The roll that I prefer—at least for holes—is to hold the paddle out of the water with your shaft hand while you do a one-hand roll with your other hand (photo 306). The roll is identical to the regular roll. You need a strong hip snap to minimize the upper-body lifting required in the second phase of the roll.

Window-shading and rolling in the hole

If you have window-shaded and the hole is big enough, it may hold the buoyant boat in the hole even with you upside down and the boat full of water. If this happens, your body will be pushed to the downstream side in an easy position to roll. As long as you're paddling on the downstream side, just do a low brace. The moving water will hold your paddle near the surface and even the sloppiest roll technique should bring you to the surface. Window-shading still has its use in a rodeo context. Throwing your paddle and upper body to the

upstream stern quarter of the boat will initiate a window-shade. As the boat flips, keep the power face of your paddle facing the green water; this will even speed up the window-shade. When the boat has gone all the way over, you'll be in a position to do a high brace to roll the boat (photo 307) or you can turn the paddle over to the conventional low-brace roll position. Essentially, this is a back-deck roll, with the hole helping to roll the boat. It will often start to flush you out of the hole or up higher on the foam pile, where you can spin more easily. If you let your body drag a little and try to catch a bit of water with your paddle, you may have turned enough when you come up to initiate your bow in an ender. The move is fast and smooth, and you can use it to impress people who don't realize how easy it is. On the other hand, some people will think you just got hammered and were lucky to roll up.

Offside window-shade and roll

If your offside is downstream, use your shaft hand to hold your paddle out of the water (upstream hand), then do a one-hand roll with the other hand. Remember to give a good hip flick and keep your head in the water until the boat is upright. You can also roll up on an offside cross-brace. You'll end up on a high brace on your offside. The offside roll is harder for most people, since it is a big stretch for the torso and offside shoulder and you have poor leverage at the beginning of the roll. The hand roll has a less awkward position and starting the tilt and controlling it are easier given the solid current under the hole, from which you can push off. After you regain the paddle, go to an upstream low brace or cross-brace.

305 Offside high brace roll.

306 One-hand roll.

307 High brace roll.

308

Maneuvers—Eddy Turns

When you first learned to do eddy turns, you probably didn't care where you crossed the eddyline or where in the eddy you would end up as long as you got there. Angle, motion and tilt were enough to think about at one time. Now you're ready to move on and desimplify this basic maneuver.

Eddy turns to exit the current (eddy out) use the same mechanics as eddy turns into the current (eddy in), so the discussion here refers to both unless stated otherwise. Incidently, we've avoided using the terms eddy out and eddy in as much as possible for the reasons stated in the terminology section that follows.

Visualize a line

You may have been told to always hit the eddies high (so that if you missed your planned route by five or six feet you'd still make the eddy). Now you should have a more precise plan as you approach the eddy. Visualize a line that includes the approach and the exact spot where you'll cross the eddyline. Include in your plan the line you'll take once you're in the eddy, whether you're heading to shore to get out on a particular rock or you're exiting the eddy downstream without losing your forward momentum.

Sweet spot

Identify the sweet spot of the eddyline, which is the zone with the strongest current differential. At this point the eddyline will be the narrowest and you'll get the most help from the river to turn the boat. In most cases this is the best zone to enter the eddy. Downriver of this zone, the eddyline is wider and the eddy is weaker. If you enter the eddy too high, you may not have enough room to turn your boat. Also, the water slows as it approaches the obstruction and the current differential is less. It will be harder to get an angle and forward motion if you're continuing back out of the eddy. If you're stopping to

rest or look, you'll have to back up to reach shore or to set your angle when you eventually leave the eddy. If you're entering and exiting the eddy without stopping, enter the eddy at the downstream end of the sweet-spot zone, and exit the eddy at the top end of that zone. The point where you leave the eddy will also be determined by what the main current is doing along the eddyline. There are great eddylines in which you can make sharp, distinctive eddy turns. If there is a lot of gradient at the point of the eddy, most of the water will keep going past the eddy and the surface of the eddy may be below the surface of the main current. Turns into these eddies are fast and fun, and sometimes a boof is in order. When you leave the eddy you will be faced with a fence, or raised wall of water. You will need to leave very aggressively to counteract gravity and make your boat climb the eddy fence to get up to the main current. It may help to leave from as low in the eddy as practical where the current differential, or at least the height differential, is not as great. If you have any choice, it's best to cross the eddyline hitting the main current at the trough of a wave, where the main current is level with or below the level of the eddy, in order to maintain forward momentum. If you hit the main current at the peak of a wave, your boat will be going up, against gravity, which reduces your momentum.

Angle

If your angle as you cross an eddyline is too small (parallel to the eddyline), you won't get turned; if the angle is too big (perpendicular to the eddyline), you'll turn too quickly, lose your forward momentum and end up on the eddyline. The default setting for an eddy-turn is 45 degrees. There isn't anything particularly magical about 45 degrees—you won't notice any difference between a 44- and a 46-degree angle—although a five-degree change in angle will make a noticeable difference.

309 Angle of your chine to the eddyline.

There are times when you should adjust this angle slightly. In general, you can use less angle when the current is stronger and more angle when the current is weaker. Although we generally visualize the angle in terms of the keel line, it is really the angle between the eddyline and the chine of the boat (which follows the gunwale line pretty closely) that is relevant. If the boat's position is the same, an outside tilt (using the outside chine) will provide, in effect, a wider angle than an inside tilt (using the inside chine) (diagram 309). So, you can use a smaller angle if you're using an outside tilt. Increasing the angle will help you get turned when you are entering a narrow eddy. If you do this, you'll need to put on the forward motion as soon as the turn has initiated so that you stay in the eddy. Closing the angle a bit will get you deeper into the eddy or farther into the main current, but it is usually preferable to do that by changing the strokes you use rather than the angle, because you'll have more subtle control as the maneuver progresses. If you close the angle up dramatically, you may end up in the eddy, facing downstream still with some forward downstream momentum. This maneuver is called a dive and is quite useful for racing.

Motion

You need forward motion to reach the eddyline. This may seem too obvious to mention when you're sitting in an

eddy, 10 feet from the eddyline, but a lack of forward motion is the downfall of a surprising number of missed eddy turns. As you're floating down the river and the eddy is getting closer, it's easy to assume that you have enough forward motion. As much forward motion as you can muster will help prevent you from turning too quickly on the eddyline if there is a strong current differential or if you've used a large angle. Eddylines are the least stable place to be on the river. Crossing them aggressively will give you stable, predictable and crisp turns. I don't mean to get you pumped up to rip and conquer every eddyline you encounter, however. By charging overzealously at a narrow or weak eddy, you may crash all the way into the eddy before the delicate opposing currents can turn your boat. If the eddy is narrow and weak and behind a rock with current on either side, you need to control your speed and aggressively turn the boat with your strokes.

Turning in an eddy

Do you ever end up facing the wrong way in a small eddy? Stick an end of the boat in the current without any forward motion and you'll spin on the eddyline. If you find yourself going down the river backward, stick your stern in an eddy as if you were doing a backward eddy turn and paddle forward off the eddyline after you are turned downstream by the eddy.

Strokes

Strokes help the opposing currents turn the boat and give you stability. You can also use them to control forward momentum and the pivoting speed.

Onside turns   For an onside eddy turn, you can reach ahead of the pivot point of the canoe as you cross the eddy line and plant a static bow draw in the current that you're entering. The opposing current will work on your boat and paddle to turn the boat, so

plant the paddle perpendicular to the current you are entering. The opposing current will also keep pressure on the blade until the boat turns around your paddle. As the boat turns, adjust the angle so the blade remains perpendicular to the current. This should leave your paddle in position to do a forward stroke at the end of the turn. This draw is a static stroke. The duffek turn is similar but more aggressive; you rotate your torso a little more and plant the paddle more than 45 degrees from your bow, whereas in the static draw the angle is around 30 degrees. Again, keep the blade perpendicular in the water and pull your shaft hand to your offside knee (with your shoulder, torso, knee and foot). Novice paddlers are sometimes encouraged to plant the blade wider and closer to the surface in a high-brace position. This is less efficient because water is spilling off the bottom of the blade, but if you plant too early or hold the stroke too late the brace position will be more stable. In all three of these variations (high brace, static draw and duffek), you plant the paddle ahead of the pivot point of the boat. For an extremely stable onside turn, use a back-sweep low-brace combination. The back sweep is very effective at helping the boat turn, and the low brace on the surface of the water is even more stable than the high brace turn ahead of the pivot point. The disadvantage is that it slows the forward momentum.

Offside turns   Fish can't tell the difference between an onside turn and an offside turn since the boat and paddle positions are the same although your hands are reversed. Of course, on a turn to your offside, you won't be able to reach quite as far and you are in a slightly more awkward body position, so your tilts may be a bit more conservative, but your average trout isn't very discriminating. A static cross-draw should be around 30 degrees from the bow, and a dynamic cross-

draw duffek should be more than 45 degrees and pulling to the opposite knee. A cross-brace during this turn has the same effect as the high brace for the onside turn, but it requires torso flexibility and a commitment to the stroke that novices rarely have. There is no offside equivalent of the onside back-sweep, low-brace turn. The cross-stern-rudder, back-sweep-low-brace just doesn't make it as a viable stroke and the sweep on the onside behind the pivot point doesn't offer any stability.

Controlling forward momentum   The onside duffek and the cross-bow duffek add forward momentum. This is useful for slalom racing or if you need to develop speed for your next move (perhaps a boof or an attainment). But you may want to slow the forward momentum. To the offside, use a static cross-draw but open the blade face and rotate as much as possible. Add an outside tilt to speed up the turn and slow the momentum even more. To the onside, you can use the static-draw equivalent of this stroke but the back-sweep, low-brace turn is much easier and more effective at slowing momentum. Slowing the forward momentum is useful if you're leaving an eddy but want to stay on or close to the eddyline or if the eddy you're entering is narrow.

Controlling pivoting momentum   The onside duffek and the cross-bow duffek are the best strokes for speeding up an eddy turn when you're slalom racing, for example, or trying to get into a narrow eddy. You may want to slow the turning momentum when you're entering a strong eddy in order to get deep in the eddy. When your boat is full of water, you need to do this type of turn to prevent the boat from pivoting quickly and staying on the eddyline. To the onside, tilt inside and lean back to delay the front inside edge from catching the eddy current and do a stern sweep to counteract the turning effect of the opposing currents. To the offside, tilt inside, lean back and do a ruddering pry to counteract the turning effect. Another option to slow the offside turn is the cross-forward sweep. It provides more forward motion but is a little more awkward if you're uncomfortable on your offside. When you use these stroke combinations to leave the eddy, you'll essentially be front-ferrying across the eddyline and then pivoting in the main current.

Tilt

When you do an eddy turn, your center of mass wants to keep going in a straight line. The opposing current wants to take the bottom of your boat the other way and couldn't care less if it sent you catapulting to the next watershed. When you tilt to the inside of the turn, you're pushing the chine down and making the cross-section of the boat sit deeper in the water. This increases the resistance to the new current so you grip that water better; it also gives you something to push against so you can stay in the boat. As you cross the eddyline, your bow will carve or displace a path of water, while your stern is pushed the other way by the opposing current. On most boats, tilting also benefits the turn by lifting the bow and stern and reducing the resistance at the ends of the boat. Tilting to the inside is the most predictable and stable tilt. Your weight is centered on your inside knee, which is pushing against the bottom of the boat. The effect of the tilt will vary, depending on the shape of the boat. The chine of a flat-bottomed, hard-chined boat will sit deeper and will offer more resistance to the current than a shallow-arched, soft-chined boat. The opposing current is more likely to slip underneath a soft-chined boat. Flat-bottomed, hard-chined boats carve more

and skid less, making them generally more responsive and faster turning. The more you tilt a flat-bottomed boat, the more vertical the bottom that hits the current first becomes and the greater the resistance.

Outside-tilt turn

The outside-tilt turn is a faster, more abrupt, turn. When you tilt to the outside of an eddy turn, your weight shifts to your outside knee, which is pushing against the side of the boat. This turn offers more resistance to the new current because the side of the hull is more vertical, than is the bottom of the hull on an inside-tilt turn.

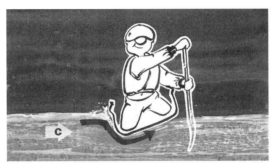

310 Outside tilt.

In diagram 310, the outside chine is on the upstream side of the boat in relation to the current

311 Inside tilt.

you're going into, and is engaging undisturbed solid water, so the effect of the opposing current is more immediate than with the inside tilt turn (diagram 311).

The outside tilt turn may feel a bit awkward at first since you are planting your paddle on the opposite side that you are tilting toward, particularly on a turn to your offside. The edge grabs more abruptly and carves more quickly, and you must be ready for the force that wants to throw you to the outside of the turn. The inside tilt is more forgiving, because if you lose your balance you'll fall on your upstream knee. If you underestimate the force in an outside tilt turn, you head into the drink.

Once you've fully crossed the eddyline and don't have the opposing currents turning your boat, the turning momentum will diminish. If you choose to do a fast dynamic turn and pull hard on the cross-bow or duffek, at some point the bow will be moving faster than the current (diagram 312). Reduce the outside tilt so you are reducing the resistance, but don't take it off completely. By keeping the leading inside edge slightly lifted, your bow will slide over the water (planing slightly) (diagram 313) rather than having to push and displace the water as with an inside tilt. As long as you have forward momentum, the stern edge will be carving while the bow is planing. You can

312 Bow moving faster but dragging, inside tilt.

313 *Bow moving faster than the current, outside tilt.*

use this technique even after initiating a turn with an inside tilt. Switch to the slight offside tilt after your initial contact with the new current.

The outside-tilt turn is very effective for turning quickly in narrow eddies and for catching eddies if you have a lot of speed. If you're forced to approach an eddy at a very small angle, you can still grab enough of the opposing current to turn with the outside tilt. Provided you have forward momentum, an outside-tilt turn works great for changing direction midstream (photo 319, figure 1). For slalom racing, it is a very fast turn. You should probably avoid this turn if you're going into a very strong current. In fact, this turn is rarely done to exit from an eddy. The inside tilt turn is preferred if you want a more gradual turn.

314 *Soft chine.*

Because a shallow-arched, soft-chined boat (diagram 314) doesn't offer as much resistance, the outside-tilt turn is more effective in a flat-bottomed, hard-chined boat. In fact, for a soft-chined boat (especially if it has a lot of flare), there is so little difference between the outside tilt and the inside tilt that it may not be worth giving up the greater stability of the inside-tilt turn for a slightly more abrupt turn.

Eddy turn on a hole

If you need to stop or get turned upstream to make a front ferry and there is no eddy nearby, you can eddy-turn on a hole. The foam pile upstream of the boil line is just like a very strong eddy–the water is rushing upstream to fill a void. Starting at the edge of the hole and going downstream, there is an eddyline separating the slower-moving water that has gone through the hole and the faster-moving main current. Stopping on a hole is a little busier than in a placid eddy, since all the water is moving one way or another. You need to pay attention to where you are or you could drop upstream into the hole or flush downstream.

Approach as you would for an eddy turn on about a 45-degree angle. If the hole is weak you may want to increase the angle. You need some forward motion to get up onto the foam pile as you turn, and an onside tilt is the most stable. The bow should hit the foam pile a foot or so in front of your knees (see photo 316). If you offer the hole too little of your bow, you'll spin quickly but be left on the eddyline, either to ferry in below the boil line or get washed downstream. If you offer too much of your bow, you'll end up side-surfing. If you're turning onside, use a little more forward motion and a low brace (see photo 317). The low brace is very stable; it will slow you down if you're going too far into the foam pile and can be switched to a forward sweep if you need forward momentum. The turn to

315 *Eddy turn on a hole.*

316

317

318

your offside is a little harder because there isn't as much adjustment available. Use a little less forward motion than you would with the low-brace turn. As you hit the foam pile, do a front sweep to help spin the boat. In these turns the duffek (for an onside turn) or the cross-draw (for the offside turn) are not very stable or effective since you would not be planting the paddle in an opposing current as you would in an eddy turn; you would be planting those strokes in the green water upstream of the foam pile. Your aim is to end up perched exactly on the peak of the foam pile. You then have the options of paddling forward to drop in for a side surf or ender, or shredding the foam pile (surf the top of the hole) to move laterally across the river, or backing off just a bit to avoid staying in the foam pile. If the boil line is flat, you can back off just below it and stay indefinitely with a slow forward stroke, to scout below or wait for traffic to clear. Even a tiny foam pile on a breaking wave will be enough to assist you in spinning around upstream to get in position for a front-ferry.

Eddy turn in slower current

You don't need an eddy or hole to do an eddy turn. As long as the current you are entering is slower than the current you are in, there will be a current differential. You can use this if you want to spin around and start a front-ferry, or if you've ended up backward and you want to spin around to see what's downstream. Approach the slower current as you would an eddy turn. Use a little larger angle, since the current differential is less. There will not likely be a distinct eddyline, but plant the strokes as you would for an eddy turn where the current differential is the strongest. There is almost always a place where the current is a little slower: the inside of a turn in the river or even along the banks of a straight channel. Even if there is no difference in the speed of the current at all,

you can make a turn just as you would practice an eddy turn on flatwater.

Shore pivots

If you're trying to find a shore eddy ("Is this the falls coming up?") and there just isn't one, you can try to make one. If the shoreline is flat and at water level, you can eddy out onto dry land. A beach or gravel bar is the perfect location for this, but as long as you don't have a steep bank you may be able to find a flat rock or shallow slope. Pretend that the shoreline is the eddyline, set an angle and power toward it; 45 degrees is still the best angle. The more forward motion, the better. An inside tilt will help you stay in contact with the shore and prevent sliding off backward. If the banks are steep and there is no eddy, use the slower current near the shore to turn upstream into a front ferry. Avoid hitting the shore before you've turned upstream because it will kill your forward momentum and send you backward away from the bank. Get as close to the shore as possible, do the turn and then front-ferry to shore; hopefully, you'll find something to grab onto. On the Urtz River in Germany, Paul and I were warned of a killer weir without an obvious eddy above it. I could tell it was coming up because the saplings on the bank were stripped of leaves.

Terminology

Eddy out, eddy in, peel out. Not only is there confusion and probably regional differences as to what these terms mean, but once you hear the definitive, proper terminology, you promptly forget it because it isn't worth remembering. For the record, the terms I use (90 percent of the time) are "eddy out" to leave the main current and go into an eddy and "eddy in" to go into the main current. "Peel out" refers to leaving an eddy to go into the main current.

Slalom racing

I would encourage everyone to try slalom racing. Usually, the race courses are on easy, manageable whitewater. Most races have a friendly, cooperative atmosphere, so even if competition is not your bag, you can have a lot of fun and learn a lot by challenging yourself with the gates. Running gates makes you develop precise lines. It can also make an easy set of rapids challenging and interesting.

A slalom course consists of approximately 24 gates. You have to go through them in a prescribed order and direction, with the green pole on the right and red on the left. You must go through "upstream gates" traveling upstream. These are usually placed in an eddy but may be placed on a surfing wave. Downstream gates are negotiated going downstream. The direction you are facing doesn't matter, and only your shoulders and head must pass through the gate. If you hit either one of the poles, 10 seconds are added to your time. If the ends of your boat go under the poles, that doesn't matter either. Decked slalom boats sit just above the water level, but open boats sit higher, so "sneaking" them under most gates is tough. If you miss a gate altogether, 50 seconds are added. Making sure you complete each of the gates is the first priority. Whether you take a conservative, perhaps slower, line or a faster line with more risk of hitting a gate will depend on the probability of your missing the move, your ability and your attitude that day. This is one of the interesting challenges of the sport.

A rule of thumb for slalom is, maintain your forward momentum. You can make up a few seconds by increasing your stroke rate and pulling really hard, but you can lose a lot more if you're off line or fighting the current. You still have a lot of options in choosing a line after the course has been set up. Before getting on the water, read where the fastest currents and the

currents that can help you turn are, then plan and memorize your line. Most touches occur when you're accelerating or turning as you go through a gate. At these times it's easy to keep the bow off the gate, but the stern can easily swing and touch before you realize it. To avoid hitting gates, try to avoid last-second lunges with your body. They usually put you off balance and then you're late for the next gate.

Upstream gates

In slalom racing, an eddy turn is the easiest place to make up time or lose it. Maintaining forward motion is the key to going fast and conserving your energy. Steering and keeping on your line are also easier when you've got momentum. Use the power of the water wherever possible. On an eddy turn, choose the line with the strongest current differential and the line that puts you in the fastest current once you've crossed the eddy line. Try to minimize the time that your boat spends turning. When a boat is turning, it's not moving forward, even though a sharp turn may feel like a powerful move. When you cross an eddyline, use the biggest angle you can without relying on a counteracting stroke to get you deep enough into the eddy to reach the fast lane. For example, on an onside turn you could go into an eddy with a really big angle, but you might have to do an onside sweep to get deep enough into the eddy to stay on your line. The sweep would counteract the turning effect and the speed of the eddy current and negate the advantage of a wide-angled turn. Also, if you can initiate turning momentum before you cross the eddyline, you will reduce the turning time further still. You can approach the eddy on an arc or initiate the turn on the stroke before the eddyline, but make this initiation subtle; otherwise it will detract from your forward momentum as you cross the eddyline.

When you are going into an eddy, use an outside tilt for a faster-carving turn unless you need the greater stability of the inside tilt or unless the abruptness of the outside tilt turns you before you reach the fastest water or your chosen line. For the initial part of the turn, the current in the eddy will push against the outside edge and help you turn. After the initial part of the turn, reduce the tilt. Your bow may be moving faster than the eddy current as it pivots, and with a slight outside tilt, the raised inside edge will plane as it completes the turn. Use a slight outside tilt again when you set the angle to leave the eddy. The more tilt you offer the eddy current, the more carving and stopping effect you will have. If you're using a wide angle into a slow current, use just a little tilt and rely on your stroke to do more of the turning. If you're forced to use a small angle or the current is strong, use a bigger tilt to rely on the current more to turn the boat.

When you're leaving the eddy and crossing the river, use an inside tilt to stretch the turn out and take you farther into the current, rather than an outside tilt, which will be abrupt and leave you turned and closer to the eddyline. As with entering an eddy, try to use as wide an angle as possible without having to counteract the turning effect of the opposing currents.

Even if you do want to turn quickly, the outside-tilt turn can be unstable going into a strong current. For a fast turn leaving an eddy, tilt inside for the initial contact with the main current, then switch to a slight outside tilt. The current will be pushing on the upstream stern edge, helping the whole boat accelerate to the speed of the current.

Downstream gates

Course designers keep the paddlers moving back and forth and using all of the river. Try to turn before you get to a downstream gate so that you're steering as little as possible as you go through the gate. The current above a downstream gate is a good place for an outside tilt turn. With downstream gates placed after an upstream gate, you have the option of turning above them and facing downstream or front-ferrying to them, backing through them and then proceeding to either front-ferry or pivot. Pivoting and going forward are usually preferred unless there isn't time in which to turn. Front-ferrying and going backward involve stopping the ferry and accelerating backward.

Downstream gates are sometimes located in an eddy or behind the edge of a hole. You can use a dive to get into the eddy while still facing downriver and maintaining forward momentum. You can make this move above the gate to start accelerating before you reach the gate, or you can make the dive with as gradual an angle as possible and aim for the gate, thus slowing your boat as little as possible.

To a spectator, you should seem oblivious to the gates when you're on your line. For those rare instances when the boat should be six inches to the left, you can avoid a lot of touches by side-slipping and making subtle adjustments to your blade angle. If you have forward momentum going into a gate and you're off line slightly, stick in a draw straight out from your hip. Start with your blade parallel to the keel line of the boat. As long as the boat has momentum, you can quickly move the boat in many different directions by slightly adjusting the blade angle. If you want to move the boat straight sideways, pull toward your hip. You'll probably have to compensate for turning momentum. If the boat is turning toward your offside, turn the leading edge of the blade outward (open the angle of your blade) and move the paddle forward to keep in a straight line (almost like a duffek). If you have onside turning momentum, close the angle and pull in (almost like a stern draw). You can use the same strokes on the offside from a cross-draw position.

Many canoe and kayak clubs have gates set up in convenient places for an evening practice. Don't be shy. Even if you initially just think of running gates as an aerobic workout, you may get hooked on how much fun it is.

Attainment

When rivers were transportation routes, adventurers went upstream as often as they went downstream. Although I can definitely do without the drudgery of going upstream, I do appreciate the challenge of outsmarting gravity. Our forebears called it exploring; we call it attaining. It's an exercise in which you progress upstream by ferrying, surfing and just plain paddling against the current. From the top of one eddy, you may be able to front ferry to the bottom of another eddy, paddle up that eddy and ferry on to another eddy upstream. You want to lose as little ground as possible, so make your ferries efficient and use every surfing wave you can find. You may end up low in some weak eddies and have to find the line with the weakest downstream current and paddle hard to make progress. However, the nifty part of attainment is making the moves where the river does the work for you. Occasionally, a wave or hole connects those eddies of different elevations. If you can front-surf or side-surf to get across the river to the higher eddy you've made an elevator move. Many attainment moves involve getting your angle just right and carrying as much forward momentum into the current as possible. These moves are fun and a good way to get a workout. They often challenge you to make your moves perfect and they make the river longer.

Dive

Normally, when you enter an eddy, the opposing currents turn your boat as you cross the eddy line—an eddy turn. The turning momentum dies and the boat ends up facing upriver. You are then in a position to relax, scout downstream and then ferry or eddy-turn back into the main current. A dive is the opposite move. Instead of turning behind an obstacle in an eddy, you counteract the opposing currents that want to turn you, cut into the eddy and end up facing downstream without losing your momentum (photo 319, figures 3 and 4). In several instances, this is a fun and useful move. You can often avoid some wet waves by cutting in behind rocks or holes and continuing downstream out the bottom of the eddy. On a steep creek, your only line might be out the bottom or the other side of an eddy but you don't want to risk the turn and end up sideways or backward. In big water if you let the current turn you, you may end up parked on a turbulent eddy line, when you wanted to get deeper into the eddy.

To do the dive you usually set up with a little less angle (facing more downstream) than you would for an eddy turn. As you cross the eddyline, lean back (photo 319, figure 3); you want to delay the edge catching as long as possible. Tilt as if you were doing an inside tilt turn (away from the eddy current). Use a strong stern draw or ruddering pry to counteract the turning effect of the opposing eddy current.

319 *Turning midstream and executing a dive.*

Ferrying

Front ferries

Ferries were probably one of the first maneuvers you learned in whitewater after being taught the golden rule of A.M.T. (angle, motion, tilt). Set an angle with the upstream end of the boat pointed to the shore that you want to get to and apply motion upstream so the current pushing against the boat moves the boat sideways instead of carrying it downstream. Tilt downstream to prevent the current from grabbing the bottom of the boat and flipping you upstream. Once you understand these basic principles, start looking for shortcuts to improve your efficiency. Surfing is one. Here, the gravity of a standing wave provides the motion upstream.

Front ferry or back ferry?

In solo playboats, you see a lot more front ferries than back ferries. Since playboats turn so easily and forward strokes are more efficient than backpaddling, it's usually more effective to turn and use a front ferry than to back-ferry. At times, however, you want to face downstream, or you just end up that way and you need to back-ferry. Plus it's good practice and fun to try back ferries when you've got the front ferry wired. Besides, you didn't get this book to find out the easiest way to get down a rapid. The principles for front-ferrying and back-ferrying are the same, so we won't make a distinction between the two here. See Corrective Strokes, pages 124 and 125, for a review of back ferrying strokes.

Angle

Angles are in relation to the current. A small angle is close to parallel to the current; a wide angle is close to perpendicular to the current. Sometimes you'll ferry from eddy to eddy; sometimes you'll set the angle and start ferrying while in the main current. If you're starting in an eddy, choosing the correct angle to cross the eddyline is important to a ferry's success. At the very moment that the upstream end of your boat crosses the eddyline, the eddy current and main current conspire to turn you. By counteracting that force, you'll be sent ferrying across the eddyline and across the current. The wider your angle, the more force there will be against the boat, the harder it will be to counteract that force and the stronger the resulting force that will send you ferrying across the eddyline and the river. Once the entire boat has crossed the eddy line, the main current will want to push the whole boat downstream and the turning effect of the opposing currents on the eddyline is eliminated. Wide, turbulent eddylines present varying problems. Sometimes you can sideslip across them; sometimes you will paddle across them with a wider angle and close it before the bow hits the main current. Almost always, approach them aggressively.

If the current is slowing down where you want to front ferry, there will be standing waves and you should use them for forward momentum (surfing). When a wave is providing the forward momentum and you're surfing, err on the side of using too small an angle. It's easier to open up the angle than to close it, and you're not wasting any energy or losing ground if you're staying in place and surfing. With too wide an angle on a surfable wave, you'll fall off the wave and go downstream. If there are no standing waves to provide forward motion or if the gradient is steep, err on the side of using too big an angle. A big angle will get you across the current quickly and if you do get swept perpendicular or even heading downstream, it doesn't matter. Keep up the forward motion, and when you reach an eddy do an eddy turn into it rather than ferry into it. You'll cross the current more quickly and lose less ground than if you had too small an angle: while you'd been paddling upstream and keeping a small controllable angle, the current would have been overpowering your forward motion, sending you downstream.

Motion

If you're starting your ferry in an eddy, the more forward motion you have, the wider an angle you can hold when crossing the eddyline. Maintaining the momentum you had coming into an eddy is easier if you don't stop but instead continue into the ferry. If, for instance, you're doing an eddy turn followed by a front ferry, pick a line where you come into the eddy low, take two strokes to get up the eddy, change the angle just before hitting the main current and ferry without stopping.

When you leave the eddy on a ferry, using a forward sweep or offside sweep stroke on the main current side of the boat will give you a stronger ferrying force and more upstream momentum. This is good if you don't have the benefit of a wave to surf or you want a fast, strong ferry. A prying stroke on the eddy side of the boat or a ruddering stroke will slow the forward momentum. This is good if you want to stay high on a surfing wave and avoid pearling.

Forward motion–surfing

Even if your objective is to get across the river and not just to hang out for hours on the same wave, use every wave you can to provide upstream motion for your ferry. If a wave isn't big enough to hold you in a static surf, it's still better to paddle on the upstream or downhill side and have that bit of gravity working for you. Avoid plowing into the downstream slope of a wave. The downstream momentum that this creates will make it harder to catch the next wave that comes along.

Ferrying

Tilt

Tilt downstream is a rule of thumb that we all learned when we started paddling whitewater. It doesn't always hold true for eddy turns or surfing, and once the whole boat is in the main current, tilt is less significant. Tilt downstream, however, pretty much still applies when you're crossing an eddyline to ferry. When you leave an eddy, it will be easier to counteract the turning effect of the main current if the leading edge of the canoe doesn't contact the water and the ends are lifted out of the water. When you're going into an eddy, tilt downstream in relation to the current you're going into–the eddy current. When the whole boat is in the main current, tilt will make the boat pivot more easily if you need to adjust the angle. With less tilt, the boat travels faster, tracks better and offers more of the upstream edge to the current for a better ferrying effect.

Front Surfing

Surfing is a static position on the upstream slope of a standing wave. The current is pushing you downstream, but gravity is pulling you down the slope, or upstream. If the wave is big enough, you'll stay on it without having to paddle forward. If it's too steep, the bow will pearl; that is, dig into the trough of the wave. To get on the wave, you can ferry to it from the side or drop onto the steepest part of the wave from above. Ferrying onto a surfing wave, ideally from an eddy, is the easiest approach since you don't need to overcome any downstream momentum.

Approach from the side This is the easiest method. In a best-case scenario, the shoulder of the wave will extend right to the eddy you are in (photo 320). Start with your center of gravity just upstream of the wave (photo 321). With a very narrow angle, paddle forward hard enough to keep your canoe slightly nose down on the wave. Drifting too far downstream, onto the back of the wave, will mean an uphill battle–literally. Until you gain the upstream slope of the wave, you'll be battling gravity and the downstream current. Controlling your angle with forward and offside forward strokes will maintain maximum hull speed and ensure that you don't fall off the back of the wave. If the wave is big enough, you may be able to control

your angle with stern correction strokes and still stay on the wave. As your canoe approaches the sweet spot of the wave, bring the canoe parallel to the current. Ideally, you are now surfing. This should happen as your stern starts to lift up the face of the wave, so that your last couple of strokes combine with a perfect angle to achieve your fastest hull speed. Still not sure if you'll catch the wave? Then it's time for one last trick. As you teeter on the crest, lean forward slightly to get your center of gravity onto the upstream slope of the wave. As the canoe slides down the face of the wave, pull yourself upright. Now you're on it!

320 *Approach from the side.*

321

322

Approach from upstream If there is no eddy beside the wave, you'll have to catch it from above. If the current is slower on one side of the wave, then start there. Remember, it's critical to avoid downstream momentum. If the current is relatively equal, drop onto the steepest part of the wave. This will give gravity time to slow your downstream descent as the current pushes your boat up the wave.

The key to a successful approach is to establish an angle to paddle against and to start paddling forward early enough. Use offside forward strokes to establish an arc toward your onside (photo 323). Switch to onside forward strokes without correction as your canoe drops into the trough (photo 324). Shorten your stroke and give it everything you've got as you ride up the face. Use the power forward stroke without correction. If you timed the end of your arc to coincide with reaching the crest of the wave, you should now be parallel to the current and set up to drop down onto the face of the wave.

The size of the wave will not change the approach. A big wave might give you enough time to paddle three to five strokes against an arc, whereas a smaller wave might give time to squeeze in only one or two. The reason is that it's difficult to maintain an arc unless you wait until you've passed the peak of the last wave upstream of your surf wave.

Approach from downstream With a slower current, paddle upstream over the crest of the wave and drop onto its face. This is a more viable approach if the wave is breaking or you've gained substantial speed in the eddy. The key is to paddle against an arc, reaching your maximum stroke rate as you climb the backside of the wave. If you can reach the crest with the balance point of your canoe, you'll then have time to throw in offside forward strokes to stay parallel to the current and drive your canoe down onto the face.

Now that you've caught the tiger by the tail, what do you do? We'll review the front-surfing basics covered in Chapter 4, as well as teach some new moves so you can really shred the wave.

323 Approach from upstream.

324

325

Front Surfing

Stern draw and pry

The two most important strokes for front surfing are the stern draw and the pry. In most situations they, in combination, will be all you need.

The stern draw will turn the canoe toward your offside. In photo 326, figure 1, the stern draw is being used to turn back toward the center of the wave. The photographer has captured the beginning of the stroke. At this point it is providing a brace to initiate a tilt. As you near the shoulder of the wave, increase the turning component of the stroke by moving the blade as far back toward the stern as possible. The stroke starts out to the side (photo 327) but quickly changes into a pure pivoting stroke (photo 328). If the boat still isn't turning back, push out with your grip hand and pull in really hard with your shaft hand while heeling the boat right over on its side. I cannot stress enough the importance of reaching your paddle back to the stern and cranking on this stroke.

Now that the canoe has turned and is headed back across the wave, it's time for a stern pry to turn the boat back before you run out of wave. Tilt downstream and place your paddle blade against the stern (photo 326, figure 2). Here are a couple of important points to note. The stern pry is easier if you have a tilt before you start the stroke. A pry will always push your gunwale down (remember the righting pry?). Setting up with your shaft hand below the gunwale will prevent you from pushing your gunwale down. Keeping your hand above and outside the gunwale also works, but you must avoid the temptation to lean on your gunwale. Sometimes on a flatter wave you'll need to keep your pry very

326 Carving with a draw and a pry.

streamlined; otherwise the drag it creates will push you downstream off the wave. In photo 326 the bow is plowing into the green water upstream of the wave, so I'm trying to back the boat up the face of the wave with a pry well out to the side (figure 3). If you look

carefully you'll notice that the braking action starts with an aggressive pry (figure 2). The paddle then stays at exactly the same angle relative to the current throughout the turn (figure 3). It is the canoe that has changed its angle. Cool, eh?

327 Stern draw.

328

Cross-draw

The reason you'd choose a cross-draw over a stern draw while front surfing is that a cross-draw has a strong braking component. In photo 329 you're surfing across the wave from river right to river left (figure 1) but need to make a major change in angle. To do that you need to pull the boat up the face of the wave so that it's balanced on top. Use your knees to radically tilt the boat downstream as you reach across for the cross-draw (figure 2). The open face of your paddle will catch the passing current. The consistent pressure on the paddle provides a bracing action so you can confidently maintain the tilt. Your paddle in figure 2 is quite far out from the side of the boat, to move the boat back up the wave, disengaging the bow from the green water. In photo 331, the cross-draw is closer to the hull, with the blade closer to parallel to the current. The objective on this wave is different. The wave is big and fast. The bow of the boat is not in danger of becoming embedded in the oncoming water, so you don't need to pull the canoe up the wave with a cross-draw stroke. You could easily accomplish this by increasing the angle of the canoe so it carves up the face of the wave. After the boat has responded to your cross-draw, you can follow with either an onside pry (photo 332) or stay offside and do an offside stern

329 Carving with a cross draw.

draw (photo 329, figure 3). The offside stern draw feels as awkward as it looks and is practical only if the canoe stays close to parallel with the current or you need forward propulsion to stay on the wave. As with an onside stern draw, for this stroke to have an effect you must keep the blade well back toward the stern. The benefit of the offside stern draw is that it combines seamlessly with a cross-draw, allowing you precise

control of your boat while you're perched on a wave. By sliding your paddle blade up to your hips, you can execute an offside back draw or a braking stroke, or you can bring the blade forward for a cross-draw. Your shaft hand will remain beside you during all three strokes. Your grip hand is what moves forward or back. To a spectator, you will appear to be using your top hand to shift gears as in a sports car.

330 Cross draw.

331

332

Inside tilt

Using an inside tilt on a small wave can greatly increase your chances of staying on it. An outside tilt relies on the chine of the canoe to carve the turn. But if the boat has a wide angle crossing the wave (photo 333, figure 1), the chine will catch the current, pushing the canoe up the wave. The solution is to flatten out the hull. This allows the boat to slide down into the trough and enables you to pivot the boat before your bow becomes embedded in the green water of the trough. In photo 333, I did not quite get turned back across the wave, so I'm pulling the boat back up the wave to free the bow. Since the canoe is now almost parallel to the current, I could revert to an outside tilt to cause the curve of the bow to push the boat through the turn.

To turn toward your onside, use a stern pry, but let the paddle flatten out a little so you can brace on it. The secret to staying on a small wave is to be efficient and streamlined. Pay attention to whether you're moving up or down the face of the wave, and time your hard turning strokes accordingly. Do hard pivoting strokes on your way down the face of the wave.

Wanting to bank off a foam pile is another reason for turning on a wave using an inside tilt. As the bow of the canoe contacts the foam pile on the top of a really big wave, the bow is stopped; by keeping the hull flat on the wave, the bow will slide down the face.

On a big wave you need to lean aggressively on your paddle during the pry turn (towards your onside), tilting the boat into the turn. To turn to your offside, do your draw way back at the stern and use your knees and hips to tilt away from your onside. Mark claims that the muscle that works hardest during the draw turn is his left cheek. (The other kind of cheek.)

333 *Turning on a wave with inside tilt.*

Dynamic front surfing

A common misconception is that once you catch a surf you'll be able to settle into a static position on the wave. This is rarely the case. Surfing waves often have microridges and weak spots, or sometimes they're not perpendicular to the current. These factors combine to move the boat across the wave, often unnoticed by you because you're looking at the water in front of

334

you. I've been quite surprised on occasion to glance sideways and find that the river has subtly surfed me off the wave. The huge pulsing wave in photo 334 is an extreme example of staying on a dynamic wave using an inside tilt.

Avoiding pearling

Pearling is what happens when you surf a steep wave with your boat perpendicular to the wave. Unless you do something evasive, the bow will submerge in the green water and push you off to one side or fill you up with water. Your response should be to angle your boat across the wave. This will cause you to ride up the face, freeing the bow. Cut back across the wave before you blow off the shoulder. Repeat the process until you're dizzy.

Exiting the wave

After finally getting on, you think, I'm going to have trouble getting off? Yeah right! True enough, falling off the wave does come naturally, but you may want to exit the wave in style or to a particular side, especially with the incentive of a big hole downstream. Initiate the exit by tilting to the outside of the turn (photo 335). The chine at the bow of the boat is now pushing you across the wave. Maintaining this tilt keeps the canoe carving as you punch through any diagonal waves guarding the eddy (photo 336).

Front hand-surfing

Front hand-surfing relies on drag to turn the boat. Therefore you'll need a big wave, so you aren't blown off it. Make the boat turn by tilting and dragging your hand (or whole arm, if more resistance is needed). This works much better if you can keep your bow free of the green water. Achieve this by braking with both hands at once on opposite sides of the hull. A variation on this is to dunk your grip hand in the water while you're still holding on to the paddle. You can alternate this with an onside stern pry, without fumbling for your T-grip each time. It's fast and fun, and it looks radical. Actually, it looks like you're using a double-bladed kayak paddle. Sometimes it's kinda' fun to cross-boat.

Shudder rudder

Getting a little bored with a bottom-feeding static front-surf? The shudder rudder can give you a whole new perspective. Lie back and place your paddle in the water directly behind you (photo 337). Now lay your head back and navigate by the clouds, or, if you've been on the wave a long time, the stars. Mark claims that this works, but don't forget to take into account the movement of the clouds and the earth's rotation, or you'll blow off the wave.

Blasting

Blasting is front-surfing on a breaking wave or in a hole. The stern of the boat is pushed under or through the foam pile and the boat rides on the green water underneath. This move is much more feasible in the short, open boats being developed specifically for rodeo paddling. When the boat gets a bit of water in it, the extra weight settles the hull even deeper into the current.

The easiest way to initiate blasting is to surf into the foam pile with an offside angle so that you are using a stern pry on the upstream side of the boat. You need a slight downstream tilt (toward the foam pile) and in bigger waves this will fill up your boat pretty quickly. Once you're full of water, the stern should settle down. As the foam pile pushes down on your boat, the bow will rise, sometimes as much as 45 degrees. Keep your body upright and lift up with your knees. You can even make the boat bob–it doesn't really accomplish anything, but it's kind of a cool sensation.

The boat will respond well to carving inside tilt turns on the wave. The same move is also possible backward. You can use the pry on either side of the boat. You'll tend to lean forward in back-blasting, but remember to keep your body upright.

335 Exiting the wave.

336

337 Shudder rudder.

338 Blasting.

Back Surfing

Fish can't tell whether you're back-surfing or front-surfing. Back surfing would be just as easy as front-surfing except for two things: you're less accustomed to the strokes needed for back surfing than to those needed for front surfing, and you're less accustomed to steering when you're not facing where you're going. You can overcome the problem of unfamiliar strokes

339 Leaving the eddy.

with a bit of practice (flatwater helps, too), and you can learn to steer by watching your bow or by looking over your shoulder at your stern. Running easy rapids backward provides good practice.

Approach from the side   Entering the wave for a back-surf is the same as in front surfing–from the side is easiest because you have less downstream momentum to overcome (photo 339). The only difference is that the backpaddling stroke is less mechanically efficient than the forward stroke (okay, that makes three things that are harder about back-surfing). To get established on the wave, you sometimes need to lean back (upstream) to get weight

and momentum on the upstream side of the crest of the wave (photo 340). Once you're established on the wave, keep your body upright or "neutral"–not leaning forward or back. A common error in front surfing is to lean back all the time, even without realizing it, rather than being upright and neutral. In back surfing, you're even less aware of your body position, and you tend to lean forward away from the water that you can't see. In the neutral position, the boat's hull performs best, your strokes are most effective and you can lean backward (upstream) if the boat is falling off the wave, or forward (downstream) to lift the upstream end and prevent pearling (photo 345).

340 Approach from the side.

341

342

343 Approach from the side.

344

345

Side-slipping Side-slipping is very useful when you're crossing an eddyline to back-surf. You use the back draw to side-slip to your onside. When you have backward momentum, plant the paddle out from your hip and angle the leading (back) edge of the blade away from you. Adjust the blade angle so the moving water keeps pressure on the blade. Moving the blade forward or backward will compensate for any turning momentum you may have, so you can control the boat angle as you side-slip. If you have turning momentum toward your offside, move your back draw toward the stern to maintain a straight side-slip. If you have turning momentum toward your onside, move your back draw toward the bow. To side-slip to your offside, use the cross-draw (photo 346). Rotate your torso a lot so you can get the cross-draw planted straight out from your hips with the paddle as vertical as possible. As with the back draw, move the blade forward or backward to compensate for any turning momentum.

Approach from upstream Dropping onto a wave to back-surf is much harder than approaching from the side or dropping onto a wave to front-surf. As you float down toward the wave, facing downstream, set an angle toward your onside so that a few hard back strokes without correction will turn you parallel to the current. The back cross-draw is nearly as powerful as the back stroke, so you can set the angle to your offside and use the cross-draw for those critical strokes if you want to end up on your offside once you are back-surfing. If there's a small foam pile that won't turn you sideways or fill you up, drop onto that and take advantage of the upstream momentum you can get from the foam pile. As you approach the wave, start stroking to slow your momentum, and as you reach the peak put in some hard strokes and lean back to stay on the wave. Leaning back is usually more important than the end of the back stroke, so shorten your stroke. If you're having problems catching the wave this way, you're normal. Try catching the same wave on a front surf. You'll realize that timing is critical with the strokes and the upstream body lean. You can't see as many landmarks when you're backward, and the back stroke is not nearly as powerful as the forward stroke. Finally, I find that I'm less stable when I'm backward on the peak of a wave and more likely to wobble and miss a backward stroke than when I'm front surfing. However, approaching from upstream is the only way to get onto some waves, so the technique is worth trying and practicing.

If you've chosen a big enough wave to surf, you won't need backward (upstream) motion once you're on the wave except for an occasional back sweep or back cross-draw should you start to fall off the wave. You can steer or rudder from either a forward stroke position or a cross-forward position, or alternate between the two. Basically, you can do a draw and pry on either side of the boat. To carve back and forth with smooth, linked turns easily and quickly, stay on one side.

Here are the strokes you can choose from.

346 Slide slipping with a cross draw.

347 Approaching a wave from upstream.

348

Backsurf Strokes

Onside strokes: back draw

With your paddle at the beginning of the forward stroke position (downstream of the pivot point), change the angle of the blade to a drawing angle (power face toward the boat) and apply as much pressure on the water rushing past as you need to turn or to keep the boat straight (see photo 349). Your grip hand will push out past your onside gunwale with a fairly straight arm. The position is not the most powerful, but if you can hold it, this stroke will give you the most stability since it feels like a high brace. This back surf stroke turns you toward your offside.

Onside strokes: static forward stroke

To turn the boat toward your onside, again start in the forward stroke position, with your paddle blade downstream of the pivot point. Change the angle of the blade to that of a forward stroke, then rotate the power face away from the boat while the shaft rests against the gunwale or hull (photo 350). Using the power face of the blade turns you toward your onside. As you adjust the angle of the blade back to a forward stroke position, you'll increase the forward (downstream) propulsion. This is the same as a prying rudder when you're front-surfing and is a very effective stroke. You can quickly switch between this stroke (which turns you toward your onside) and the back draw (which turns you toward your offside) by changing the angle of the blade.

Offside strokes: static forward stroke

To turn toward your offside, put the paddle shaft on the gunwale and the paddle in the cross-forward stroke position. Rotate the blade slightly so the power face is facing away from the hull. As you change the blade angle to a cross-forward position, you will increase the resistance on the paddle, and therefore increase the turning effect to the offside; you will also provide some forward (downstream) momentum. Although this feels awkward, it is very effective.

Offside strokes: cross draw

You can turn in both directions from the cross-draw position, too (photo 351). In fact, it's sometimes easier or more efficient to turn from this position than from the onside position. To turn toward your onside, use a cross-draw. As with the bow draw, angle the paddle blade so that the water rushing past holds the blade in

349 Back draw.

350 Static forward stroke.

351 Cross draw.

352 Cross bow pry.

position, and apply as much pressure as required. Because your torso is twisted to reach the offside, you can use it as well as your lower arm and shoulder to pull toward the opposite knee.

Offside strokes: cross-bow pry

Keep the same paddle angle as the cross-draw, put the shaft on the hull or gunwale, and pry with the back face of the blade (photo 352). Paul and I call this the cross-bow pry. Changing back to a cross-draw is quick and subtle. Putting on a downstream tilt is also easier than if you are doing the alternative, an angled cross-draw stroke. However, you can't switch to forward propulsion as easily with this stroke as with the cross-forward pry.

I generally prefer to use the offside strokes because the angled cross-forward stroke has much more leverage than the bow draw and the cross-draw is as effective as the angled forward stroke. However, it's harder to keep your balance with the offside strokes. This may depend on the wave, though. At high water on our "home wave" in Ottawa, you need to be angled slightly to river right. For a righty that makes the downstream side the onside, so there I favor the onside strokes. Another key is to use forward or downstream propulsion to pull you up the wave toward the crest. This releases the stern from the trough of the wave and allows the boat to turn more quickly. As with front surfing, tilting the boat (downstream) releases the ends and makes the boat easier to turn. Again, this is something that just takes some time to get used to.

Backsurfing is fun on its own, improves your back-ferrying, is a building-block skill for 360s and flat spins, and improves your general boating awareness and skills.

Back hand-surfing

Not many boaters know this, but it's actually easier to back hand-surf than it is to use a paddle. You can keep both hands in the water at once and your brain has to translate simpler directions. Compared to front hand-surfing, if you lean forward onto the front deck you can reach the water more easily. Mitts—or webbed fingers—help with the stroke; but you've still got pretty good leverage without them, since you can dunk a good part of your arm in the water. Choose a wave that needs only a light touch for steering. Once you get established back-surfing, stick your paddle under the airbag ropes. Lean forward and dunk both hands in the water (photo 353); you should come up the wave. Sit up and lean back and you'll go down the wave. Use one hand at a time and you'll carve (photo 354). Since your weight is on the downstream end of the boat, once you've initiated the turn, tilt to the inside. If you're falling off the wave, you can furiously back-paddle with your hands or lean backward, but don't count on any miracles. If the stern is digging in and you can't change the angle, dig both hands into the water and hope you can pull the boat up to the peak of the wave, where it will be easier to turn. You need to rely on finesse for back hand-surfing because you won't be able to hide any mistakes. If you smile and make it look easy, everyone will think it isn't.

353 Back hand-surfing.

354

Flat Spins

Flat spins or 180-degree, front-surf-to-back-surf spins on a green, nonbreaking wave are possible in open boats. (Yes, the wave in the photo is breaking, but I'm spinning on the shoulder, which is green.) For this maneuver, you need a short, flat-bottom hull. Because the water flowing under a flat-bottom hull (planing hull) is a relatively flat surface itself, the planing hull can spin without disrupting the water flow beneath it. Since there is some resistance at the edges, some boats are slightly beveled to create turbulence and reduce the chance of the edge catching as the boat spins and slides around.

Find a steep green wave and establish a front-surf. This move will be easier if the wave occasionally breaks, but if you use the break, that's not really a flat spin. You can do a flat spin from any position on the wave (down low or up high near the crest) or from a completely static position. It will help a bit if you can carve your way up to the top of the wave and then initiate your spin as you start down the wave with a bit of upstream momentum. Make sure that your body position is upright and balanced over your boat.

You can spin in either direction but on some waves it is easier to go in a particular direction. If the wave is not quite perpendicular to the current or not of uniform steepness, you'll have better luck staying on the wave if you initiate the spin toward the upstream end of the wave or the steeper part of the wave. In photos 355 through 360 of "Baby Face" on the Ottawa, I am spinning towards the river right shoulder of the wave since that side of the wave curves upstream and the wave is flatter towards river left just beside the foam pile. That means initiating the spin with a cross-draw and spinning to my offside. This is slightly harder than initiating with a back sweep since the cross-draw gives you a bit of downstream momentum and there is a tendency to tilt the boat to your offside. Keep your boat perfectly flat and do a strong, quick cross-draw. The more rotation and further back you can reach, the better (photo 356), since this will be pushing the stern around and down the wave rather than lifting the bow up the wave. Once you have spinning momentum, it is easier to continue the spin rather than stop and initiate again. However, be aware of where you are on the wave. If you are starting to fall off the wave, it is better to readjust and then initiate the back to front spin. From the back surf position, photo 358, the front sweep is

355 Flat spin on a wave.

356

357

358

359

360

used to continue the spin. Again, keep the boat flat and use a strong, quick forward sweep. Start the sweep close to the hull so you maximize the turning effect and minimize the downstream momentum. Notice that I am looking in the direction that I am spinning, photo 359. Leading with your head will initiate and encourage shoulder and torso rotation.

To spin to your onside, initiate the spin with a back sweep. Start with your blade as close to the hull as possible. This minimizes any downstream momentum that would pull you off the wave. Keep the boat flat, use a strong, quick back sweep and look in the direction you are spinning. To continue the spin in that direction from a back surf position, you will be using an offside forward sweep. Start with the blade right next to the hull and sweep outwards. This stroke is difficult because you should still try to lead with your head towards your onside.

With these stroke combinations you can flat spin in either direction. A front-to-back flat spin followed immediately with a back-to-front flat spin in the opposite direction is called a *shuvvit*. This is easiest done with a back-sweep and front-sweep combination. A full 360-degree spin with just one stroke is called a *clean 360* or just a *clean*. For a *clean*, start the spin as you would for a 180-degree flat spin but use a very strong cross-draw or back sweep. Keep the spinning momentum going for the second 180, by keeping the boat flat and leading with head your shoulders and torso rotated. In order to do a clean, you need a hull that spins very easily.

If you want a job teaching flat spins, stand on shore and every time your student blows off the wave yell, "Your boat wasn't flat," then motion something about body position. You'll be giving good advice 99 percent of the time.

Here's something for those breaking waves that are not sticky enough to do 360s on and too wet and steep to front surf. Shred the foam pile! When you're front-surfing the top of a breaking wave, the ends of your boat will be out of the water. You can cut back and forth really quickly across the fall line of the wave. The maneuver is graceful yet dynamic, and very useful in many different river-running, play and rodeo situations.

The key to the move is balance and timing. You will literally be balanced on the peak of the wave. It will take some time to get the feel of where the balance point is. When you're front-surfing in the trough of a wave, you can reach an equilibrium between gravity pulling the boat down the wave (upstream) and the current pushing it downstream. This equilibrium is much more elusive on the top, or peak, of a breaking wave; here, you also have gravity pulling you down the downstream side of the wave and the action of the foam pile breaking and falling to the wave's upstream side.

Getting there

Very often, you can reach a breaking wave by front-surfing the smooth wave beside it (see photo 361). Get yourself just upstream of the peak of the smooth wave by using turns back and forth and the backward momentum of braking strokes. Ferry to the foam pile with a fairly wide angle, 45 degrees or more. A wide angle will keep you up high on the wave, whereas a small angle will give the boat forward momentum upstream and down the wave. The wide angle will also move you quickly across the break to give you enough room to cut back and still stay in the foam pile. When you hit the foam pile, be ready with your first turning stroke. If you're dropping onto the foam pile itself from upstream, drift backward with a 45-degree (or wider) angle. The angle is wider than what you would

use to drop on to a smooth wave, because you want to reach the top of the wave. Also, the upstream effect of the foam pile (and gravity) will provide more momentum upstream than just the gravity of a smooth wave. Angle the boat so you're paddling on the downstream side; in this position, your next stroke will be a forward stroke rather than the less powerful cross-forward. Take a couple of cross-forward strokes before you hit the foam pile to slow your downstream momentum and to set up an arc to paddle against. When you feel your boat near the peak of the wave, put in a hard front sweep to overcome your downstream momentum and start your first turn.

Angle

It's extremely difficult to stay on that balance point without moving, so we'll put in turns back and forth across the fall line of the wave—this is called *shredding*. Each turn will go to within 15 degrees of being perpendicular to the current (I'm just choosing a number for the sake of description). You can stall here for a split second (almost side-surfing), then turn the boat back the other way. You need to move quickly when you're parallel to the current, since stalling then will send you down the wave to get wet or to pearl your bow.

Strokes

Face upstream just as you would for front-surfing. When you start to fall off the back or downstream side of the wave, quickly paddle forward to provide a little forward momentum. If you start to slide forward, down the upstream side of the wave into the trough, you need to provide backward motion or braking to slow yourself and move the boat back up the wave. Your strokes will be instrumental in providing forward and backward motion as well as steering left and right.

Shredding the Foam Pile

The most important element of this move is reacting quickly with either forward or backward motion in combination with a turning stroke.

Turning toward the offside To do this, choose either a forward sweep or a cross-draw. For forward momentum, use a sweep out to the side (photo 363). A draw or sweep behind your body (as you might do front surfing) will be a slower transition to the next stroke and provide less forward momentum. To include backward momentum, choose the cross-draw (photo 364). It's a little awkward initially because you plant the paddle on the upstream side while you tilt downstream. The stroke is very powerful and you need to commit to it quickly; being tentative puts you in a vulnerable position. You can rotate the paddle blade outward (thumb away from you) to get even more backward motion or braking. You could expose your shoulder to possible dislocation or strain if you commit to the cross-draw on your offside, but the boat keeps ferrying to your onside.

Turning toward the onside To do this, choose between a cross-forward and a pry (stern rudder). For forward motion, use a cross-forward or, even better, put the blade out wider for a cross-forward sweep.

This cross-forward obviously has less power than the forward sweep; try not to let yourself fall back so far that you need a lot of forward motion. For backward motion, use a pry on the upstream side. Keep your blade close to your hip (photo 365) and not back toward the stern, the way you might for front surfing. This stroke is sometimes referred to as a rudder, or stern pry. To increase the backward motion, rotate the blade to a stop position (grip hand thumb out, pushing with the back of the blade). You can even move the paddle to slightly ahead of your hips. This stroke, too, is very powerful. Use your shaft hand as a fulcrum for the pry or sometimes the hull of the boat, but don't pry against the gunwale or rest your hand on the gunwale, because this will push the gunwale down and affect the tilt.

The pry and the cross-draw are more powerful strokes for both turning and slowing momentum. I try to be just slightly to the upstream side of the peak so that I'm always turning and using backward motion, rather than switching between forward and backward momentum, as Paul is shown doing in photos 366 and 367. It also helps to make the turns consistent and to develop a rhythm of turning back and forth. I think this makes the move quite aesthetic: cross-draw, pry, cross-draw, pry, in a steady rhythm.

Tilt

The proper tilt helps, but not as much as timing and strokes. While you're front-surfing, a tilt helps you turn by releasing the ends. In shredding, the ends are already out of the water, so there is less advantage. Tilting downstream will push your boat up the wave (especially boats with edges), while tilting upstream improves your forward momentum a bit. Generally, I try to tilt downstream and change the tilt once I initiate the turn. This means that you will be tilted away from the side on which you plant the pry and the cross-draw (the upstream side), as shown in photo 365, and tilted toward the side on which you plant the front sweep (the downstream side), as shown in photo 363.

Body position

Keep your upper body upright. When you're perched exactly on the crest of the wave, leaning forward will give you forward momentum to prevent you from falling off the wave. Don't overuse that option. Leaning forward too much puts you in a poor paddling position.

Ferrying on the foam pile

Sometimes you'll want to use the foam pile to front-ferry across the river. When you're balanced on top of the foam pile, set an angle and ferry. You won't ferry as

361 Shredding the foam pile.

362

363

364

quickly as you would on a smooth wave, since the foam pile provides resistance to moving sideways while you're ferrying on the green water underneath. A significant downstream tilt will improve the contact that your boat has with that green water. If the foam pile is big, you may have to add a bit of a side-slip to the ferry. This fits well with the strokes you're using to steer the ferry and stay balanced on the foam pile.

Ferrying onside–draw

Using a static draw to ferry toward your onside will give you constant sideways pressure. Start with the shaft vertical and the blade out from your hip. Your blade will be in the solid green water under the foam pile. To increase the ferrying angle and come up the wave, move the blade forward. To close the angle or to avoid falling off the wave, move the blade back into a bit of a sweep and lean forward slightly. The mechanics of this stroke are the same as if you were side-slipping with forward motion on flatwater. Tilt to your onside.

Ferrying offside–cross-draw

You can use either a cross-draw or stern pry to ferry toward your offside. The cross-draw has a stronger side-slipping action than the stern pry. For the cross-draw, rotate your torso a lot so your shaft can be vertical straight out from your offside hip. To increase the ferrying angle and come up the wave, move the grip hand back and the blade forward. To close the angle or to avoid falling off the wave, move the grip hand forward and the blade back. This is getting close to the position for a cross-forward sweep. Tilt to your offside. For ferrying to my offside, I prefer the cross-draw to the stern pry. I feel I have more subtle control of the angle with it and when I get to the end of the foam pile I'm already in position to continue the ferry with cross-forward strokes or to turn downstream with a cross-bow draw.

Ferrying offside–stern pry

You can also use the stern pry to control the angle while ferrying to the offside. To increase the ferrying angle, reduce the pressure on the stern pry. To decrease the ferrying angle, apply more pressure on the stern pry. Tilt to your offside. So far you're just controlling the ferrying angle with the stern pry. This will move you sideways as long as the foam pile is small and you're getting good contact with the green water. To increase the side-slipping effect with the pry, you need to get the paddle shaft more vertical and against the hull of the boat near your hip. This move is difficult, because to adjust the ferry angle, you need to move the blade forward and backward. It's hard to make those subtle adjustments while you hold the shaft against the hull under pressure.

Back-shredding

I find back-shredding to be fairly hit-and-miss. But it's worth experimenting; it will only help your back-surfing and 360s.

What's next?

Shredding will work on a breaking wave or hole of any dimension—from six inches to bus size. The flatter the gradient downstream, the wider the peak and the easier it will be to find the balance point. You can use it to set up for an ender or to lead into a side-surf or 360. In fact, I've often used it to avoid some nasty spots on a river or creek. This move also works on a smooth wave. However, you'll fall off the wave more often and spark the casual spectator comment, "That boater just can't stay on the wave."

365

366

367

368

Hole Riding

369 Dropping in from upstream. Rodeo hole, Petawawa River, Ontario.

Dropping in from upstream Little instruction is needed for you to ferry out above a hole and then let the current carry you in. The drawback is that you'll be stuck in a side-surf position right away. Better to put some thought into how you drop in, so you can keep your options open. One way is to drop in sideways but let the hole turn the boat so you can set up for a maneuver. Another is to approach the hole sideways with forward speed (photo 369). This momentum will determine where you'll end up: on top of the hole, near the shoulder or in the center. Contact the hole with the front two-thirds of the boat. The foam pile will stop the bow, while the downstream current pushes the stern around. Not enough boat hitting the hole will turn you upstream but leave you sitting on the shoulder of the hole too far downstream. On the other extreme, if the whole boat contacts the foam pile, the boat won't pivot and will end up side-surfing. The Petawawa Rodeo uses the hole pictured here. It pulses a bit, making it hard to gauge how much boat to stick into the foam pile. Even after a couple of hours of practice, I still caught the hole only four out of five runs–good enough for third place but not good enough to beat Mark. Some things never change.

Entering from the side   The smoothest way to begin your hole ride is to enter from the side. There is a transition from riding on the shoulder of the hole to sliding into the meat of the hole. You can spend this time sizing up the hole.

Approach the hole on a front ferry (see photo 370). Aim for the face of the hole. You want the front two-thirds of your boat to catch the foam pile. This will cause your boat to turn upstream. The amount of speed you carry into the hole will dictate whether you cross the face and exit the far side or settle in for an extended side-surf. You can adjust your momentum with forward or braking strokes, but it's easier if you anticipate how much lateral speed you will need.

Entering from downstream   Consider this approach if the edge of the hole nearest the access eddy is ugly. Ferry across just downstream of the boil line, then pour on the power to cross the boil line and slide into the hole. Sometimes the hole may create a mid-stream eddy that you can ferry out to. This allows you more time to landmark your position before you drop in. Once you leave the relative calm behind the hole and cross the boil line, don't loiter. The foam pile will likely be sliding you subtly to the left or right, making you miss your target area. Compensate for this before you cross the boil line, since working against this current as you drop into the hole is very difficult.

370 Entering from the side.

371

Some paddlers become comfortable with a small hole and then experiment with progressively larger holes. That's me. Other paddlers jump right into a meaty hole, get thrashed and figure that's the worst it can get so let's do it again. That's Mark's approach. The next paddler may have the same experience and promptly vow to take up golf.

To advance your hole-riding skills, you must become accustomed to letting the hole lead. You're using the hole to perform maneuvers, but you will at times be just along for the ride.

Being able to maneuver in a hole will open up all kinds of new lines down a rapid. Riding a hole can allow you to traverse a rapid where the current would be too strong for a front ferry. Some holes make excellent eddies and smaller ones can assist you in pivoting your boat. So find a hole where you feel comfortable–or shall I say just a little uncomfortable–and try the techniques covered in the next few pages.

You can do the moves that follow in slab or pour-over holes and, with a little more difficulty, on curling waves. The moves will be helpful whenever you find yourself in a hole–whether you're trying to rack up points in a rodeo or you've inadvertently dropped into one and you just want to get out of it. These moves, along with shredding the foam pile, will help you set up for vertical moves.

Side-surfing

Side-surfing is a stationary position down in the deepest part of the hole or curling wave. Your boat is perpendicular to the current, with the foam pile pushing upstream against the side of your boat, while the smooth green water pushes downstream on the bottom of the boat. Those two forces often conspire to flip you upstream in a window-shade. Although you can get stable by tilting downstream and by bracing on the downstream side, you'll have more maneuverability by keeping the boat as flat as possible, your body upright and balanced on your knees, and the paddle ready to brace only if you need it (see photo 372). Tilt downstream just enough that the upstream edge won't catch. With a lot of tilt, the foam pile will fill up the boat more quickly and the edges will dig in and prevent the ends from releasing as easily into a spin. When you're comfortable with this, get rid of your paddle. You'll become much more conscious of your body position and balance. If you still haven't window-shaded, it's time to try something different.

Moving back and forth

When you're on the downstream side, you can ride back and forth along the hole by doing forward or back strokes. If your paddle is on the upstream side, rotate your torso past the cross-forward position to a cross high brace, with the blade out to the side (power face down) as shown in photo 373. A cross-draw that starts as far back as possible will move you backward and a cross-forward sweep will move you forward. Instead of a cross-brace, you can do a low brace on the upstream side (see photo 374). Keep the same tilt; that is, as flat as possible, with a slight downstream tilt to avoid catching the upstream edge on the green water. Use the low-brace position but keep the blade behind you and close to the hull, instead of out to the side. Lift the upstream edge of the blade so that it stays on the surface of the green water. The advantage over a cross-brace is that you're in a less awkward body position so that the tilt is easier to control with your knees, and instead of resting your paddle on the turbulent aerated water of the foam pile, you're bracing on the solid, predictable, green water. However, there is a tendency to tilt upstream and, most important, you have fewer options for moving the boat from this position–you can only back up.

Exiting the hole

When you want to leave the hole, choose the end of the hole that is the weakest, or is angled downstream, or has a strong downstream current beside the hole. Head along the hole with speed, burst out the end and grab the downstream current with your paddle.

372 Onside surf.

373 Offside surf.

374 Upstream surf.

Hole Riding

Flat spins in the hole

You can start your spin either from a static side-surf position or a dynamic position just on top of the foam pile (photo 375). You'll be using a tongue of downstream water beside the hole to help turn the boat. Sometimes you'll find a strong enough tongue of water in the middle of the hole, but the corners are the easier spin locations. You can spin either way and initiate with the bow or the stern.

Spinning toward your offside In photo 376, the spin is toward the offside, leading with the bow. Use a slight downstream tilt. Use a cross-draw to initiate the turn (see photo 377). Turn your head in the direction you're spinning to help shoulder and torso rotation. You will also be moving the boat sideways back onto the foam pile and off the tongue (see photo 378). With the cross-draw, you can add a little backward motion if you're starting to flush downstream and off the peak of the foam pile. If the hole is strong, gravity will pull you upstream and into the trough of the hole. You want to keep your center of gravity up near the peak of the foam pile so the stern won't pearl as you spin. You can switch to a forward stroke, with the power face angled away from the boat and the shaft prying against the gunwale, as you would in a back-surf. This stroke will also turn the

boat and move you laterally back onto the foam pile (photo 379).

Soon after the boat is parallel to the current, you'll need to change the tilt of the boat. Wait until the end has cleared the green water, even if you're past parallel. Be sure to change the tilt before the green water hits the upstream edge of the boat. After the end has cleared, use the momentum and keep the spin going (see photo 380). If you hesitate at this point, the boat will settle into a side-surf and you'll have to start over at initiating the spin. Use the gravity pulling the boat down the foam pile and a stern draw to get the stern going in the direction of the spin. This stroke serves the same purpose as the cross-draw in the first half of the offside spin. If gravity is pulling you upstream into the trough, adjust the stroke into the beginning of a compound backstroke, then switch to a cross-draw. Rotate more and open up the angle of the cross-draw for a greater backward effect. This mirrors the forward stroke in the first half of the offside spin. Change the tilt when your bow has cleared and you'll be into the second 360-degree spin. Adjust it to a cross-forward if you need to move forward to the spinning tongue, then cross-draw to help the current spin the boat. The mechanics of the offside spin are very similar to cartwheeling but on a horizontal rather than a vertical plane.

Onside spin When you're spinning toward your onside, a forward stroke will take you to the tongue. Use a back draw to help the spin and pull the bow back onto the foam pile. Because the back draw is not as strong as the cross-draw used in the offside spin, you'll have to consciously draw hard enough to get back on the foam pile. If you're falling off the foam pile, lean back and add a little backward motion to the back draw. If the hole is strong and you're starting down the foam pile into the hole, adjust the blade angle to a bit of a forward stroke to pull downstream. When the boat is nearly parallel to the current, switch to a cross-forward stroke. You want some prying effect with this stroke, so rotate the power face of the blade away from the boat as you would in a back-surf. Stay on the back-draw longer if you're likely to need upstream motion to avoid blowing off the wave. Once you're past parallel, change the tilt and adjust the cross-forward to a cross-forward brace and you've completed a 180-degree spin. Let the stern go down the foam pile and contact the green water tongue. At this point you can either stay on your offside or switch to an upstream low brace.

Completing the onside spin with offside strokes

From the cross-brace position, you can make a lot of subtle adjustments. For more backward motion to travel to the tongue, move your grip hand back and

375 Flat spins in the hole.

376

377

shovel water toward the bow. When the stern contacts the tongue and the boat starts to spin, a cross-forward sweep will help the spin, move the stern sideways onto the foam pile and provide forward motion if you're falling off the wave. When you get past parallel, switch to a low brace or forward stroke to control your motion toward the tongue and your second 360-degree spin. Now let's back up 180 degrees and try that last half-spin with the upstream low brace.

Completing the onside spin with an upstream low brace

To initiate the second 180 with an upstream low brace, switch from the cross-brace or cross-forward to the upstream low brace when your stern is heading down the foam pile and toward the tongue. When the boat starts to spin, increase the pressure on the brace and make the blade more vertical, with the back face pushing out in a stern pry. This will aggressively spin the boat and lift the stern onto the foam pile. Stay on the low brace until the boat spins past parallel and you're on the downstream side. You've completed the spin and are ready for the next 360 with a forward stroke on the downstream side. The upstream low brace can be effective on holes that have a soft corner (a corner that's hard to stay in). Because it's such a powerful stroke, you can initiate the spin before the stern even reaches the tongue. This means you can stay closer to

the middle of the hole, where the foam pile is stronger. You can also try the upstream brace if you're having trouble getting out of a hole or initiating a spin from a static side-surf.

Some fine points of spins in the hole

Initiating Side-surfing is a static position. If you try to start spinning from down in the trough of the hole, one end will hit the foam pile and the other will hit the green water preventing the spin. From the side-surf position initiate a spin by sticking an end into a green-water tongue. To clear the end that is still in the hole, you have to go farther onto the tongue than you would from the top of the foam pile. That's why it's easier to start from the top of the foam pile or continue a spin without settling into a side-surf. Stay aware of where your center of gravity is on the upstream slope of the foam pile. Try to keep it near the peak. Use the gravity pulling you down the slope to move laterally toward the tongue. Find a rhythm and keep the boat moving. To avoid flushing downstream if there is a strong tongue or a weak hole, emphasize the turning effect to pull the leading end back onto the foam pile. If the hole is strong, get onto the second stroke (the one on the upstream side) as soon as possible. If the foam pile is steep and strong near the tongue, it's even more critical to stay near the peak,

where you'll remain drier and won't get pulled down to a side-surf. Initiate more aggressively with turning strokes, rather than relying on the tongue to turn the boat. In a hole the foam pile is pushing back upstream, but the hull is also in contact with, and being supported by, the green water moving downstream underneath it. That's why you can ferry on the top of a foam pile.

Tilt Use just a slight downstream tilt. As with flat spins on a green wave, the flatter the boat the better it turns.

Body position Generally, you should keep your body position upright, just as in front surfing. If you are teetering on the crest of the foam pile, putting your weight to the upstream end of the boat (by leaning forward or backward) will help to keep you in the hole.

No-paddle 360s Find a hole that is sticky enough to hold you side-surfing but isn't too strong. Do one or two spins with your paddle, and when you have a smooth rhythm going, try it without the paddle. Concentrate on keeping the boat flat and using your body position (weighting the bow or stern) to initiate the spin.

378

379

380

Vertical Moves

381 *Big boat equals big air! Farmer Black's rapid, Ottawa River.*

Getting your boat to go vertical is one of the most exciting moves in whitewater, and even though more difficult or intricate moves exist, your plain old ender in an open boat is one of the best feelings and turns a lot of heads.

Facing upstream, let your boat slide down the upstream side of a breaking wave or hole. Gravity and the water breaking back upstream will push the boat down towards the trough. If everything is just right, the bow will hit the green water at the bottom of the trough and keep going deep. The downstream current will push the bow farther down; the stern releases and the boat rotates to a vertical position. Trapped buoyancy, in the float bags, will lift up the boat in that vertical position—hence the other common term for this move, the *pop-up*. Many difficult and intricate moves start from this vertical position, or "station," so honing the skill needed to get into it will be helpful later on.

Type of boat

If the hole is big enough, you can ender anything, including a 16-foot Prospector. Unfortunately, for ender aficionados, not all of the current and popular open-boat designs are built with verticality in mind. Full, bulbous ends, with lots of rocker and depth, will lift and float when they hit the trough of a wave, rather than allow the end to initiate. Longer boats are more likely to span the crest of the hole and the pillow or wave in front of it. The bow may go down, but it's hard to get the stern to release and go vertical if the center of gravity of the boat is still settled in the crest of the foam pile. You'd expect that boats that ender well would, by definition, be wet for running rivers, but these shorter boats are lighter, and respond more quickly to paddle strokes and weight shift. They are also less likely to span the crests of waves, so the bow of a short boat will lift and go over the wave rather

than through it. Therefore, they can be just as dry as a longer, more rockered and full-ended boat.

If you're looking for a boat that will ender, start under 12 feet and find something without the fullness in the bow of, for instance, the Dagger Rival. The Mohawk Viper 11 (see photo 381) and the Dagger Ocoee were the first open boats to perform consistent, predictable enders in reasonable-sized holes. The narrow ends of Frankie Hubbard's Edge racing designs endered, but the length made them unwieldy. Since the water must contact the deck of the boat, less end depth will initiate an ender sooner. Most open boats have nice deep ends that look reassuringly dry. If you have a boat that has trouble endering, get out the jigsaw and cut the depth at the ends. For example, with an Ocoee just trim a bit if you still want some dryness (two to three inches), or trim a lot if you're using the boat mostly for playing (six inches for a rodeo cut). Even on my creek boat I've cut a moderate amount off the end depth so I can get some vertical performance while retaining sufficient dryness (two inches off the bow and three inches off the stern).

A design opinion

The shorter boats that ender well happen to be boats that are more performance-oriented, with harder chines. These boats are not as forgiving to the less experienced paddler. I hope to soon see a stable and forgiving boat aimed at first-time owners of solo open boats that will ender as easily as the higher-performance designs do. The nine-foot roto-molded designs that are just emerging show promise as boats that will flat spin, perform well in a hole and be forgiving enough for beginner/intermediates.

Dry-land simulation

If any of this section gets you excited, you're going to spend some time in the vertical position or station. That time will go by very quickly and you'll probably think of many things at once. Spending some time in that position without the world going past fast will help when you get on the river. So if you're really bored at the lake, get your friend on the dock to lift the stern of your boat, and put you in the vertical station. After you've read about pirouettes, you can try onside and offside flatwater pirouettes. If you remove your bow float bag, you can wallow around practicing more pirouettes and lots of rolls.

The ender

Choose a hole that isn't too sticky, yet has enough green water going into it to easily push your boat vertical. A nice big eddy beside the hole will make the setup easier and

382 Station practice.

shorten the time you take to empty the boat and try it again. The best and easiest holes to ender from have a wide crest on which it's easy to sit and set up. Look for the sweet spot of the hole–the spot with the best distinction between green water and foam pile. Front-ferry out to the crest or boil line of the hole. Line up parallel to the current. If the hole is diagonal, key off the angle of the green water coming into the hole. Let the foam pile carry you down the upstream side of the hole and keep the momentum of the bow going downward when the bow initiates into the green water. This is the most important point in the ender. Maintain the angle parallel to the current and the deck perpendicular as it contacts the green water. If the angle or tilt is off, the buried end will pop up to the side prematurely. Leaning forward slightly, yet distinctly, as the bow hits the green water helps drive the bow down and release the stern (see photo 383). There is a tendency to overplay the forward lean. Timing is important. Think of a boat on a lake. When you lean forward, the bow bobs–down, then up. If your timing is early, the bow may be rising when you reach the bottom of the trough. Once you've initiated, get back to an upright body position and let the force of the river continue to drive the bow down and the boat vertical. For an ender or pirouette, your aim is to get the boat to a vertical and balanced position or station. You'll end up with your back against the float bag, but think of keeping your body upright and standing on your knees as the boat rotates underneath you to a vertical position.

Location, location, location

You can get enders on breaking waves, very steep standing waves or pour-over eddylines, but the most common and predictable ender spots are holes. The size of the foam pile, the steepness of the upstream side of the foam pile and the distance from the crest to the bottom of the trough are important variables. See River

Morphology for the differences between breaking waves, holes and sticky holes. The ideal location for an ender is a hole with a substantial foam pile and a long, angled slope (say, 30 degrees) on the upstream side of the foam pile. There must be sufficient depth of green water coming into the hole and below the hole or else the bow will hit bottom. Because I don't heed this advice, the most common repair I do to my boat is on the stem near the deck. Some rodeo open boaters attach an impact-resistant skid plate of plastic or even rubber before the damage occurs.

Too little slope on the upstream side will make it difficult to initiate the bow and you'll end up just front surfing. If there isn't enough distance down to the green water from the crest, the bow may initiate, but the stern will be settled in the crest or boil of the hole and won't release. Your boat will end up pearling (the bow will bury), but the boat won't go vertical. The bigger and steeper the foam pile, the more difficult to control the boat on top of the crest and the quicker and more violent the results. Also, the bigger and steeper the foam pile, the more likely you are to remain in the hole after the first ender. This attribute of holes earns them the adjectives of "sticky" and "retentive." These holes or waves are preferred if you are linking a number of vertical moves rather than just hoping for a flashy ender or pirouette before you continue downstream.

383 Ender.

Vertical Moves

Stern ender

The stern ender is identical to the bow ender, except that you enter the hole backward. It is harder because you're probably less used to steering backward and you can't see when the stern initiates. Try one where you have an easy approach. If the sweet spot of the hole is right beside the eddy with an easy eddyline, you can line up in the eddy and slide sideways onto the foam pile. Another approach is to spin on top of the foam pile into a stern ender position. Concentrate on the angle and tilt for the initiation; lean back slightly when you think you're about to hit the green water. Lean forward when the boat starts to go vertical and you've got a stern ender.

Ender to exit a hole

An ender can be a survival move in a creek or river-running situation. If you're side-surfing a big hole and having trouble exiting it, get some lateral movement toward the weakest corner of the hole. Try to move the end of your boat into the green water going past the hole. If you can't use that water to climb out of the hole, use it to initiate a spin. If you can get the end up onto the foam pile, keep the boat parallel to the current and let the boat ender. If you're doing a bow ender, lean back as much as possible. Push backward and downstream if you can keep your paddle in contact with the water (see photo 385). Leaning forward or not leaning back aggressively enough will result in a retentive move (see photo 386). Avoid any rotation, as you want to land upright. With luck you'll be squirted out in the same way that a bar of soap squirts out of your hand.

384 Stern ender.

385 Ender to exit.

386 Ender to retain.

Pirouette

From the vertical station, the boat will rotate on its long axis. A 180-degree pirouette will leave you facing downstream. Although 360-degree pirouettes are much more aesthetic, you take what you can get. Pirouettes past 360 degrees are not uncommon but require lots of rotating momentum, just the right balance and, for me, a bit of luck. You can rotate either to your offside or onside. The angle of the hole or the flow sometimes makes it easier to go in one direction or the other, but your repertoire should include both onside and offside pirouettes. If you're playing at an ender spot and bailing is difficult or time-consuming, don't bother. Although controlling an empty boat for the ender or pirouette setup is easier, you can start an ender or pirouette with a boat full of water.

Onside pirouette   Set up and initiate as you would for an ender. Stand on your knees as you rise to the vertical station (photo 387). For maximum rotation, initiate the rotation before you reach the apex of the vertical station. For an onside pirouette, you'll be doing a back sweep. Reach down to the water and slightly behind you. It's more important to plant the paddle where you'll be balanced and comfortable, rather than reach far back behind you. Keep the blade near the surface and fairly close to the boat. The blade angle can be somewhere between a back-sweep position (vertical) and a low brace (flat). The vertical aspect will give more rotational momentum, while the flat aspect can lift the boat for more height or prolonged verticality.

The stroke is a quick push just as the boat reaches the apex of verticality. Lift the paddle out of the water at the end of the stroke and rotate your head and shoulders toward your onside. This upper-body rotation is very important (photo 388). You also want to stay balanced over the vertical axis (photo 389). If your upper body leans, you'll fall over sideways. For a controlled, upright landing, straighten your upper body when you start to lose the rotation momentum (photo 390). For an onside stern pirouette, do a front sweep as the boat goes vertical in a stern ender. The front sweep will help you keep your balance as well as initiate the pirouette. Lift the blade out of the water and reach your upper body toward your onside to increase the rotation of the pirouette.

387 Onside pirouette.   **388**   **389**   **390**

Vertical Moves

Offside pirouette   Set up and initiate as you would for an ender. As the boat nears the vertical station, reach across your body and plant a cross-draw fairly close to the boat (see photo 392). For maximum rotation, plant your blade perpendicular to the current. Pull on the cross-draw and lift the blade out of the water. As you do so, rotate your head and shoulders toward the pirouette (photo 393). Remember to rotate and stay balanced rather than lean your upper body. Rotating to face the cross-draw starts the rotation and this body position gives you better leverage for a stronger pull than does the back sweep, so there is potential for greater rotation with the offside pirouette. As with the onside pirouette, straighten your upper body to stop the rotation for a controlled landing (see photo 394). If the pirouette is near completion and you're feeling greedy, don't straighten your body but keep reaching with your upper body. As the boat goes past vertical, reach under the boat. With the leading edge of your blade up, push the paddle around in a high-brace position. Once your body is out from under the boat, and before the boat flops over, do a high brace to right the boat. This is a bow screw-up exit.

Wing over

This move will give you one vertical end and keep you in the hole side-surfing on your onside. Set up as you would for an offside bow pirouette (see photo 395.) Reach around and plant the cross-draw, but don't pull on it or lift the blade out of the water. Rotate your upper body, but instead of staying balanced as you would in a pirouette, lean your upper body toward the paddle (see photo 396). This will pull the stern down sideways into the hole, upstream of your planted paddle (see photo 397). Keep holding the cross-draw plant and it will become a high brace on the downstream side of the boat (see photo 398). It's not as flashy or difficult as the pirouette, but it is a retentive, controlled vertical move. Be sure you recognize the difference between the balanced upper-body rotation of the pirouette and the slight lean of this move. Don't let it start bad habits when you revert to the pirouette.

391 Offside pirouette.   **392**   **393**   **394**

395 Wing over.   **396**   **397**   **398**

Wiper

A cool variation of the ender is the wiper. It's like an ender, but it starts with the boat upside down. There is no rotation or pirouette, but the boat finishes right side up. For a bow wiper, set up as you would for a bow ender (see photo 399). When you start to go down the foam pile and just before the end hits the green water, lean back, reach back with your paddle and flip over quickly toward your offside as if doing a back deck roll (see photo 400). It's best to flip to the offside because your paddle won't be in the way to delay you from getting right upside down. The only time you'd flip the other way is if you were near the edge of the hole and flipping offside would put you into the green water going past the hole. Lean back so your body won't catch as much of the downstream current under the boat. When you feel the boat going vertical, push down with your blade to help you balance and get the boat vertical. If you just let the boat land, you'll be parallel to the current and facing downstream. If the hole is retentive enough, you'll land on the foam pile setup to do a back ender. Go for it!

You can also do stern wipers. Set up as you would for a back ender, lean forward and flip to your offside (unless this flips you away from the sweet spot of the hole). There isn't much to do with your paddle but keep leaning forward. If the hole is retentive enough, you'll come up in position to initiate a bow ender.

Loop

A loop is a bow ender that flops you upside down while still in the hole and is followed by a stern wiper. To qualify as a loop, the two moves must be linked without a break in form. The move is a difficult one: when you're upside down after the ender, your upper body is hanging into the green water; this tends to drag you downstream and out of the hole. You need a hole powerful enough to make the boat go past vertical and hold you in the hole upside down.

Set up as you would for an ender. Try to initiate as shallow as possible into the green water tongue. The deeper you go, the more downstream pressure you'll

get from the green water. You can control this by going down the foam pile slowly and leaning forward early and hard. Instead of sitting up as the boat goes vertical in the first ender, thrust your upper body upstream. You want the boat to go past vertical and you want to create upstream momentum. The ender has to go past vertical and land upside down and parallel to the current in the same position in which you would be setting up for an upright ender. Just before the boat lands, tuck your upper body down against the bow float bag. When you're upside down waiting for the wiper, keep your upper body leaning forward and your paddle parallel to the current. You want as little drag as possible. Now it's just a matter of waiting and hoping that the upside-down end will initiate. When it does, get ready to initiate your next vertical move. The loop is not a high-percentage move, especially for longer boats (over 10 feet), but as boat design and techniques advance, it may become as common as the ender or pirouette.

399 Wiper. *400* *401* *402*

Cartwheel

A cartwheel is two vertical ends that are linked without a break in form. Think of it as a flat spin, but with the boat spinning on a vertical plane. With low-volume ends, rodeo kayaks can do controlled multiple cartwheels at any elevation between flat and vertical, or even past vertical. The larger buoyant ends of the open boat are hard to keep under on an angle, so for the most part open-boat cartwheels must be vertical. You'll need a hole that is retentive with a pretty big foam pile. Kayaks can use the corners of the hole, but open boats usually need to use the strongest part of the hole and have the whole boat in the foam pile to avoid flushing out of the hole.

Bow-initiated cartwheel
To keep a blade in the water for stability while each end is vertical, you need to cartwheel to your offside; that is, start the cartwheel with a cross-draw. Set up as if you were going to do an ender, but set up with an angle 5 or 10 degrees toward your onside rather than parallel to the current. With your offside move you'll pull the boat back to parallel the current or just slightly beyond parallel as you go vertical. In an open boat, that angle must be much more subtle than with a rodeo kayak, where the initiation is typically at one o'clock or 11 o'clock; that is, 30 degrees off parallel. The larger buoyant ends of the open boat will resist being pulled or sliced back toward 12 o'clock. As the boat goes vertical, rotate exactly 90 degrees to your offside and lightly plant your blade in the foam pile. The thwarts should be parallel to the current now and your body should be horizontal. Your upper body leaning out of the boat horizontally will counteract the boat's being not quite vertical. This is the most difficult phase of the cartwheel. Keep a light touch on the paddle until the boat has come past vertical. As the bow starts to lift, rotate your head and shoulders upward and around to

the hole, and thrust your offside hip around and down toward the hole. The head and shoulder rotation is critical in initiating the second end of the cartwheel. With some balance and luck, the stern will line up in the hole. The more rotational momentum you've created by leading with your head, shoulders and hips, the better your chances of going vertical, even if the boat position isn't perfect. That is a two-point cartwheel (or two ends).

Stern-initiated cartwheel
Set up as you would for a stern ender. Unlike the cross-draw bow cartwheel, your angle should be parallel to the current. Use an onside high brace near the bow to control the angle and tilt as the stern initiates. Look over your offside shoulder upstream and toward the hole and tilt to your onside. Allow the head rotation to change the boat angle slightly toward your onside. As the stern initiates, push downward on the high brace to help the boat go vertical and then lift the blade out of the water and rotate toward your offside. The key is to get off the brace quickly and get your head, shoulders and paddle rotating ahead of the bow. After the stern is initiated, you can use a lot of tilt (up to 90 degrees). This means that your head, shoulders and paddle will be rotating skyward and then upstream and toward the hole. Since your head and paddle rotation is leading the boat, you will be able to plant the paddle in a cross-bow position before the bow comes down. Plant the cross-bow beside your boat rather than upstream of it. Make sure your blade is grabbing the greenwater under the foam pile. The paddle will help stabilize you and help pull the bow through the vertical station. If all is going well, the stern will still be parallel to the current and falling back toward the hole. The cross-draw will have pulled through to a high brace just downstream of the boat. Now you're back to the starting point except that the boat is tilted on its side

and you already have rotational momentum. As the stern initiates, get a last push on the high brace, then rotate your head, shoulders and paddle to your offside. Keep going until you get dizzy.

At this point you're on your own. I linked a three-point cartwheel in a shortened Ocoee during a training session for the 1995 World Championships and I don't think I even got two ends during that competition. With newer boat designs and improved skill levels, these moves may become more common. You may find it easier to learn the cartwheel in a decked boat. With less volume, balance is easier since you're not as high out of the water. Paul won't condone this, so as soon as you've got the basics, transfer these skills to the open boat.

Splitwheels

Splitwheels and cartwheels are very difficult and rare moves for open boats. A splitwheel is a directional change in between the vertical ends of a cartwheel. During a cartwheel your body stays in pretty much the same position while the boat spins vertically end to end. In a splitwheel your head will be closest to, for instance, the right shore as the first end goes vertical. Between the first and second end you rotate the boat on its long axis and end up with your head closest to the left shore. You can initiate this move on either the bow or the stern.

Bow-initiated splitwheel
Set up as you would for an onside pirouette. Go vertical and initiate the pirouette. Reach farther back than you normally would for a pirouette and keep the blade in the water rather than lifting it out. Rotate your head and shoulders toward your onside. Just before you reach 180 degrees of rotation, lean back to flatten out the boat. The objective, is to land the boat upright on the foam pile with the stern going down the foam pile to initiate the second end. Your blade can stay in the water throughout

the back sweep and now controls the boat as the stern initiates. Continue the move as you would for the stern ender or if you're still balanced and thinking ahead, try a stern-initiated cartwheel.

Stern-initiated splitwheel Initiate with the stern, tilt toward your onside and put out a low brace. Keep the brace loaded, or near the surface, with the blade angled behind you (upstream) so you're ready to do a back sweep as the boat goes vertical. Look behind you over your offside shoulder to see when you will initiate and to get your body in the proper position–balanced over your boat. As the boat goes vertical, do a back sweep, rotate your head and look for the water over your other shoulder (the onside shoulder); sit up to keep balanced over the boat. Get your blade off the back sweep quickly and follow your head as it rotates around on the upstream side of the vertical boat. As soon as you're on the other side of the boat, get your blade onto a low brace. You should be in a position to get an onside bow end. Use the brace to stabilize yourself and drive the bow down to a vertical position. To be considered a splitwheel in rodeo scoring, at least one of the ends must be considered vertical; that is, between 70 degrees and 130 degrees. One of the ends can be off vertical (20 to 70 degrees elevated).

Miscellaneous Moves

Here are a few moves that may prove useful or are simply fun to do.

Rock 360s

Paddle downstream toward a rock that is just out of the water. Drive the boat up onto the rock so that the pivot point (directly under your body) is directly over the rock and the rest of the boat is out of the water and not touching the rock. Just as you arrive and

before you come to a stop, do an aggressive back sweep. If you didn't make it completely out of the water, keep the boat flat so the current won't grab the upstream edge. Your objective is to spin all the way around. Before your momentum stops, lean forward and slide off the downstream side of the rock. The ideal kind of rock for this is smooth, slippery and rounded, and sticks out of the water only a few inches. The upstream and downstream side should be sloped. You could use a front sweep, but that doesn't provide as much spinning motion. You can also use a sloping rock on the shore. Drive onto shore as if you were doing an eddy turn, back sweep, then lean forward when you're facing the water again. You can do this, as well, while you are traveling down a slide. It is, however, preferable to hit the water facing forward. While you're spinning, hold your paddle in the air and do an offside gunwale grab, and you'll be stylin'.

Rock a baby

When you're in a big hole side-surfing, try bouncing your weight forward and backward. Keep the upstream edge lifted just slightly so you won't window-shade. When you lean back, the weighted stern digs into the green water and gets pushed down farther, the buoyancy takes over and the stern pops to the surface. As it does, bounce the bow down and you'll be doing a Rock a Baby. I've sometimes had one end go up as much as 45 degrees.

Cross-over

For Paul and I, the edict "weekday rules" at our local surfing wave in Ottawa means we don't have time to park out on the wave for a perma-front-surf. We allow ourselves to back-surf, spin on a breaking part of the wave or do cross-overs. For cross-overs you need a big smooth surfing wave and another boater. As you and

the other boater surf toward each other, one person stays low on the wave, while the other person stays high. It's best if both boats are ferrying, rather than one boat being stationary. The low paddler leans back to get his or her boat down low on the wave. The paddler high on the wave should try to balance on the crest of the wave or shred the top of the wave. Since the high paddler's bow is up off the water because he or she is shredding and the low paddler's stern is weighted and deep in the water from him or her leaning back, the high paddler can cross right over the low paddler's back deck. I don't just mean close. When I'm the high paddler, I aim my bow at the back of the low paddler's head. The person needs to sit up as I go across the back deck. There is definite contact between the two boats, but as long as you're both on big angles you will pass quickly and manage to straighten out your boat. When you've mastered this, you can try it with one boat backward. It's easier with the low boat back-surfing and the high boat front-surfing.

Rocket moves

Instead of floating down big standing waves, you can try boofing off the peaks. You get a more dramatic ride, and as long as the wave length is long and the peak smooth, you can stay pretty dry. I've never seen an open boat get totally airborne this way, but that's what you should visualize. You'll get more air if you cross the grain and go off the shoulder of the wave. You can go off either side, but for righties, it's simplest to go off the right shoulder, since his or her boat will be deflected upward by the peak of the wave. This force is counteracted by a strong onside forward stroke. Treat the launch into orbit as you would a boof.

River-Running Skills

If it's worth trying once it's worth trying twice

Cruising down a river, trying to make difficult ferrys and catching all the surfing waves and eddies, is a real blast. You and your friends can take turns scoping out the next "impossible" move. If you actually do make the move there's a good round of cheering, and if you blow the move everyone shrugs and assumes it wasn't really possible anyway. Much can be learned by trying difficult moves that offer a small chance of success. But you'll learn even more by trying that "impossible" move repeatedly. At the same time, make the most of every move. Have a plan, concentrate and put as much energy into the move as you think it will require to succeed. To stay focused on succeeding, try pretending that there's a waterfall located 10 feet downstream. Psychologically, this is good practice for when there actually is a waterfall just downstream.

If this sounds a little like work, consider this: if you're in shape, you'll get a lot more out of a day of paddling. Of course, paddling with this kind of intensity is a great way to get in shape. For competing athletes, being in shape so you can train hard is just as important as being in shape for the actual competition.

The really tough moves usually involve boat control, precise power strokes, timing and reading the water to make the move even possible. With so many factors at play, trying a move once and failing only tells you it's a tough move. You won't have learned much about your skills and weaknesses. Incidentally, giving it one more try may mean anywhere from two to five more tries. It's like surfing, where "one more surf" means one more good surf. You can't quit on a bad surf, and if you had a great move you'll be so wired you have to repeat the performance. This explains why paddlers are never off the river when they said they would be.

The Unknown

A new river has a certain allure. This mystique drew three of us in to driving around looking for some intense whitewater on the Quyon River in Quebec. No one had actually told us about any rapids, but by studying a Quebec road map, we determined that the river must have good gradient. After all, a waterfall and a rapid named Ragged Chute were on the map, so there had to be more stuff upstream. Several hours later we found what looked like the Quyon's headwaters. We asked a local what lay downstream. He painted a foreboding picture: "Oh, it's bad down there, real dangerous. You can't see 'em comin' and the current's really strong. Back a couple years ago, two guys almost drowned. Yup, ran right into a deadhead before they even saw it. Deadheads everywhere." We thanked him, then drove a mile or two away before tumbling out of the car in laughter. Deadheads are logs with one end resting on the bottom and one end at the surface. They usually come to rest in slow current moving over shallow water. He was right. Real dangerous to a motorboat. Now, any time the flatwater gets a little tedious, just mentioning the deadhead episode brightens our day.

Please note our other discovery: that a provincial road map is a lousy source of information about a river; the deadheads were the highlight of that day.

403 A real sweet boof when it counts.

404 Approach, launch and land. Bagging verticality.

The Boof

You use the boof to run waterfalls, ledges and rock pillows. If you can go off a drop and land flat on the water, you'll stay dry, be able to land in shallow water and will have propelled yourself away from the obstacle causing the drop. On top of that it is a cool move. The name comes from the sound of a flat landing. The ideal place to learn is a four- to eight-foot straight drop with a straight, deep approach and big deep pool below.

Sunshine on the Green

I ran the Narrows of the Green River in North Carolina for three consecutive days one November. Most of the rapids were pretty challenging, but I was led down the river by Scott Sullivan, Beau Bethel and the Kern brothers, who knew the river well. Although a lot of the lines on it are very tight, with consequences if you screw up, the river is beautiful, with some very aesthetic lines requiring classy, totally committed moves. Sunshine is one such place. It can be a dangerous rapid, and some near-fatal injuries to expert paddlers have occurred there.

At Sunshine, there is a drop of about 20 feet onto a jumbled rock pile, with another eight-foot broken ledge directly below it. At the bottom of the big drop is an eddy on the right. You must get into the eddy. The required move into this eddy is a boof; not just close to the eddy or onto the eddy line, but *into* the eddy. The approach is fairly straight, with a slight curve to the right. You need to either scrub-boof (we'll explain this move shortly) or boof off the outside vein of water with a very wide angle and a lot of speed. There is an eddy 20 feet above the drop on river left and a tiny curling wave just above the drop most of the way across the narrow river. The common line is to come out of the eddy low, catch a bit of the curling wave and

ferry with a wide angle and a forward sweep on the left, then open up the angle with a duffek on the left and take a strong boof stroke on the left. I paddle right. A lefty or a kayaker can get the last stroke out on the lip and in deep water, but I was forced to have my boof stroke earlier and on the inside, where the water is shallow. (I didn't think I could get enough power from the shorter offside boof stroke, and with a dicey landing area, I wanted more control of the tilt than I would have had in that awkward position.)

The first day I ran it, my paddle blade was delaminated from a mishap upstream, so I was missing a bit of power. Instead of taking the eddy on the left, I decided to go direct, with a large inside-curving charc, reasoning that I needed the extra approach distance to develop speed. I may not have had sufficient speed anyway, but I lost a bit of it opening up the angle as I approached the boof stroke. I made it onto the eddyline, but that wasn't far enough. The water pushed my stern down and pinned my boat to the bottom. My bow was in the eddy and I tried to shake and pull myself forward into the eddy, but nothing was moving. I bailed and was flushed down the broken ledge—luckily, with just a few bruises.

The next day I started from the eddy on the left. I decided to come out of the eddy aggressively on a wide angle above the curling wave. I crossed the grain quickly but reached the other side too early, had to turn downstream to get to the drop, then close the angle up again. This killed my speed, and although I got as good a boof stroke in as possible and came off the drop fairly flat, without the speed I needed I landed on the eddyline. I bottom-pinned again, bailed out and swam down the now-familiar broken ledge. To have made the run successfully, I should have come out of the bottom of the eddy, dropped onto the curling wave on my offside at the very lip of the drop, taken a

cross-forward stroke to cross the river with a wide angle and then gone to my right for an onside boof stroke. Unfortunately, the next day I blew out my bottom thigh straps pitoning the drop upstream at Gorilla. My upper straps were enough to run the rest of the river, but I didn't want to try this difficult move without the lower straps. This is one of the coolest boofs that I've attempted. It is a sweet line that requires timing and commitment.

Approach and choosing a line The line you take will vary at each drop, depending on the obstacles and water depth above and below the drop, the angle of the current in relation to the lip of the drop (not always perpendicular) and the height of the drop. When you're boofing a drop, look for the area of the drop with the steepest and most abrupt lip. You'll also want enough water to avoid grinding to a halt at the lip.

Angle at the lip of the drop If you have a nice deep launch (by "deep" I mean enough to float the boat and plant your paddle), a straight approach and a clean landing, it is easiest to boof perpendicular to the lip of the drop. In a shallow boof spot, getting outward momentum with your boof stroke may be more difficult. If you go off the lip of a drop at an angle (rather than perpendicular), your center of gravity

doesn't have to get as far out from the lip before the stern clears the lip and it will be easier to land the boat flat (photo 410). However, it is a little harder to keep the tilt flat when you're boofing on an angle (photo 409). Photos 405 to 407 show a more perpendicular approach. Notice how the bow drops a bit more than in the second series, where the angle is greater. Also, if you are crossing the grain of the current, rather than going parallel with it, you'll have less inertia to overcome and it will be easier to release the boat from the falling water and lift the bow. The line of the approach and landing and the turning momentum are factors in determining the angle going off the drop. The current may not be going off the drop at a 90-degree angle, as is the case in these photos, and there may be obstructions to avoid. For boofs over 20 feet you may want to consider that aerated water will

absorb the shock of a flat landing better than the solid green water of an eddy.

Turning momentum at the drop Because the boof stroke is a long, powerful, forward stroke without a corrective pry, it will normally have a dramatic turning effect—even more than on flatwater, since there will be less boat in the water. This can be particularly useful in shallow or difficult approaches where you need to change the angle at the lip of the drop to clear your stern (photo 411). If you need to maintain a straight line from your approach or be angled toward your onside, you can counteract the turning effect to your offside of the last stroke by approaching with an arc toward your paddling side to create inside turning momentum, just as you would for the forward stroke without correction. More speed in the approach will also help maintain a straight line or turning momentum to your onside.

405 Straight off the lip.

406

407

408 Angled off the lip.

409

410

Boofing

411 The boof stroke.

The boof stroke

The most important part of the boof is the last stroke. Timing and power are critical. Delay that stroke as long as possible and plant the blade where you'll get the last possible grip on something solid (either water or rock) before starting the downward free fall. Visualize the plant on the vertical face of water with your blade below the lip. Where the water curves over the lip of the drop is where the water is more vertical than horizontal. It is surprising how effective a late boof stroke is and how ineffective an early boof stroke is. With the stroke, think about pulling your boat forward to the lip. Thrust your hips and boat forward as if you were going to take flight. At the point where the water is still supporting all of your weight and gravity takes

over, you want to leave with lifting momentum on your bow to keep the boat flat, and with forward momentum to propel the boat outward from the drop. You now plunge downward and land flat on the water below with an audible *boof*. Without this lifting momentum in the bow, the boat will stay connected to the falling water and "pencil" into the surface; that is, pierce the water in a vertical position, still in contact with, or close to, the falling water. We used to think that speed in the approach was critical. It certainly makes it easier to develop that outward and lifting momentum for the final stroke, but shorter and lighter boats and a powerful boof stroke allow you to boof drops that have shallow or tricky approaches.

Tilt

As you thrust your hips forward and leave the edge, it is critical to control the tilt of the boat. You may or may not have a slight onside tilt when you plant the paddle, but your knees and hips should be driving the boat to a flat tilt at the end of the stroke. The usual tendency is to allow the boat to tilt toward the paddle side. There isn't much you can do about the tilt when you're in the air and on high drops; that tilt will continue to rotate and you'll land on your side or on a low brace. (For every action there is an equal and opposite reaction.) In shallow water this can be hard on knuckles, shoulders or paddles.

Boofing vs penciling

The water and your boat will absorb a lot of the impact of a flat landing (see Outfitting), but you may not want to land totally flat at heights much over 20 feet (due to the risk of spinal compression). You may want to let the bow penetrate the surface of the water, at which point the rocker will return the bow to the surface. You'll end up taking on a bit more water, but

with less stress on your body. While a vertical entry leaves you susceptible to hitting rocks beneath the surface or popping up backward into the falls, hitting the water at a 45-degree angle will absorb some of the shock and allow you to maintain control and get you away from the drop. Plant the last stroke at the lip as you would for boofing and pull as you would for a forward stroke, but make it a shorter stroke and keep your weight forward. This will carry you out past the lip without creating the lifting momentum on the bow that will result in a flat landing. The shorter the stroke, the more vertical your entry will be. The higher the drop, the more vertical your entry should be. Gauging how much hip thrust to use to achieve a certain angle is difficult. A clean 15- to 20-footer is a good place to practice this since you'll have time to see what is happening to the boat on the way down, but a really flat landing is still manageable. The depth of water you need depends mostly on the angle (boat to surface) but also on how aerated the water is and the height you've dropped. From 20 feet, you may draw only 3 to 4 feet of water with a 45-degree entry or less than a foot with a flat boof. A flat boof will still keep you drier and require less depth at the landing and is more aesthetic, but learning to control the angle at which you hit the water is a useful skill.

If you know that the landing is deep and the falling water is a steep-angled ramp more than a straight drop, forget the boof stroke and hip thrust and ride the tongue and lean back as it plunges into the pool below. You may even completely disappear below the surface to dramatically resurface downstream. Plunging below the surface is kind of cool but popping back up as the buoyancy takes over is even better. Be very sure that the hole at the bottom isn't powerful enough to stop and hammer you.

Other useful boofs

As well as ledges or waterfalls, you can boof off rock pillows sticking only a few inches up in the air. In addition to making an easy section of water interesting, boofing into the eddy behind the rock may avoid some wet standing waves in the current (see photo 412). Try aiming at the shoulder of the pillow on an angle toward it. Having your paddle on the upstream side of the boat so that the turning effect of your boof stroke will land you parallel to the current downstream of the rock works best. Another type of boof is executed from a raised vein of water or ramp dropping past an eddy. If you are crossing the grain, you can boof off this current into the eddy. You'll probably land on an angle to the eddy current, so correct your tilt accordingly as you land. This move is often used in conjunction with a dive.

Scrub boof   You will sometimes encounter a drop where the water falls onto some rocks or into a hole, or somewhere that you just don't want to be. You can sometimes boof with speed and a large angle to land in the eddy or away from the hazard. If the lip of rock beside the water is smooth and rounded, you can often drive your bow out of the water and onto the shoulder of the rock to completely avoid the current

in the landing area. We call this a *scrub boof*. Essentially, you will be boofing off the rocks to the side of the flow of water. This move is easiest to make with the paddle on the downstream side of the drop (for right-handed paddlers that would be angled left). Contact with the rock will slow the descent of the bow, while contact with the falling water will take the stern down so you can get a really flat landing. You want to lightly contact and slide off the rock. If you hit the rock too high (where it's more horizontal than vertical), you risk grounding out, spinning and penciling backward into the hazards you were trying to avoid—a cheery thought. Contact with the rock will want to roll the boat away from the rock. A slight tilt toward the rock will counteract this and help the boat to slide off the rock. Too much contact with the rock or snagging on an uneven surface and you might catch an edge and flip in midair. The best line of approach is to cross the grain from the other side of the river with speed. This will make it easier to slide on the rock and maintain your forward momentum to get as far into the eddy as possible. Starting on the same side of the river as you will be boofing will require you to turn more at the lip of the drop, which will reduce your forward momentum.

Scrub and slide   Limiting yourself to paddling only lines that actually have water will restrict the number of options available in a rapid. Using a scrub boof to leave the water and slide down the backside of a rock results in a really dry boat and avoids obstacles. Photo 414 shows that you can slide down the sloping rock to miss the rock in the foreground. Visualizing your intended route, including the part without water, will help convince you to hit your launch target aggressively. The old saying, "Look where you want to go, not at the obstacle," holds true here. Generating speed in little or no water is difficult. This makes it important to have a good arc to paddle against during your approach. Once you're sliding, controlling the boat's angle may be possible by dragging your paddle, but you must establish the angle before leaving the water. Using scrub boofs to slide down rocks and land in an eddy is my favorite river-running trick.

Offside boof   The boof stroke on your offside is awkward, a lot less powerful and, most important, can make it difficult to control the tilt with your knees and hips. In most cases, it's still best to stay onside.

412   Boofs keep you dry.

413   Scrub boof.

414   Scrub and slide.

How to Hit Rocks

In three words, hit 'em hard. Here's why. Sometimes hitting rocks is unavoidable, either because they are in the way or because they offer the driest line down the rapid. Mark drew the short straw, so he got to demonstrate how not to hit a rock in the first series of photos.

Slowing the canoe down, or even freezing when a collision is imminent, is quite natural (photo 415). Natural, but not good. The canoe stops when it contacts the rock, allowing the current to push the stern around so you are now sideways against the rock. If the boat doesn't actually become pinned, it will roll off to one side, dumping you into the water (photo 417).

The alternative is to boof right over the rock. The bonus here is that you'll land in the eddy behind the rock, an ideal position to boat-scout from. To make this work you need speed. Once you realize you need to go over the rock, set an arc to paddle against just as you would for any other maneuver, and paddle! Accelerate toward the rock and plant a boof stroke as your bow contacts (photo 418). This will help to lift the bow so that you skip over the rock. Just because scraping over the rock slows you down, doesn't mean you should stop paddling. Continue to pull yourself up and over the rock before your boat stalls out (photo 419). Control your landing and continue in the direction you were trying to go.

This skill becomes a real asset when you're confronted with a rock-studded rapid but is really only applicable if you're paddling a plastic boat. Staying on line if you had to go around every rock, pillow and hole would be very difficult. By aggressively boofing over them, you can straighten out your route–much the same way a good skier runs a straightish line through moguls.

Coming from a canoe-tripping background, where we treated our cedar canvas or Kevlar canoes like art objects, I was a little disconcerted about dishing out abuse to our new ABS playboats. But I took comfort in the idea that in playboating, boat abuse is not misuse if you're learning something. I'll frown right along with you at the sight of someone mindlessly bouncing off the rocks as he or she wanders down a rapid. But I'll be the first to cheer the paddler who hits those same rocks with a purpose, using them to bounce in the direction he or she wants to go or perhaps just learning how different-shaped rocks affect the canoe. After all, it's better to learn how to go over rocks in an innocent Class 2 rapid than to suddenly find that last-chance eddy guarded by rocks and have no idea how to get over them. Many well-planned lines in difficult rapids involve purposefully hitting or going over rocks.

415 Hitting a rock slowly.

416

417

418 Boofing over the rock.

419

420

River Reading

421

River Reading

Reading the river and choosing a line are essential skills for river running. Being able to predict what will happen to your boat just from looking at the surface of the water is an ongoing educational process. This is even harder when you don't have a good view of the rapids. The first step is to recognize that without a full view, you may be missing some crucial information. Sometimes you can't even tell that your view is obscured. With experience, though, you should be able to pretty accurately predict what the water is doing, even if you can't fully see the rapid.

Garvin's Chute on the middle channel of the Ottawa River is a favorite rapid of mine that is responsible for a few memorable moments. The Dragon's Tongue pictured in photo 422 is one of four channels, each with runnable lines at various water levels. The tongue is long, classy and inviting–so long that you actually have time to enjoy it as you paddle down its smooth contours: that is, if you can ignore the confused eruptions below. The river-right side drops into a fairly massive-breaking wave followed by a hole. The hole is the turbulent and dynamic kind–not like some holes, where you check in and the hole just locks your boat down in its depths until you give up and swim. There's too much happening in this hole. It's more like a blender making margaritas. Like a margarita, this hole has a kick. The left side of the tongue fans out over a granite ledge. Just below is an island with a very sticky hole extending 40 feet out from its upstream end. This hole is the kind I mentioned earlier–the kind that locks your boat down until you give up and swim. It is broken by a tongue near the shore. The island offers the best vantage point for taking photos and for observing what the water is really doing in the Dragon Tongue channel. Because you'd have to portage or run the rapid, paddle over to the island and climb the bluff, most people think only of scouting from there with hindsight. I was one of those people. The rock that defines the left side of the channel offers a good view but is difficult to reach. The small island on river right is the usual scouting spot, and from there you have a good view of the steep wave and the hole on the right.

The first time I ran this channel I was buoyed by Rob McClure's enthusiasm. Advice from our companions ranged from "Don't do it" to "Run the meat." Rob thought the best ride would be to run the meat–the biggest, steepest part of the rapid. I'm not sure of the exact meaning of that term. Vegetarians might interpret it as "inefficient" or "difficult to digest," but I think it means you've got a good chance of ending up as hamburger. Rob's reasoning was that since the wave was green at the bottom of the trough (before exploding into a confused breaking wave), his momentum would get him through it and the hole following. Rob, at 6'3", is a very sturdy and strong guy paddling a big XL-13 solo boat, and I knew from playing hockey with him that the momentum he could develop was not insignificant. However, the wall of water turned out to be too steep to climb. The break rejected him and he finally resurfaced below the hole. The ride down the tongue looked so exhilarating that it may have been worth the trashing at the end. His line at least put him far enough right to avoid the very sticky hole.

I chose a more conservative line. The left side of the tongue is not as steep and extends farther downstream. The conventional line runs far left, where the tongue fans out. The hole created as the water drops off the four- or five-foot ledge is substantial but can be boofed or punched with speed coming off the tongue. That day, I chose a narrow line just to the left of where I am shown in photo 423. I wanted to be right of the ledge but left of the steep wave, where there appeared to be a break in the hole. I thought I'd run down the tongue, then angle slightly right to find the gap between the holes. When I reached the tongue it looked completely different. It fanned out much wider than I'd thought, and instead of there being a break in the hole, the hole was diagonal and quite sticky. Still, my lot was cast, so I charged onward on my planned route. I managed to punch through, narrowly skirting the meatiest part of the hole to my right. After collecting my wits, I found that I was just above the island hole, and barely managed to get around the corner of that lower hole.

I've run that line quite a few times. On several occasions, like the one shown in the photo series below, I've been too far right and have been stopped in the upper hole. We've since named that the Rodeo Line. I've always ended up coming out of the hole in an ender–sometimes back and sometimes forward. Once I traveled the entire length of the hole in what seemed like a split second and was spit out on the river-right side. I've also spent some quality time in the lower hole. While Paul and I were shooting for a television broadcast, I agreed to run Garvin's with a waterproof camera strapped to my bow (something I wouldn't have done with my own camera). I ran the top part of the rapid fine but was too close to the lower island hole when I punched the left tongue. I was pulled into it on my offside. After window-shading a few times and trying to move around on a cross-brace, I finally gave up and swam. That ride yielded some interesting footage.

So, the whole point of this (other than it being an excuse to tell a longwinded story about my summer vacation in Garvin's Chute) is that rapids are not always as they appear. From a low angle off to the side, detecting the direction of flow is difficult. Your subconscious usually reports that the current is running parallel to the shore, but remember some of the fixes that your subconscious has gotten you into. There have certainly been times when I ran rapids that I couldn't see fully from one side of the river, rather than going to the other side of the river to check things out, but I was able to see that there were no hazards and the drop was within my comfort zone. Don't be shy about checking from the other side or portaging to scout from below. That's a lot quicker and safer than a lengthy rescue. I often scout rapids that I know I can make it down, when I want to see if there's a great move to be made.

Sometimes bubbles that float downstream from a hole or wave near the top of the rapid give you a clue to where the current is going and something to landmark on when you get into the rapid. We call them bubble streets. Look for where the water flows out the bottom of the rapid. It won't tell you what's happening in the rapid but can indicate general direction or if the current has split. Look at the surrounding geomorphology (that's rocks). Are there shallow limestone ledges, irregular granite bedrock or undercut sandstone boulders, etc? The rock formations that you can see may continue under the water. Imagine what the forces of the river might have done to the riverbed over its lifetime. Obviously, most of this is educated guessing if you can't get a good view of the water. But it may at least serve to warn you not to trust your assumptions and to be ready to adjust; or, if you're not sure, to shoulder your boat and take the dry line. Watching kayakers and other debris floating down the rapid also helps. However, it's considered bad form to toss in logs, kayaks and such for that purpose.

422 *The rodeo line, Garvin's Chute, Ottawa River.*

423

424

Visualizing

Visualizing is an extremely useful tool for scouting a rapid, remembering the line of a blind move and practicing a difficult move or series of moves.

In scouting a rapid from a vantage point onshore to decide whether to run it, start by mentally drawing the precise line that your boat will follow, then see yourself paddling down the rapid. Your mental image should include placing each stroke throughout the run and anticipating the reaction of the boat to each wave and new current. Try to be honest: if a wave or something pushes you off-line, observe all the gory details. Replay the tape in your mind until either the line looks realistic and you're convinced you can do it, or the run doesn't look feasible, at which point you'll look for a different line or you'll visualize yourself on the portage trail. Watching a few people run the rapid and seeing what actually happens to boaters of various skill level on different lines can be advantageous. But it can also be distracting and misleading if you're not quite sure of their skill level or what line they intended to do.

If you're running a rapid that you can't see top to bottom or with closely linked moves, then visualize the run as you will see it in your boat. This is a little harder, especially if you haven't run the line before. Go upstream a bit and crouch so your view will be more like what it will be when you're in the rapid. Look for prominent features or landmarks that you'll be able to recognize from your boat. Visualize the run again, stroke by stroke, but this time *feel* yourself making each stroke. It helps to orient your body and go through the movements at least with your torso, if not your arms. Now step aside, close your eyes and play the sequence through in your mind. You should be able to see the whole rapid and the line you're taking, and feel each stroke as it will be when you're running the rapid. At a slalom or downriver race or rodeo, you'll see athletes onshore, eyes closed or unfocused, going through body contortions as they visualize the course or moves they will make. This is a highly effective technique. Replaying these moves in your head when you are not actually boating is an effective technique and provides an enjoyable distraction at work.

With practice you can improve your memory for rapids—a very useful skill that some people perhaps have a predilection for. I do not. If you're known to have done a particular river before, people will often ask what the next rapid is like. Before I realized this personal failing I would describe some half-remembered rapid that may or may not have been in the same province. Now I just shake my head, "Haven't a clue," and endure their stares afterward when halfway down the rapid I remember a real cool move or an ugly undercut you have to avoid. On the other hand, Willie Kern has a renowned memory for rapids and can describe most of the rapids (the good ones at least) on a creek he ran once, last year. On a section of the Petite Nation in Quebec, we had scouted a series of five or six rapids, the last of which was a difficult drop. After scouting, we slowly worked our way down to the last drop. It was over an hour and quite a few distractions since we had scouted and when we finally got to the last drop the rest of us got out to set up safety and cameras. When I asked Willie if he was going to have another look before running it he drawled, "I've got all the information I need."

Visualizing can help you figure out and learn those difficult rodeo moves or a series of moves on rapids where you don't have time to stop and think about what to do next. Your body needs to memorize the body positions and movements so that they can be smooth and efficient, just as a musician learns a difficult piece of music by playing it over and over slowly. Go over the move in your head, in slow motion, making sure that you can see and feel the ideal body position throughout the stroke and the rest of the move.

425

426

427

Punching Holes

Novice paddlers tend to shy away from holes—with good reason. The aerated foam pile can fill up an open boat and a strong hole can flip you if you end up in it sideways. Staying dry and staying upright are the interesting challenges of open boating. While even the biggest holes offer sport for the open boater (participant and spectator), at times you don't want to hang around side-surfing, or get filled up. The best strategy then is to give holes a wide berth. This is easy to say, but not always practical. If you're faced with the choice of going through a hole or almost going around it (but not quite), your best strategy is to approach it aggressively and perpendicular, as shown in photo 430. If you try to go around the hole (see photo 428) but don't make it, you'll end up going into it sideways. If you hit the foam pile on an angle or sideways, you're offering quite a bit of your boat to the foam pile that is crashing back upstream. It will turn you sideways and you're in for some quality side-surfing (see photo 429). If you're going to hit the hole, attack the foam pile perpendicularly. Hopefully, your bow will pierce the foam pile. If you've approached with the proper angle to get through the hole but lack forward speed, the aerated water rushing upstream will slow you down and perhaps fill up your boat.

Downstream momentum is the second key ingredient in punching a hole. You can increase that forward momentum by timing your stroke to take a hard pull as the bow strikes the foam pile. Make sure that your blade is down in the green water going underneath the foam pile (see photo 431). With a pourover-type hole, you can also take a boof stroke as the boat clears the pillow above. Even if the drop isn't steep enough to catch air, the stroke will give you increased momentum. Of course, this is entirely the wrong strategy if you want to stop and play—and why would you want to miss an opportunity to practice spins and vertical moves?

428 Trying to avoid the hole.

429

430 Punching the hole.

431

432 Prime creek territory, Upper Tellico River.

Rodeo or play boating is a lot of fun, but you spend a lot of time at the same rapids, looking upstream. In creek boating you're paddling forward and going downstream. In terms of boating moves, there's no legal distinction between creeks and rivers. You may do "creek moves" on the biggest-volume rivers, and sometimes a narrow creek exhibits pushy currents characteristic of rivers. Most people think of creeks as fairly shallow and channelized, with a constant, somewhat steep gradient. On creeks you might encounter waterfalls, slides and slot moves–narrow channels barely big enough for a boat between boulders. Rivers have more volume, standing waves, playspots, boils and, in places, deep water.

Boat scouting

You'll probably do a lot less scouting from shore when you're on a creek–not that you should charge downstream without knowing what's around the bend. While creeking, you often boat-scout or plan your route as you go downstream. If you scout each rapid, you may not have time to finish the run in daylight, and in some long, complicated rapids you may not remember what you scouted anyway. However, you must *always, always, always* have an eddy that you know that you can reach before the next unseen section. Since there may be logs or traffic, this is a good strategy even if you know a creek well. Once you get close to an eddy, you may see a clear path to another one farther downstream so you won't have to stop. If you can't see a safe spot beyond, eddy out; and if you still can't see one from the eddy, get out and scout from shore. Several of us were running a creeky section of the Doncaster River in Quebec and got out to scout when we couldn't see around the corner. An ice bridge blocked the lower part of the rapid. I'm glad we stopped. Many paddlers have similar stories about logs or a paddler stuck in a hole downstream.

Forward momentum

Generally, forward downstream momentum is a good idea on a creek. When the creek is shallow and steep, ferrying and surfing aren't too effective. If you blow it and end up heading for a rock, pretend that that was part of the plan and hit the rock with speed. This will give you a better chance to get around or over it, rather than have the current push you against it from behind. Forward speed helps you boof rocks and drops. Maintaining forward momentum also helps you avoid being treated like debris. River debris collects on the outside of the corners. If you're boat scouting, favor the inside of the bends. It's easy to reach the faster-moving water on the outside of a bend in the creek, but it's hard to move from the outside of the bend to the inside.

Sideslip, or pivot and go

If you're running a rapid with a lot of rocks, you'll find yourself doing a lot of draws and cross-draws to get around them. If just a small adjustment in the line is required, side-slip. If you need to move sideways a lot, pivot the boat and go forward to get around the obstacle. Both these moves require forward motion. To side-slip to your onside, get forward motion and do a draw straight out from your hip. If you start with turning momentum to your offside, open the angle of your blade (rotate the shaft so the leading edge of the blade is out from the hull) and move the blade forward as necessary to keep the boat moving sideways. If you started with turning momentum to your onside, you'll be closing the blade angle and adjusting the blade back (into a stern draw or sweep) to keep the boat moving sideways. If you are side-slipping to your offside and you have onside turning momentum, plant a cross-draw out from your hip, open the blade angle and adjust the blade forward as necessary. With turning momentum to the offside, you can use an offside sweep (it provides more momentum) or an onside stern pry (make sure there's enough water for your blade) to side-slip toward your offside. For pivoting, use a duffek or cross-draw duffek to maintain forward momentum.

Crossing the Grain

Crossing the grain is explained on pages 86 through 89 in the solo classic section. This technique is critical for short playboats. For playboating we generally recommend an aggressive style of maintaining momentum. If you are not actively going somewhere, *anywhere*, then as Jeff Snyder says, "To the river, you're just a piece of debris." Practice always crossing the current (crossing the grain), going where *you* want to go. If you change your mind mid-stream, you will only need to adjust the angle of the boat, your forward momentum will carry you on this new course.

How do you learn the precision required for the tough drops? Well, try searching out tight technical moves without serious consequences. Ideally, there will be some features to slap you around a bit if your line is sloppy, just to keep you honest.

The photos on this page show a rapid named Little Trickle, located on the Ottawa River in Ontario. I spent quite a few years bypassing this rapid before I noticed its possibilities. It looked like it contained a really technically tight line with reasonable consequences. So one sunny day, Mark and I decided that it was time to give it a shot. A friend, Garry, accompanied us to the scouting spot. After studying the rapid briefly, Garry said he was going to run it. Mark and I exchanged glances, both of us thinking, "Oh, good. A probe!" Garry promptly demonstrated that it was possible to slam into the major crux rock and run the rest upside down with only a bruised bum and a torn drysuit to show for it. Armed with this information, Mark went out and ran it clean. After seeing a bad line and a good line, I inadvertently compromised, smacked the rock with my boat and swam the outwash. Ouch! Kinda shallow. Garry still claims that he thought we always ran that rapid and didn't know he was breaking new ground. Since that day, I've run that line more than a dozen times. Making

it clean is never a sure thing, as a broken paddle and the odd dent in the canoe can attest to.

These photo collages illustrate the differing results you get when similar angles are used but the speed of the canoe is increased. The faster a canoe is traveling, the more it will cut across the grain, which translates into being pushed sideways less.

The first sequence shows Mark lining up well (see photo 433). But without enough speed he is also moving sideways down the tongue. To stay aimed at the slot, he's forced to open the angle of the canoe—in other words, to turn more broadside to the current. The current now has more of the side of the canoe to push on, compounding the problem. The split second it takes to correct the angle slows forward momentum and *crunch!* He hits the rock that the water is pillowing off. (We've enhanced the visibility of

the rock so you can see it in the photo.) The impact throws him forward, but by maintaining a low brace, he stays upright and grinds down off the rock. I'm happy to say that in the second photo sequence I fare better. Guessing that Mark's speed was too slow, I really start cranking it from farther upstream. I'm paddling against an arc as I crest the lip, ensuring that all my strokes are power strokes. This brings me closer to the landmark rock on my right (see photo 434). Fortunately I've visualized my route correctly, and my speed carries me into the slot), landing me in the foam pile beside the pillow rock, then straight into the eddy so I can tell Mark all about my great run. One footnote: before you start bragging about your run, make sure you're securely holding your buddy's boat so there's no escape from your glorious, full-color instant verbal replay.

433 Crossing the grain (almost).

In drops like Little Trickle, the key is to visualize your route before you reach the lip. Cresting the lip, you are confronted with some seriously disturbed water. Being able to landmark in a fraction of a second is crucial. Aiming at the slot would allow the water to sweep you into the ugly rock, whereas confidently aiming at the landmark rocks and rooster tails on your right ensures that you will be in the correct position when you do reach the slot.

434 *Crossing the grain.*

435

Iron Ring

By my third trip down the Upper Gauley, West Virginia, I was anticipating the major rapids with some degree of enthusiasm. The mention of rapids with names such as Lost Paddle and Sweets Falls no longer caused an instantaneous urge to pee. The one exception was the notorious rapid called Iron Ring (photo 435). It features sharp rock that loggers in a past era blasted with dynamite to improve the channel. If this is "improved," we can only imagine how challenging it must have been in its natural state. It now boasts a mammoth hole that reportedly hides a table-sized rock that makes the thought of hitting the hole truly ugly. Iron Ring used to be considered a Class-5 rapid and indeed still is, unless you use the technique of crossing the grain.

Let me describe the scene. The water is flowing downstream—no big surprises yet. Most of the river goes through the hole or at least really close to it!

Some does go left of the hole, but all the dynamited rubble should scare everyone off that line. The remainder goes to the right of the hole, offering at least a 25-foot-wide path. No problem, you're thinking. Most paddlers could hit a tongue that wide if they were hand-paddling—which might work if not for the diagonal reactionary waves just upstream. These steep curling waves would like to feed you to the hole, and might if your canoe were pointed downstream. All the vigorous finger pointing and gesturing boils down to being able to cross the river above the hole, skirting two small holes in the process, while maintaining lateral momentum as you drop down the tongue with your bow pointing directly into the right-hand reactionary waves.

After arriving at Iron Ring, I scampered down the left shore to scout. I ruled out the far-left sneak slot partly because I wanted to challenge myself in the meat of the rapid and partly because the scar on my thumb from my last run down that channel two years ago is still visible. I'm pleased to say that I ran the right line perfectly. Good forward speed, just avoiding the landmark holes on my left at the top, then punching the apex of the V still angled right. The whole time I was thinking that I had blown it and was headed for the hole. The rapid was a blur—half the time I was trying to blink water out of my eyes. I did not feel in control.

The next day I did some more schoolin' on my open-boat buddies. Ghyslaine Rioux was the one who caused me to realize that actually ferrying upstream slightly during the approach would slow the action, allowing me to read the water, yet still giving me plenty of lateral motion. Plus I could be sure of avoiding the holes on my left because I could ferry away from them. If you've read my father's book *Path of the Paddle*, then this is probably starting to sound familiar—"slow the descent of the canoe" is a common phrase in the book. If we'd chosen to do a back-ferry, it would have been impossible to generate the forward speed necessary for the latter part of the rapid, plus we would likely have gotten ourselves into an uncontrollable back-surf, since the smaller playboats want to surf everything. A slight front-ferry slows the playboats' descent but maintains some forward speed.

The rapids you'll encounter while playboating have much greater topography than what you'd run during a trip in your classic canoe. This alone necessitates more forward speed to carry you up over the waves.

Sneak Routes

A sneak route is any line down a rapid that avoids the crux of the rapid. This usually makes the rapid easier, although not always. Typically, a sneak route is closer to shore and involves dealing with shallows, slots and possibly trees. The sneak route often requires that once you're over there you may be committed to the sneak route if a portage or return upstream is not feasible. After you sneak past the tough part, you'll rejoin the main current. Are you launching into an eddy or directly above a hole? As well, you will likely be running this route alone, out of sight of your companions. Don't mess up!

The other side of the coin is that sneak routes can offer some really fun creek moves on a big-water river. The best example has to be Pillow Rock on the Gauley River in West Virginia. The usual line is down the middle, threading your way between holes and finishing the run with a big wet smile. The sneak route on river right is a whole different world. It has some micro-eddies, a slot and a mandatory slide down a sloping rock to avoid a pinning rock. If I had never tried the sneak route, I would have missed all that cool stuff.

Photo 436 depicts a sneak route on the Ottawa River at Colliseum. You need to approach a sneak route with the same conviction that you would a creek move. Generate any speed you will need while you still have water to paddle in. Don't be afraid to brace on rock (see photo 437); it beats flipping over. Note the elbow pads as added insurance. When choosing a sneak route, remember that there is no such thing as not enough water.

Slots

Although there may be little room, you still need to be crossing the grain as you enter the slot. This means good forward speed angled in the direction you want to go. It's important to carry speed into the slot to avoid being pushed by the current into ugly places you don't want to be in. A prime example of this is shown in photo 438. Forward speed enables you to cut through this slot without being pushed into the undercut boulders on the left and right. Momentum will also allow you to boof any unseen obstacles such as rocks and pour-overs. Make sure, however, that no trees are lodged in the slot before you commit to going through.

Test yourself

It's a sunny warm day in August—the perfect day to put your newly acquired skills to the test on this major rapid. Scout it, then pencil in your route. Our version of a good line is on page 186, no peeking!

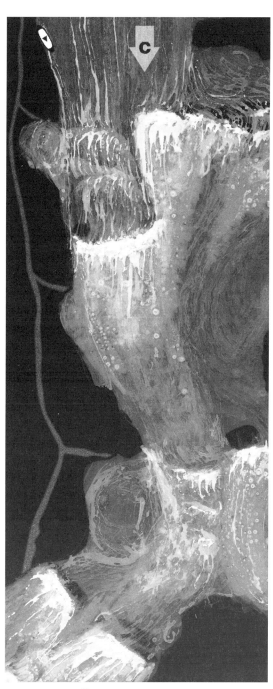
439 *Test yourself.*

436 *Sneak route.*

437

438 *A slot.*

Hair Boating

440 Morilla, Bottom Bottom Moose River, New York.

Hair boating means running rapids with significant consequences if things don't go as planned. Playboating is perhaps the antithesis of hair boating. In playboating, you can try the same hard move over and over until you get it right or get too tired to try it any more. In rodeo paddling, you add the pressure of *having to* perform that difficult move on a run or there are the consequences of not making the finals or not winning the first-prize T-shirt or gold medal. In easy rapids, you can look for hard and aesthetic lines. In hair boating, you have the challenge of a physically difficult move along with the mental pressure of knowing you *have to* make that move. Consider dealing with the fear and adrenaline a skill.

Assessing the risk and the decision-making process in hair boating is different for everyone. If you're taking a long time scouting a potentially dangerous rapid, assess what you're spending your time thinking about. You might be working out the move, but if you are thinking that long about its consequences, it may be a sign that you should shoulder your boat and consider running the rapid another day.

Recognize other factors that may influence your decision. You may be in a rush, and not spend sufficient time scouting; or you may want to run a rapid because it's faster and easier than portaging. There may be pressure from others or yourself because someone else has run the rapid. Hair boating is no place for an ego. No one respects a successful run if your decision to run was a bad one and you just got lucky.

Safety and responsibility

As well as assessing the consequences of missing a move, you must consider safety. Consider the consequences of a rescue and the responsibility that you are placing on members of your group. The decision to run a rapid is yours alone. The decision that you shouldn't run a rapid is partly a group decision.

Mental and physical conditioning

When the consequences are injury or worse, you really want to be sure that you can make the move. Being in shape and paddling regularly are essential to hair boating. You want to be in good physical shape so you can meet the physical demands of a hard move. If you've been boating regularly, all your skills will be honed. Your timing and stroke efficiency will be good and, perhaps most important, your skill in reading the water will be at its peak.

Rewards

The rewards of hair boating are significant. On a practical level, if you're willing to run difficult rapids, you will have more rivers and rapids available to you, with less portaging. Everyone experiences some adrenaline from the power of gravity and water. The possibility of severe consequences adds to the adrenaline flow. Plus, when you're hair boating you're meeting the challenge of mastering skills on several different levels. For some people, these additional skills can make the paddling experience more complete.

The Holtzbox, Inn River, Austria

I should have seen this situation coming. If you ever have the feeling that everything is happening too fast and something is lurking in the shadows, eddy out, pull your boat right out of the water and pretend you're scouting until the bad karma passes. After the '95 Rodeo Worlds, we were paddling with a large group near Landau in Austria. On our first full day of paddling after the competition, we ran a section of the Inn River. At the takeout after a great day, we had the option of running another section, which included the Holtzbox Rapid–likely a portage for most of us. Our group of 40 or so had spread out during the day and traveled at a leisurely pace down the river. I recall Phil Foti giving this last section a miss, saying that it would be busy, crowded and crazy. It was late in the day and the 30 or so who were continuing on to the next section were bunched up and starting to think about dinner and leaving the river. Ahead of me, a number of boaters were starting to walk, but Jeff Richards was just climbing back in his boat and heading downstream.

"Are you going to run it?" I asked. "There's another takeout downstream" he informed me.

The fact that he had stopped to scout the upcoming entrance rapid and that a dozen or so of the world's best rodeo paddlers were portaging from there didn't really register, and off I went in his wake. I went around the next few bends, and by the time I had gathered my wits I had swamped in some big waves and was moving toward a horizon line. A lot of boaters stood onshore looking at the rapid below. Ahead of me, Jeff neatly tucked into an eddy on river left just above the drop. I started to do the ferry to join him but realized that, being full of water, I would have no chance of making the left eddy. I had already passed the last eddy on the right, but to the right of the drop, I spotted two large boulders. Paddling hard, I wallowed over to the boulder just right of the drop and managed to balance my boat against the boulder as the water divided and swept around both ends of the craft. Peering over my shoulder, I could see that the first drop was about 10 or 15 feet, followed by a long rapids that was steep and messy. The boulder was too steep and smooth for me to get out and I wasn't happy where I was, but I really, really didn't want to be going down that drop backward full of water. I wasn't sure my boat would fit in the slot between the two boulders in front of me and I couldn't see what was happening in the bigger channel to the right. It turned out to be a nasty spot with a few logs stuck in it. The narrow slot seemed to be my only choice, so I stuck my bow in the slot between the boulders. It was wide enough for my boat to go down but narrow enough for me to reach both sides with my hands. As the bow descended over the lip, the water poured out. Relieved of the weight of water in the boat, I was able to do an iron-cross kind of thing with my boat attached to me; I managed to push the boat back up and somehow jam it between the rocks so I could get out. I eventually arrived with boat, paddle and myself intact on top of the boulder closest to shore. I waited until someone tossed a line to get my boat to the river-right eddy above, and then, with a rope in my hand, I dove in and swam to safety.

No matter how large or experienced the group is that you are on the river with, if you mess up, you are initially on your own. How quickly your group assists you will depend on their expertise. But never run something counting on assistance. The limiting factor of what you will personally run should be your own intuition of what consequences you will be able to deal with on your own. The possibility of rescue is just insurance.

442

443

Test Yourself: Solution

Of course there are many different ways to get down this rapid, which you may notice bears a striking resemblance to McKoy Rapid on the Ottawa River, Canada. The line we are proposing is the easiest if you can confidently perform the individual moves that you've been practicing.

Loosen up those muscles–here we go.

Start well away from the river-right shore (figure 1). Our objective is the small eddy on river right above a substantial hole. No! Don't look downstream at the hole. Focus on the eddy. Concentrate on hitting the eddy line high and hard. You need good forward speed to break through the reactionary wave guarding the eddy.

Congratulations. By counteracting the boat's tendency to turn on the eddy line, you ended up deep in the eddy, clutching a tree. Pull your canoe out onshore and take a second look at that really big hole, the one you're about to ferry above. When you are back in your boat don't look behind you–the mist

coming off the hole will not help your concentration. Plan B is to punch the center of the hole if you blow the ferry, but put that out of your mind; otherwise, that's exactly what you'll be doing. Leave the eddy with lots of speed and little angle. Okay, don't linger on the wave; keep your lateral momentum going. As you surf off the shoulder of the wave, turn downstream (figure 2). Aim to punch the curling wave coming off the hole on river left. Made it. Now peek at the hole on river right (figure 3). Ease up so that your stern just catches the hole, pivoting the boat for the next move, a ferry back to the river-right shore (figure 4). Take a break in the eddy and enjoy the feeling of being below the hole. The next step is to do an eddy turn directly below your present spot. Don't be lulled into just cruising down the shore; make sure to get out into the current (figure 5) so you can set an angle and develop motion to cross the next eddy line. A strong diagonal wave looks to be guarding it so punch it hard, just as if

you were trying to boof off it. Again, fight the turning effect of the upstream current in the eddy so that you drive far into the eddy (figure 6).

The last stage of this rapid has a big hole on each side with a tongue down the middle. These holes offer some juicy rodeo potential, but on this run we'll just go for the tongue. The trick here is to leave the eddy on a wide ferry angle and stay angled across the current (figure 7) until you drop down to the tongue. This ensures that you won't end up just going with the flow. Since the river is turning so dramatically, it's very difficult to read the currents and boils to line up the tongue farther upstream. When you're on line, turn your boat downstream and paddle. Remember to plant a forward stroke as you hit the apex of the tongue, to pull you through and stabilize the boat.

You made it! Wow, this must be a really good instructional book, eh?

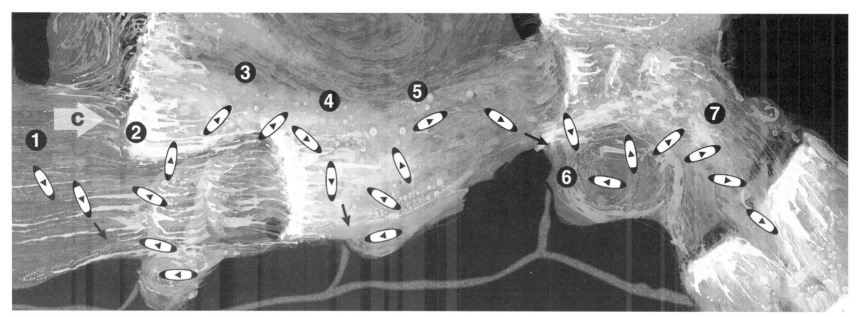

441 The solution.

GLOSSARY

We use nine names describing different kinds of water. So we thought a glossary might not be a bad idea.

Attainment Working your way upstream utilizing eddies. Fish could teach us a thing or two about this.

Attila spinning your paddle around your neck to show off. It has the opposite effect if you drop it.

Back surfing Surfing your canoe with the bow pointed downstream parallel to the current, usually performed on a smooth wave.

Back wash What happens when you drink straight from the bottle with a mouthful of crackers. Or, more relevantly, the water flowing upstream into a hole.

Black attack To resurface from under water with the boat vertical.

Blast To front or back surf with your bow or stern buried under the foam pile.

Boat Canoe, kayaker sit-on-top used primarily for whitewater.

Boof attitude Refers to whether the bow of the canoe is up or down while airborne.

Boof tilt Horizontal plane of the canoe from side to side.

Bottom feeding A static front surfing in the trough of a wave.

Bubble street A line of bubbles leading into a steep drop that you can use as a landmark.

Carve To tilt the boat on edge while turning with forward speed.

Classic canoe A canoe suitable for wilderness canoe camping.

Clean 360s A flat spin that is initiated with one stroke and carried through with body english alone. The next stroke ends the clean portion of the spin.

Correction strokes Strokes that propel the boat forward or backwards but also change its direction of travel.

Cut A static turning stroke in which the paddle blade is placed in the water near the bow but angled at approximately 45 degrees away from the end of the boat. A reverse cut is the same stroke but used by the stern paddler with the paddle pointed towards the back.

Destination paddling Going to a playspot and not running the river.

Ender A vertical move that results from the bow of the boat being submerged in the green water upstream of a hole.

F-150 pick-up truck A tool for straightening gunwales, much bigger than a hammer.

Foam pile The white aerated water on top of a wave or in a hole.

Front surfing Surfing facing upstream, parallel to the current.

Goon stroke What a sloppy pry at the end of a forward stroke used to be called.

Grabby A hole that produces a violent ride caused by the green water catching the upstream chine of the boat.

Green water Undisturbed water usually flowing downstream.

Grip hand The hand that is holding the top end of your paddle.

Gunwale/rail Trim that caps the top of the canoe hull, usually vinyl, aluminum or wood.

Juicy A challenging rapid or move that involves powerful currents and holes.

Landmark A river feature that you can use to determine whether you are on line during your descent of the rapid.

Lid Expensive helmet.

Olie A dynamic front surf during which the whole boat becomes airborne on the face of the wave. The secret is to let the water pile up under your boat then lean forward to quickly release the stern. I've managed this once, by accident.

On it Paddling really well.

Punch a hole To aggressively drive your canoe through the foampile of a hole with the intention of continuing downstream.

Pig To blow off a hole or wave after the opportunity to do the move presented itself but you passed it up because you thought it would get better.

Pirouette While vertical, as during an ender, the boat rotates on its long axis.

Piton Hitting a rock straight on, usually the result of a poor boof off a steep drop.

Pivot strokes Strokes whose major function is to turn the boat.

Playboat A canoe or kayak designed exclusively for performing maneuvers in white water.

Pothole A depression caused by water swirling grit and stones in a circular motion. Can be as small as a tea cup or as big as a boat.

Pour over An abrupt drop in the river that causes a sticky hole. The lip is often not sharp enough to enable you to boof successfully. The falling water is green or undisturbed.

Probe Someone who voluntarily or otherwise runs an unknown rapid first.

Rail slides Driving the boat up onto a log or vein of rock that runs parallel to the current; this causes the boat to slide sideways down this impromptu railroad.

Retendo Performing a vertical move but landing and staying in the hole.

River rescue The rescue techniques that are particular to rivers.

Rocket move Launching off the shoulder of a wave in a quest to become airborne.

Scrub To hit a rock a glancing blow with the boat. A commonly used technique to prevent the bow of the boat from diving during eddy turns and boofs.

Scrubby Shallow steep rapids.

Shaft hand The hand that grasps the shaft of your paddle.

Shudder rudder While surfing on a wave or in a hole lean back and steer with the paddle directly behind the boat.

Sidesurf The boat is perpendicular to the downstream current, held there by the foampile of the hole.

Sieve A jumble of rocks in the current that allows water to flow through but traps debris, like swimmers.

Sneak route A line on a rapid that avoids the major obstacles.

Solid water Not aerated. Also meaning to make use of any microcurrents available during a stroke.

Stick Expensive paddle.

Strainer A tree that has fallen into the river that is partially submerged but still attached to the bank.

Stylin' Being cool. Needless to say, you're not if you had to look this up.

Suckhole A hole between or through rocks that has current flowing through it.

Swim Yard sale, quick trip to the fish store, nasal flush, throwing you into the suds.

Treads Gloves with webbed fingers for hand paddling.

Undercut A rock that has been eroded by the water to form an overhang.

Waterfall Usually higher than a pour over, hopefully it has a sharp defined lip and the falling water does become aerated on the way down.

Whitewater pry What an efficient corrective pry at the end of a forward stroke is now called.

Windmill An exceptionally sloppy forward stroke during which the recovery phase takes place high in the air.

Windowshade Flipping upstream in a hole.

BIBLIOGRAPHY

The following is a list of books, magazines and videos that we recommend for additional reading and viewing.

Bechdel, Les and Ray, Slim. *River Rescue.* Boston: Appalachian Mountain Club Books, 1989.

Ford, Kent. *Solo Playboating.* The work book. 67 Performance Video, 55 Riverbend, Durango, CO 81301

Foster, Tom and Kelly, Kel. *Catch Every Eddy. Surf Every Wave.* Massachusetts: Outdoor Center of New England, 1995.

Lessels, Bruce. *AMC Whitewater Handbook.* Boston: Appalachian Mountain Club Books, 1994.

Mason, Bill. *Path of the Paddle.* Toronto: Van Nostrum Reinhold Ltd., 1980.

McKown, Doug. *Canoeing Safety and Rescue.* Calgary: Rocky Mountain Books, 1992.

Ray, Slim. *The Canoe Handbook.* Harrisburg, PA: Stackpole Books, 1992.

Walbridge, Charles and Sundmacher Sr., Wayne A. *Whitewater Rescue Manual.* Camden, Maine: Ragged Mountain Press, 1995.

Whiting, Ken. *The Playboater's Handbook.* Clayton, Ontario: The Heliconia Press, 1998.

Magazines

American Whitewater, New York: American Whitewater.

Canoe and Kayak, Kirkland, Washington: Canoe American Associates.

Kanawa Magazine, Joseph Agnew, Box 398, 446 Main St. W., Merrickville, ON, K0G 1N0.

Paddler, Springfield, Virginia: Paddlesport Publishing Inc.

Playboating Magazine, Gunn Publishing, PO Box 694, Maidenhead, Berkshire, England, SL6 8UT.

Rapid Magazine Inc., Scott MacGregor, Box 115, Quadeville, ON, K0J 2G0.

River Magazine, Box 1068, Bozeman, MT 59771.

Voyageur Magazine, 92 Leuty Ave., Toronto, ON, M4E 2R4.

Videos

Drowning horses, Messing around in boats, 1997 White water rodeo world championships, Greenhouse Productions, Box 12, Foresters Falls, Ont. K0J 1V0

Heads up, River Rescue for river runners, America Canoe Association, 7432 Alban Station Boulevard, Suite B226 Springfield, VA 22150 and Walkabout Productions, Inc. 632 Harberts Ct. Annapolis, MD 21401

Just add water. Joe Holt Productions, Box 97, Almond, NC 28702

Solo playboating, Drill time; Solo playboating 2, Take the wild ride, Retendo, Whitewater Self defense. Kent Ford, Performance Video, 55 Riverbend, Durango, CO 81301.

Websites

Paul Mason at www.wilds.mb.ca/redcanoe

Canadian Whitewater Freestyle web site at www.synapse.net/~scriver/frsty1.htm

INDEX

Amoeba rescue, 18
Attainment, 140
Back cross-draw, 125
Back deck roll, 132
Back draw, 58, 65, 71, 80, 106, 124, 150
Back ferry, 66, 71, 141
Back paddle, 58, 124-125
Back surf, 64-65, 71, 79-81, 104-106,
    148-151
Back sweep, 55, 58, 59, 71, 125
Blasting, 147
Boat scout, 109, 179
Boil, 11, 13, 14
Boof, 90, 109, 168-173
Boof stroke, 109-113, 172
Bottom feeding, 100
Bow pry, 65, 106
Bracing strokes, 72, 126-127
Breaking wave, 11
C-stroke, 120
Canoe design, 20-26, 160
Cartwheel, 166
Carving turns, 62, 76-78, 100-102,
    144-146
Catch, 95, 119, 123
Chine, 20, 115, 121, 134
Compound back stroke, 59, 71, 124
Controlling momentum, 135-136
Correction strokes, 56, 118
Creek boat, 23
Creeking, 179
Cross-bow pry, 151
Cross-draw, 55, 58, 65, 71, 77, 80, 94, 101,
    106, 116, 117, 121, 145, 150
Cross-over, 167
Crossing the grain, 66, 86-89, 180-182
Current differential, 10
D-ring, 45, 49-51
Deadhead, 168
Decks, 51
Diagonal wave, 89
Dive, 134, 140
Downstream gates, 139

Draw, 55, 102, 115
Drysuit, 32, 53
Duffek, 27, 94, 116
Flare, 20
Eddy, 10
Eddy turn, 121, 134-140
Eddyline, 10, 134
Ender, 103, 161-162
Flat spin, 69, 108, 152-153, 158-159
Flotation, 43, 49-51
Foam pile, 11, 13, 14, 103
Foot braces, 45-46, 48-49
Foot entrapment, 18
Forward stroke, 70, 95, 118, 122-123
Forward sweep, 118
Front ferry, 141-142
Front surf, 60-63, 74-78, 92, 98-102, 141,
    142-147
Gunwale, 53
Hair boating, 184
Hand roll, 132
Hand surf, 147, 151
Helmet, 38-39
High brace, 57, 72, 83, 127
Hole, 11, 12, 14, 67
Hole riding, 82, 156-159
Ice, 15
Inside tilt, 78, 94, 115, 116,134, 136-137, 146
J-stroke, 56, 118, 122
J-lean, 94
Knee pad, 45-46
Ledge, 14
Loop, 165
Low brace, 57, 72, 82-83, 127
Nose plug, 36
Offside boof, 173
Offside bow pry, 65, 81, 106
Offside forward stroke, 119, 120, 121
Offside forward sweep, 119, 120
Offside high brace, 83, 133, 157
Offside roll, 97, 132-133
Offside static forward stroke, 65, 81,
    106, 150

Offside stern draw, 77
One-hand roll, 133
Outfitting the canoe, 43-51, 73
Outside tilt, 78, 94, 115, 117, 134, 136-137
Paddle, 27-31
Paddling against the arc, 120-121, 123
Pearl, 146
Pencil, 172
Perk, 120
Personal flotation device (PFD), 19,
    40-41
Pirouette, 163-164
Pivot, 68, 115-117
Pothole, 16
Pour-over, 14, 18
Pry, 55, 78, 81, 100, 144
Punching holes, 84-85, 178
Rating rapids, 8-9
Reactionary wave, 10
Repairs, 52-53
Reverse J-stroke, 58-59, 71, 125
Righting pry, 72, 126
River morphology, 10-12
River reading, 175-176
River rescue, 15
Rock, 360, 167
Rock a baby, 167
Rocker, 20, 54
Rocket move, 167
Rodeo, 22-23
Roll, 60, 73, 96-97, 130-133
Royalex, 52
Saddle, 45-46
Scout, 109, 175-176
Scrub boof, 173
Self-rescue, 128
Shoulder of a wave, 13, 167
Shred, 153-155
Side slip, 149, 179
Side surf, 68, 82, 107, 157
Sieve, 17
Skid plate, 52
Slalom race, 138-140

Slide, 11
Slot, 183
Snag line, 19
Sneak route, 183
Splitwheel, 166-167
Standing wave, 11
Static forward stroke, 65, 80, 106, 150
Staying dry, 85, 157, 170
Steering strokes, 118-121
Stern draw, 76-77, 144
Strainer, 16, 19
Strong swimmer rescue, 19
Suck hole, 17
Sweet spot, 13
Telfer lower, 19
Test yourself, 183, 185
Thigh strap, 45, 47
Throw line/throw bag, 18, 42
Tilt, 83, 120-121, 136,142, 154, 172
Tongue, 10, 175-176
Torso rotation, 70, 122-123
Towline, 40-42
Trimming the canoe, 44
Tripod rescue, 19
Trough, 11, 13
Tumblehome, 21, 54
Undercut, 17
Upstream gates, 139
Upstream low brace, 83, 157
Urban boating, 8
V, 10
Vinyl adhesive, 51
Visualize, 177
Waterfall, 14, 18
Wetsuit, 33
Whirlpool, 10
Whistle, 37
Whitewater pry, 122
Wing over, 164
Wiper, 165